THE REAL NAPOLEON

THE UNTOLD STORY

JOHN TARTTELIN

M.A. History
Fellow of the International Napoleonic Society
(Legion of Merit)

DEDICATED TO THE MEMORY OF
BEN WEIDER

(1923-2008)

Founder of the International Napoleonic
Society

Cover picture Napoleon in Egypt by Gerôme - 1868

Sunburst, representing the Enlightenment and Napoleon's love of knowledge, added
by the author

THE REAL NAPOLEON

Bust by Houdon

"The great works and monuments that I have executed, and the code of laws that I formed, will go down to the most distant ages, and future historians will avenge the wrongs done to me by my contemporaries."
Napoleon at Saint Helena

CHAPTERS

PREFACE

"But be not afraid of greatness: some men are born great, some achieve greatness, and some have greatness thrust upon them."
(William Shakespeare: *Twelfth Night*)

And one man was the product of all three.

Napoleon Bonaparte was both a man of his times and yet one who rose above the circumstances that prevailed around him. Compared to the other rulers of his day he was in a league of his own – the only one who promoted careers open to talent, the only one really open to the new ways of the Enlightenment. The fact he took 177 scientists and experts with him to Egypt proves that he was more than just another conqueror. Only a man with a mind like Napoleon, as he stood next to the Great Pyramid of Cheops in 1798, would speculate that it contained enough stone to build a wall around the whole of France.

Napoleon was born with a phenomenal memory, one of the greatest of all time, and he possessed an incredible ability to concentrate on the task in hand. His capacity to work astounded his ministers. He had visions beyond the ken of his contemporaries and the willpower and sheer application to make those visions come alive. As William Hazlitt said in his essay *On the Disadvantages of Intellectual Superiority*: "The chief disadvantage of knowing more and seeing farther than others, is not to be generally understood." To this day, Napoleon is often seen as but a caricature of his real self. Many do not want to *understand*, they prefer the propaganda of their own nation and the self-delusion that they alone, and their valiant army or their heroic navy, were the ones that were always in the right.

In an age of persecution, it was Napoleon who first conceived the idea of a Jewish homeland in the Holy Land and only he allowed the Jews the same rights as every other person in his

Empire. And he was the only ruler to employ those that disagreed with him. He once said to Caulaincourt: "I know you don't like me, but you always tell me the truth".1

The *truth* was the last thing that George III, Tsar Alexander, Francis of Austria and Fredrick William of Prussia wanted to hear. Those feeble monarchs believed they had a divine right to rule - even though they all proved to be pretty incompetent at the task. Their forbears had found it easy enough to carve up Poland between them, and they expected to continue in the same old way. But they did not know what to do when, as they repeatedly attacked France, Napoleon defeated them time after time. There wasn't enough gold in the vaults of even the Bank of England to buy Napoleon's genius. Thus, in a military sense, did he have greatness thrust upon him.

On a personal level, he put those arrogant fools to shame. As Felix Markham has said, to his servants and secretaries: "he was naturally kind and considerate".2 And he was perhaps the only exception to the rule that 'no man is a hero to his valet' as Marchand proved so admirably at Saint Helena and afterwards. He even allowed his staff and officials to get away with things that would have led to imprisonment or far worse with any other ruler. One example is a letter he wrote to Decrès, his Minister of Marine:

'I regret that you should have lost your temper with me;
but in a word, when once the anger is over, nothing remains;
I hope, therefore, that you feel no ill-will towards me.'3

That was a letter *from* Napoleon to one of his staff. For decades in England, Charles James Fox was denied a place in the Cabinet because George III *did not like him*. Had Fox been in the English Cabinet, there would probably have been peace between England and France. Napoleon did his best to entice even former enemies into his government in order to do the best for France.

Napoleon was the epitomization of the New Age, a living example that through hard work and constant endeavour, even those from more humble beginnings could make it to the top. In this book he is shown for what he was, not as his enemies constantly portrayed him.

We shall see his passion for intellectual enquiry, the kindness he showed to men of all ranks and stations, and his ability to identify with and personify the hopes and dreams of his soldiers and the nation as a whole. With the aid of Coignet's and Bourgogne's testimony we shall see the Emperor up close and personal and how he came across to the common man.

In a review of his career as depicted in the recent English Press and by English 'historians' in general, we shall see how Napoleon has been constantly maligned and misinterpreted and a forthright rebuttal of their accusations duly follows.

Napoleon would have loved the Internet – so many facts available at the mere press of a button. Its overwhelming sweep has enabled me to glean information from 'forgotten' historians like Abbot and Runciman who have a completely different take on the supposed Corsican Ogre and many other germane facts from a multitude of websites. In particular, the information on the Tamboran eruption of 1815 ought to fascinate anyone who has ever argued over the details of that much debated battle - Waterloo.

Recently, information on the weather conditions prevailing during the year 1812, in particular the lack of sunspots, which indicate particular cold spells here on Earth, and even a study of the El Niño phenomenon – which also adds unusual turbulence to the global climate – show that in 1812 Napoleon was incredibly unlucky to have both these adverse weather conditions to contend with at the same time.[4]

In particular, I hope a new generation of readers will take a fresh look at the history of Napoleon Bonaparte, without that dead weight of bigoted tradition that smothers his achievements and his deserved claim to greatness.

John Tarttelin,

Conisbrough, South Yorkshire, England, 2013

NOTES

1. Felix Markham *Napoleon* (New York: Mentor 1963) 138

2. Ibid. 140

3. Ibid. 140

4. See http://www.elnino.noaa.gov/
and Cesar Caviedes book *El Niño in History: Storming Through The Ages*
(University Press of Florida: 2001) Also
http://www.unisci.com/stories/20013/0904016.htm

THE REAL NAPOLEON

"Will there ever be an adequate life of Napoleon?" wrote Lord Roseberry in 1900.1 Nearly a hundred years later, David Hamilton-Williams stated that: "History has yet to record her final judgment on Napoleon."2 Stendhal enthused: "The more that the complete truth becomes known, the more that Napoleon's greatness will be evident."3 Yet, David Chandler called him a "great, bad man."4

There appear, at first glance, to be many Napoleons, almost as many as that legion of writers who have executed a non-stop campaign over the past two centuries to blacken his name and destroy his reputation. Most have begun with obvious antipathy towards him and have not allowed facts to come between them and their bile. In their partial accounts they have barely scratched the surface of his complex personality and their angry pens have failed to drown his achievements under their lakes of bitter ink. Over eight generations, more than 300,000 books have been written about Napoleon, so wherein does his fascination lie and why do so many poor historians keep returning to the scene of their crimes, fascinated by the person they despise?

"Here's a man!" exclaimed Napoleon when he met Goethe at Erfurt in 1808.5 Having once favoured a literary career, for he himself was a novelist long before he was a warrior, Napoleon the life-long romantic, who had read Werther at least seven times, was happy to bestow upon its author the prestigious Legion of Honour.6 And when he parted from him the Emperor said: "Come to Paris!"7 Here was the man who, with a little help from Marshal Davout, destroyed the Prussian army at Jena-Auerstädt, honouring German culture by saluting its greatest living exponent. Simply a meglomaniac military dictator? Far from it. Napoleon was much deeper than that.

Goethe wore his ribbon proudly for the rest of his life. In Kolbe's portrait of May 1822, the French rosette is prominent amongst Goethe's other decorations – exactly a year after Napoleon perished in exile on Saint Helena.

Napoleon was a voracious reader and a discerning one. On campaign, if a book did not take his fancy, it was apt to be slung out of the window of his speeding berline. Such a missile was a hazard of war that his duty squadron of Guard cavalry learnt quickly to accept. Napoleon was fascinated by other great minds and learned men and he sought them out on the most unlikely occasions.

In 1812, the year after the passage of a spectacular comet, Napoleon was poised to conquer Lithuania, a whole Russian province, after barely firing a shot. Its capital Vilna lay at his feet. Yet half an hour before his triumphant entry into the city, he sent his aide Count Roman Soltyk on a mission to find one Jan Sniadecki, the Rector of the University. His reputation as a famous astronomer was well known to Napoleon and he wanted to talk with him. Sniadecki began to put on his silk stockings and dress for the occasion. Soltyk told him: "Rector, it does not matter. The Emperor attaches no importance to exterior things which only impress the common people. Science is the dress of the wise."[8] The Count knew his master well.

At the onset of his career, Napoleon exhibited both a passion for ancient history and the Orient. Although he admired Frederick of Prussia, his real hero was Alexander the Great. The Macedonian's empire seemed to shine through the haze of centuries with particular fascination for the young French general and, in a real way, its brilliance could be said to have illuminated his own path and guided him to his own place upon the world stage. The French Revolution had swept away the barriers to men of innate talent and ability and Napoleon harboured romantic dreams of his own. To him it was 'the best of times' when anything might be possible to a man prepared to seize and control his own destiny.

The expedition to Egypt of 1798 demonstrated his intellectual grasp, his quest for knowledge and his love of adventure. It was a roll of the dice, for the British navy controlled the Mediterranean, but it was a gamble that was to bring prestige and honour to the whole of France. With this in mind, no less than 177 scientists were given places in the flotilla that set its sails for the mystical East, the land of the Arabian Nights. Napoleon had bemused the Directory by insisting that the expedition should seek to advance the "Progress of Knowledge and the Development of Science and the Arts." As General Michel Franceschi has written: "what distinguished this military operation from all others was the cultural and scientific dimensions which few historians accord its proper value."9

Talleyrand, who would later betray Napoleon time after time, played a pivotal role in getting the necessary political support in Paris for the whole project to be given the go ahead. It resulted in the discovery of the Rosetta Stone, the decipherment of Egyptian hieroglyphs, the study of Egyptology, and the eventual uncovering of Tutankhamun's tomb.10 The rest, as they say, is history. Can anyone seriously consider Wellington, Kutozov or Archduke Charles engaging in such a mission? It wasn't just as a military leader that Napoleon was in a league of his own.

The awe of the Orient held even the common soldier under its spell. At the first sight of the pyramids of Giza, one of the seven wonders of the ancient world, the French Army burst into a spontaneous round of cheers and applause. They were sons of the Enlightenment, some more sophisticated than others, but they were all adventurers and conquerors too, in the intellectual sphere as well as in the martial arena. Napoleon played to the national love of drama and spectacle when he declared on the eve of the Battle of the Pyramids: "From the top of these monuments, forty centuries are watching you!" They were each about to have their moment in history.

Many of Napoleon's officers were intelligent, cultivated men, not at all the second-raters he was supposed to surround himself with according to some disparaging historians. Furthermore, Caulaincourt, his Grand Equerry, never spared the Emperor his most forthright opinions and he was respected all the more by Napoleon for it. Caulaincourt's manner was so gracious that even the Tsar became his friend when he served as ambassador to Russia. Narbonne, the former Minister of War for Louis XVI and a major confidant, was another Napoleon listened to carefully. He nearly always asked for the opinions of his chief subordinates and even if he didn't follow their advice, he weighed it all carefully. And his reading was so comprehensive that he knew of historical precedents for most of the paths he was to tread.

Napoleon inspired confidence in his men and in France at large. The outburst of popular joy at his return from Elba attests to this. Yet this support is often ignored by British historians who see his return simply as a declaration of war upon the Allies! The same Allies who were almost at war amongst themselves thanks to Castlereagh's machinations and especially his betrayal of Prussia. This could have had calamitous consequences at Waterloo, because Gneisenau detested the British thanks to such treachery and only Blücher's hatred of Napoleon and his sworn word to support Wellington at Mont Saint Jean led to over 40,000 Prussians engaging upon a very dangerous flank march between Grouchy at Wavre, and Wellington and Napoleon at Waterloo, just in time to save the Duke.

Blücher had been knocked off his horse at Ligny and Gneisenau wanted to retreat back to the Prussian homeland. Had his bruised and battered superior not turned up, Wellington would have been scuttling back to Brussels under cover of the 17,000 British troops he had posted at Hal for just such an eventuality. The man with the brass-plated smile nearly put the final nail in the coffin of Anglo-Prussian relations. His squalid suicide draws a veil over the unfortunate British Foreign Minister and the masque of Castlereagh.

Napoleon had a human touch, he was happiest when he was amongst his soldiers unlike the monarchs of the ancien regime who lauded it over all they surveyed with their arrogant adherence to the doctrine of divine right. On the eve of Austerlitz, Napoleon astounded his Marshals and aides by discussing – literature.

After a few hours' sleep, he made the final inspection of his troops only to stumble on the way back to his tent. A startled grenadier lit a straw torch to reveal the mud-splattered Emperor standing before him. "Vive l'Empereur" rang out and soon dozens more torches were lit on either side, and the acclamation swelled to a crescendo. Napoleon smiled. "This is the most beautiful day of my life! You are my children!" he said, but then his expression changed. He knew that within hours, many of them would be dead.11

The victory at Austerlitz was total and complete. It was said after the battle that: "The English are merchants of human flesh. There can be no doubt, in the quarrel with England, France is right."12 But this wasn't said by Napoleon, it was the remark of the Austrian Emperor Francis II who had been lured into declaring war against France by a huge English bribe. Francis II knew that he had been duped by the British. It would not be the last time. Even when he was a grandfather to Napoleon's child, he allowed the sparkle of English gold to outweigh both his common sense and his national interest.

Napoleon led from the front, he literally put his own life at risk alongside that of his men. This physical bravery they could all identify with. It was a matter of honour not to flinch when under enemy fire. At Borodino, French cavalry withstood an intense artillery barrage, without hope of retaliation, for hours, in order to hold the line - Napoleon's Grand Army had been much reduced in numbers during its march into Russia. A third of the men and horses were blown away. Foot soldiers charged into battle for him under withering fire, to the accompaniment of admonishing cries by their officers with comments like: 'Raise your heads lads, those are bullets not turds!'

At Fère-Champenoise in March 1814, Pacthod's 3,000 men had been repeatedly assailed by 20,000 Allied cavalry. After covering four miles under constant artillery bombardment and repeated cavalry charges, what was left of his squares finally surrendered. It was a brilliant display of courage under fire, worthy of the 300 Spartans. Pacthod offered his sword to the Tsar who had been stupefied by what he had seen with his own eyes. Such an example of fortitude against overwhelming odds amazed him. When Alexander returned the sword as a mark of respect, his aide enquired: "Are you Napoleon's Imperial Guard?" The reply will echo down the centuries: "No sir, you were lucky, we are only the National Guard!"13

After all, these men were fighting for Napoleon, their legitimate Emperor, acclaimed by the French people and sanctified by the Pope himself. The fact he wasn't there in person that day did nothing to reduce their stalwart adherence to his cause.

The mere presence of Napoleon had an electrifying effect upon his troops. In 1812, lost in the snowy wastes of Russia, demoralized and freezing to death, Bourgogne and his friend Picart, the regimental marksman, were almost in despair. But they were men of the Guard. Picart said: "Cheer up, mon pays... if we are lucky enough to find the Emperor, it will be all right."14 They did, and along with the other survivors of the Imperial Guard they fought at the Battle of Krasny where, as the Denis Davidov said: "The Guard with Napoleon passed through our Cossacks like a ship armed with a hundred guns passes through fishing boats."15

Vastly outnumbered, exhausted, beleaguered, their courage never deserted them, for they fought for such a man, and he in turn, was lucky to enjoy such loyalty and devotion.

Napoleon was ever approachable by his men. Often his aides and superior officers were shocked at the familiarity he allowed them to express, especially his Guard. His 'grognards' – grumblers – could do no wrong and he seemed to know them all individually. Bourgogne records an episode in regard to a Sergeant Pierson. On July 4th 1812 at Vilna, Pierson was on guard over big ovens being constructed to bake bread for the Army. Napoleon came to see how things were getting on. Pierson took advantage of this to ask for a decoration. "Very well," the Emperor replied, "after the first battle." It wasn't until March 16th 1813 that Pierson was able to remind him of his promise. "True," Napoleon smiled, "at the works at Vilna."16 Pierson did have a distinctive ugly face but Bourgogne adds: "What a memory the Emperor had!"17

Captain Coignet gives other examples of the closeness Napoleon felt towards his Guard. During the Waterloo campaign he was baggage-master-general and quartermaster of the palace – a big title for the smallest member of the Immortals. Sent on horseback to reconnoitre troops on a distant hill by Napoleon himself, he killed an English officer in a cavalry duel and returned to his Emperor. "Well, old grouser, I thought you would be captured... You have done well." Turning to a Marshal he added: "Make a note of this old grouser. After the campaign, we will see him."[18] Sent later on another mission to find General Gerard at Ligny, he is addressed as if he were a personal friend of the Emperor's. This rapport with the common man was unheard off amongst the rulers of Europe at that time.

At the end of that long day of June 18th 1815, the last glimmer of twilight was fading on the brilliant empire of Napoleon Bonaparte. Coignet relates how Napoleon wanted to enter the square commanded by Cambronne, but the Generals protested: "What are you doing?" they cried... His design was to have himself killed. Why did they not allow him to accomplish it? They should have spared him much suffering, and at least we should have died at his side; but the great dignitaries who surrounded him were not anxious to make such a sacrifice."[19]

It was like a throwback to the mythic times of the Dark Ages and the belief that a lord's retainers should die with their master or else face unending shame. Little Coignet was prepared to die by Napoleon's side. Such was the loyalty commanded by Napoleon, the one-time writer whose romantic nature and multi-faceted genius overawed his contemporaries. Here's a man! The real Napoleon.

NOTES

1. Lord Rosebery *Napoleon The Last Phase* (London: Arthur L. Humphreys, 1900) 1
2. David Hamilton-Williams *The Fall of Napoleon* (London: Arms And Armour, 1994) 12
3. General Michel Franceschi *Bonaparte in Egypt* (International Napoleonic Society publications, 2006). Quoted on inside back cover.
4. David Chandler said this in the *Great Commanders* video series about Napoleon. The original quotation comes from Clarendon's description of Oliver Cromwell in his history of the English Civil War.

5. Horst Hohendorf *The Life and Times of Goethe* (London: Paul Hamlyn, 1967) 52

6 *The Sorrows of Young Werther* was written by Goethe in 1774.

7. Horst Hohendorf 52

8. Antony Brett-James 1812 (London: Book Club Associates, 1966) 45-46

9. General Michel Franceschi op.cit. 15

10. Without Napoleon's expedition to Egypt there would have been no real understanding of Egypt. His campaign made the Orient fashionable and turbans became all the rage for the ladies of Paris. More importantly, because of the discovery of the Rosetta Stone, Champollion was able to decipher hieroglyphics for the first time. The famous 'forty centuries look down on you' remark was said just before the Battle of the Pyramids. Franceschi Ibid. 30

11. General Michel Franceschi *Austerlitz* (INS publications: 2005) 26

12. Ibid. 35

13. David Hamilton-Williams op.cit. 91

14. Sergeant Bourgogne *Retreat From Moscow* (London: Folio, 1985) 128

15. Paul Britten-Austin *1812 The Great Retreat*, 179. Colonel Denis Davidov was a leader of Russian partisans.

16. Sergeant Bourgogne op. cit. 254

17. Ibid. 254

18. Jean-Roch Coignet *Captain Coignet* (USA: Leonaur, 2007) 268

19. Ibid. 272

NAPOLEON'S ACTS OF GENEROSITY AND KINDNESS

"I shall punish no one; I want to forget all such incidents."
(Napoleon before leaving Elba, 1815)*

It is often said that the child is the father of the man. As a small boy, Napoleon was pugnacious and feisty, but he had a marked sense of justice and a strong loyalty to his family. He was also very open-handed. Cronin remarks that: "He had a generous nature and would share his toys and sweets with other children without asking a return."[1] A lot of nonsense has been written about Napoleon having had few friends. In fact, he had many friends throughout his life and he never forgot them. Above all else, he never forgot a kindness shown towards him.

Eleanor Roosevelt said that: "The basis of all good human behaviour is kindness."[2] Napoleon instinctively knew that and, on many occasions, he demonstrated it with great liberality and genuine personal warmth.

For the women in Napoleon's life the look of love became the *luck* of love, for he was generous to them all. To his old wet-nurse, Napoleon returned the milk of human kindness. Corsican Camilla had doted on him as a baby and became an honorary member of the Bonaparte clan. She was very religious and when Pope Pius VII came to Paris to crown Napoleon Emperor, she begged to see him. Napoleon dutifully arranged it. Camilla's little Napoleone did her proud. How many divine right monarchs would have personally dealt with such a matter – and for a mere commoner?[3]

For his mother, Madame Mere, Napoleon had the utmost respect. She had already had thirteen children by the age of 34 when her husband Carlo died – only eight survived. She was faithful to his memory for the rest of her long life. Stern but loving, her nature was reflected in Napoleon's own behaviour. She was also very careful with money, a trait her son shared.

When he heard of the death of Carlo, Napoleon wrote to console his mother:

"Dear Mother,

Only today has calmed my first sorrow a little, and I hasten to tell you how grateful I am for all the kindness you have shown us. Be consoled, dear mother, circumstances demand it. We shall redouble our attention and our kindness to you, and we shall be happy if by our obedience we can to some extent make up for your dreadful loss of a dear husband...

Your affectionate son Napoleon di Buonaparte."[4]

The writer was just fifteen years old.

When he met Caroline du Colombier in Valence, the youthful Napoleon found that his young heart was bursting. Still very shy, it remained a platonic relationship. In 1792 she married a retired army captain and went to Lyon. He had not seen her for twenty years, then, in 1805 he got a letter from her. The once gauche young suitor was about to be crowned King of Italy. Nevertheless, he found time to meet her at Lyon on his way to Milan. As Kemble relates: "In later years her husband was granted an official government post, her brother a lieutenancy, and Caroline herself was appointed lady-in-waiting to Madame Mere. In 1810 her husband was made a Baron of the Empire."[5] Not a bad return for a few stolen kisses.

Another early flame was Mademoiselle de Lauberie de Saint-Germain. Many years later, she too was made a lady-in-waiting, this time to the Empress and her husband was made a Count. Napoleon liked to be surrounded by people he knew, and particularly dear to him were the friends and loves of his youth.[6]

His best friend at the École Militaire in Paris was Alexandre Des Mazis. He was a year older than Napoleon and his drill instructor. After the storming of the Bastille, Alexandre became an émigré. Years later, on 26 April 1802, Napoleon granted an amnesty to Frenchmen living abroad. Forty thousand émigrés returned, and Alexandre was amongst them. Cronin says: "Guessing he was penniless, Napoleon sent him a treasury bill for 10,000 francs and a word in his own hand: 'Des Mazis, you lent me money once, now it is my turn.' "[7]

Napoleon demonstrated his physical bravery long before he went to war. In 1792, on a hot day in August, he was a witness to the massacre of the Swiss Guards at the Tuileries palace. The National Guard went on the rampage slaughtering up to 800 men. Sickened at the sight of well-dressed women abusing the bodies, Napoleon saw men from Marseille killing the survivors in cold blood. When one of them pointed a musket at a helpless victim, Napoleon intervened: "'You're from the south? So am I. Let's save this wretch.' The Marseillais either from shame or pity, dropped his musket, and on that day of blood one life at least was saved."[8]

This courageous action encapsulates the essence of Napoleon. It demonstrates his sense of justice, his hatred of the mob, his feeling for his fellow man, and his incipient qualities of leadership. Despite all the slanderous words written about his supposed bloodthirsty nature, he was often deeply moved by the butcher's bill after a great battle – usually caused by subsidies from the English Cabinet – and equally, at the plight of an individual caught in the cross hairs of a seeming implacable fate.

Robespierre was to opine that: "Clemency is barbarous,"[9] while as First Consul and then Emperor, Napoleon offered clemency even to barbarians – men who would be classed as traitors and rebels by the majority of his fellow citizens.

In 1793, he was posted to Portet. He took part in an attack against National Guardsmen from Marseille who had seized Avignon. Frenchmen blasted away at their countrymen and civilians were killed. Such atrocities made a mockery of his youthful ideals of equality and liberty. Deeply upset, he had what, in effect, was a nervous breakdown and he went to Beaucaire to recuperate. There he wrote *Le Souper de Beaucaire* – a personal tract against the brutality of civil war.[10]

That same year, the British navy was supporting 18,000 foreign soldiers who had seized Toulon. Thanks to Napoleon's well-placed cannon, the invaders withdrew. The bestial Stanislas Fréron had purged Marseille, now the reptilian Fouché was let loose on the unfortunate inhabitants of Toulon.

The latter wrote in a veritable ecstasy to the Committee of Public Safety in Paris: "We have only one way of celebrating this victory; this evening 213 insurgents fall under our thunderbolt. Adieu, my friend, tears of joy flood my soul... we are shedding much impure blood, but for humanity and for duty."11 Years later, Fouché tried to arrange for Napoleon to be captured by the vengeful Allied armies after Waterloo. He nearly succeeded. Back in 1793, Napoleon for his part was demonstrating his humanity.

A family of noble birth, called de Chabrillan were imprisoned by fanatical revolutionaries in Toulon and their prospects were grim. Napoleon brought up some empty ammunition boxes in which he secreted the terrified victims and sent them to Hyeres from where they emigrated. Had their absence been discovered, citizen Bonaparte might well have taken their place.12

With the Whiff of Grapeshot in 1795, Napoleon effectively saved the gains made by the Revolution. As a reward he was given command of the Army of the Interior. "Now our family shall lack nothing," he wrote. He gave his mother 50,000 louis (a million francs); had Joseph made a Consul in Italy; Lucien a Commissioner in the Army of the North; Louis became his aide-de-camp; and Jerome went to a good school. Napoleon wrote to Joseph: "You know, I live only for the pleasure I can give my family."13

Eventually, he made his brothers and sisters kings, queens, princes and princesses. Joseph, the eldest, became King of Naples and then King of Spain. Napoleon was proud of his family even though they all let him down in one way or another. Joseph, for example, abandoned Paris at a crucial time in 1814, leaving the city in the scheming paws of Talleyrand. As always, Napoleon forgave his siblings. He told Las Casas at Saint Helena: "Joseph would be an ornament to society wherever he might happen to reside; Lucien, an ornament to any political assembly; Jerome, had he come to years of discretion, would have made an excellent ruler; I had great hopes for him. Louis would have been popular, and a remarkable man anywhere."14

Nepotism yes, but loving one's family is not a crime; forgiving their errors is a mark of maturity and compassion. And his brothers and sisters were far better rulers than the odious Bourbons they usually replaced. And what was the former monarchy if not nepotism enshrined?

Napoleon was also generous to strangers and even enemies. In 1800, he crossed the Alps via the Great Saint Bernard Pass on a mule guided by Pierre Nicholas Dorsaz. The mule slipped and nearly took him over the edge of a precipice – but Dorsaz saved him. Finding that the peasant's dream was to own a farm, a field and a cow, enough for him to get married, Napoleon ordered 1,200 francs paid to him for his "zeal and devotion to his task." The normal fee for a guide was three francs.[15]

In a review at the captured Austrian palace of Schoenbrunn in 1809, he recognised a soldier who, nine years before at the siege of Acre in Syria, had risked his life to recover Napoleon's hat. He was given 50 francs.[16]

When Captain Goedeck, a popular commander of the garrison of Wrietzen, was given a gift by thankful citizens, he suggested that the money be spent on five paroled Prussian officers who were in extreme want. When Napoleon heard of this he said: "Express to him my satisfaction and let me know what I may do for him."[17]

Nothing impresses a generous man like the generosity of another.

After the great victory of Austerlitz, the Emperor adopted the orphans of dead soldiers. He arranged for places to be found for the boys when they grew up and marriages were arranged for the girls, their dowries paid for by the state. When the Bourbons returned to power in 1814, they shut down the Invalides because it cost 700 francs a year to provide for each veteran, and sent them back to their own villages with 250 francs instead. Similarly, the orphans were kicked out of their boarding schools and sent packing. Of course, many of the children had no homes to go to. Such was the beneficence of the great house of Bourbon. They really knew how to take the biscuit.[18]

At Wagram in 1809 Napoleon promised impressed Austrian boatmen 6,000 francs each for ferrying a scouting party across the Danube, then in spate. When his men returned with three Austrian prisoners, Napoleon doubled the reward - 12,000 francs, a colossal sum in those days. He ordered their release remarking: "that it might not be said that any soldiers, even enemies, had spoken to the Emperor of the French without receiving some benefit."[19]

In his will, he left '20,000 francs to a brave inhabitant of Bocagnano' in Corsica who rescued him from brigands during his time there in 1792-93.[20]

Bravery always impressed Napoleon. When the siege of Mantua in Italy ended in 1797, in Cronin's words: "The Directors wanted Napoleon to shoot Wurmser, a Frenchman who had taken (up) arms against France, but Napoleon, who respected Wurmser's courage, disregarded the order, and allowed him to return to Austria."[21] Not for the last time, Napoleon was magnanimous in victory. This was a quality which the so-called Allies utterly lacked.

Time after time, they attacked him: "In 1800, 1805, 1806, 1807, 1809, and 1814 his enemies struck first..."[22] After he had destroyed their armies, Napoleon replaced the arrogant, divine right monarchs back on their corrupt thrones. As Runciman states: "The Allies pursued Napoleon to his downfall. Their attitude during the whole course of his rule was senselessly vindictive...The exile of St. Helena acted differently... He made what he wished to be lasting peace, and allowed the sovereigns to retain their thrones. How often did he carry out this act of generosity towards Prussia and Austria..." When defeated, they became "grovelling supplicants for mercy, which he never witheld."[23]

As Napoleon himself said to Caulaincourt, his ambassador in 1814: "These people will not treat; the position is reversed; they have forgotten my conduct to them at Tilsit. Then I could have crushed them; my clemency was simple folly."[24]

Even those who betrayed him spoke of Napoleon's generosity. Elting mentions that: "In his Judas memoirs,

Marmont confessed that Napoleon never forgot any kindness done or service rendered him."[25]

To his own soldiers, he could be very tolerant. When Lannes spent 300,000 francs too much on uniforms, suckered by the criminality of the clothing contractors, Napoleon forced him to repay the money himself. Augereau bailed him out, but he was still disgraced. Napoleon, having made his point, then sent Lannes to Portugal as his ambassador, a very lucrative role indeed. Jean Lannes swore at Napoleon on occasion and the Emperor liked him all the more for it. But His Majesty was a great stickler where money was concerned as his old friend Bourrienne found out when he embezzled funds. Bourrienne was given a second chance but let Napoleon down again, after which he wrote some very unreliable memoirs about his former master for royalist readers, before going mad. Bourrienne is often quoted today as telling the gospel truth and is loved by one-sided British historians. Elting thought him so unreliable he refused to use any of his 'memoirs' which are "mendacious and worthless."[26]

Napoleon gave new generals 20,000 francs, and 1,000,000 francs to all the marshals in the 1809 Austrian campaign. He also gave gifts to deserving soldiers. Elting adds: "Part was natural generosity: a man who lived simply and saved his money, Napoleon could be imperially munificent."[27] Sadly, those to whom he gave the most, were usually the ones that betrayed him. But even Ney, who led the marshals' rebellion in 1814 was given another chance at Waterloo, despite him bragging to Louis XVIII about bringing Napoleon back to Paris in an iron cage. Before Mont Saint-Jean, it was Ney's talent that had gone rusty and he threw the French cavalry away.

The rapport Napoleon had with the common soldier is legendary. At a review, a corporal of the Guard stepped forward and asked his Emperor for an advance in pay of 300 francs for the benefit of his sick mother. Napoleon suggested 1,000 francs instead, in the form of a treasury order. French bureaucracy being what it was, his old mother might be dead long before she saw a sou of it the corporal inferred. With some choice language, the Emperor of 20 million French and the overlord of tens of millions of others, dug into his own pockets, grabbed a handful of gold coins and told him to be off.28

Before he died, Napoleon remembered everyone in his Will who had ever done him a favour and all the children and families of those that had died in his service.29 And with the utmost self-control, tolerance and generosity, when still in charge of his vast domains, he refused to execute men like Talleyrand, Fouché and Bernadotte, self-seeking, grasping traitors that were not fit to be in the same room as him. Even though he had evidence of their double-dealing and treachery, Napoleon let them live. Why? Because Bernadotte was married to Desiree Clary whom Napoleon had once loved, and her sister was married to his brother Joseph – so 'Pretty-Legs' Bernadotte was a member of his family, and gained sanctuary thereby. Talleyrand had once been his friend and had helped him in his early career. And even Fouché who, if kept in solitary confinement in a locked room, would have started to scheme and plot against himself, had done his duty on occasion.

So, Napoleon stayed his hand – and those three brought him down. The common soldier and the mass of the French population could hardly believe it. It is hard to believe even to this day.

NOTES

* Vincent Cronin   *Napoleon* (Harmondsworth, England: Penguin Books, 1971) 491

1. Ibid. 18
2. Quotation from a flier for the new Oxford History of Quotations Folio Edition 2008.
      See www.foliosociety.com
3. James Kemble   *Napoleon Immortal* (London: John Murray, 1959) 22
4. Ibid. 23   Napoleon's letter of March 28, 1785, Paris.
5. Ibid. 37
6. Ibid. 38
7. Cronin op.cit. 254
8. Ibid. 74
9. Ibid. 83

10. Ibid. 83-84
11. Ibid. 91
12. Ibid. 91
13. Ibid. 104
14. Walter Runciman *Drake, Nelson and Napoleon* (London: T. Fisher Unwin Ltd., 1919) 128

    From http://www.gutenberg.org/etext/15299 128 (When printed off)
15. See http://en.wikipedia.org/wiki/Pierre_Nicholas_Dorsaz
16. John Elting *Swords Around a Throne* (London: Weidenfeld and Nicolson, 1989) 596
17. Ibid. 596
18. Ibid. 596 and 635-636
19. Ibid. 572
20. Kemble 66
21. Cronin 150
22. Elting 529
23. Runciman 136
24. Ibid. 136   Runciman himself quotes Napoleon here.
25. Elting 596
26. Ibid. 735
27. Ibid. 178
28. Ibid. 205
29. Alex de Jonge *Napoleon's Last Will and Testament* (London: Paddington Press, 1969)

    See this for a lot more details of his generosity from beyond the grave.

ENGLAND'S WARS AGAINST NAPOLEON

John Abbott said he "admires Napoleon because he abhorred war, and did everything in his power to avert that dire calamity..."1 What to some may seem revisionism can, nevertheless, be the truth. The misnamed Napoleonic wars were caused, fostered and prosecuted by England against Napoleon. Not only were they expensive in terms of human life and British gold, they were not even necessary. Napoleon wanted peace with England and he tried repeatedly to get the British Cabinet to come to terms. But fate shot Napoleon's Fox. Had that illustrious statesman lived a little longer, England and France would have become friends and allies.

Abbott remarks that: "The reason is obvious why the character of Napoleon should have been maligned. He was regarded justly as the foe of *aristocratic privilege.* The English oligarchy was determined to crush him. After deluging Europe in blood and woe, during nearly a quarter of a century, for the accomplishment of this end, it became necessary to prove to the world, and especially to the British people, who were tottering beneath the burden of taxes which these wars engendered, that Napoleon was a tyrant, threatening the liberties of the world, and that he deserved to be crushed."2

Abbott, an American, was writing in early 1850s at a time when many of the people who had known Napoleon had only recently died. Marmont, who went over to the Allies in 1814, and gave the word 'raguser' – to betray – to the French language, died in 1852. Soult, who wasn't up to Berthier's former job as Chief of Staff at Waterloo, died in 1851. Many of Napoleon's Young Guard and the 'Marie Louises' who fought in the 1814 campaign of France, were only middle-aged. Abbott's aim, his mission indeed, was "to rescue one of the greatest and noblest of names from unmerited obloquy."3

The campaign of slander and vilification engaged upon by Napoleon's detractors has gone on for over two centuries. The warmongering of Pitt and Canning and the lies spoken by both have yet to be brought fully out into the open. Most English people know nothing about the seedy, low machinations of the British Cabinet, the pathological hatred for the French people felt by Pitt and Nelson, nor the dire, merciless retribution prosecuted upon the Bonapartists by Lord Liverpool after the Battle of Waterloo.

Just like the Japanese still refuse to teach their children about the atrocities of their soldiers during WWII, so British historians ignore, deny and obfuscate the truth about Anglo-French relations at the beginning of the C19th. Napoleon wanted peace, the British Cabinet did not.

Colonel John Elting's book *Swords Around a Throne* was the product of thirty years of research. He comments upon the doomed Treaty of Amiens: "England repudiated the Treaty of Amiens (signed March 27, 1802) and declared war on France, following the ancient and very profitable English practice of authorizing its warships to seize French merchant vessels before issuing the formal declaration."[4] So much for the supposed British virtue of 'fair play'.

Elting mentions ' "la perfide Albion" (treacherous England)'[5] and notes that "the English spent lavishly to hire and bribe."[6] He points out that "After the Treaty of Luneville with Austria (February 9, 1801) much of the French Army had been put on peace footing."[7] So much then, for Napoleon being an inveterate megalomaniac crazed by a lust for conquest. Had Britain not reneged on the Treaty of Amiens, there could have been peace between the two nations.

It was not just with England, that Napoleon wanted peace. Of 1812, and conflict with Tsar Alexander, Elting says: "Napoleon did not want war, but it obviously lay in his path."[8] And in regard to Austria in 1809: "Anxious to avoid war, Napoleon told him (*Davout*) to keep his cavalry several miles west of the (*Austrian*) border."[9] (My italics). As for the English, Colonel Elting adds: "England in 1805 hired Russia and Austria to attack France from the east..."[10] Then there were the "repeated attempts by the Royalists (with British assistance) to assassinate Napoleon."[11]

What was Napoleon's response to all this? He wrote to George III on January 2nd 1805:

"My dear brother

Since I was called to the throne of France by Providence and by the suffrage of the Senate, the people, and the Army, my foremost and most earnest desire has been for peace. France and England are squandering their prosperity. Their struggle may continue for centuries. But are their governments discharging their most sacred duty? Is not their conscience troubled by such a useless effusion of blood with no real end in view? *I count it no dishonour to be taking the first step in this matter.* (My italics). I fancy I have shown the world that I am nowise daunted by the hazards of war; indeed, war holds no terrors for me. Peace is the dearest wish of my heart, but war has never diminished my deputation. I charge Your Majesty not to reject the happy opportunity of yourself conferring peace upon the world..."[12]

Napoleon was almost beseeching George III when he adds: "If the moment passes, how can this war reach an end, when all my efforts have failed to bring it to a conclusion?"[13]

This impassioned plea went unacknowledged and unanswered. The British Cabinet wanted war, and war duly followed, paid for with British gold.

William Napier, who wrote the *History of the War in the Peninsula*, sets the record straight in the first sentence of his account: "The hostility of aristocratic Europe forced the republican enthusiasm of France into a course of military policy, outrageous in appearance, in reality one of necessity; for up to the treaty of Tilsit, her wars were essentially defensive."[14] He goes on to add that it was "a deadly conflict to determine whether aristocracy or democracy should predominate, equality or privilege be the principle of European civilization."[15]

Napier, probably the foremost English historian of his day (he, like Wellington, was actually born in Ireland), speaks of "the wonderful genius of Napoleon" and how "the privileged classes of Europe consistently transferred their implacable hatred of the French revolution to his person; for in him they saw innovation find a protector, and felt that he only was able to consolidate the hateful system..."[16]

Napoleon was a steady beacon around which chaos swirled. He alone was strong enough to bring order, to quell the anarchy all around him. He was the light at the edge of the world to which all moderate men turned. Napoleon forged republican and émigré, peasant and soldier, into one people, one nation. With his foresight, application, and sheer strength of character, he tamed the disparate political forces and brought peace and security to the people as a whole. Beyond Louis XIV's wildest dreams, Napoleon was France. Above all, having lived through the horrors of the Terror, he wanted peace at home and abroad.

Returning to the country that remained his inviolable foe, here is Runciman on Nelson and Napoleon: "It would be futile to draw a comparison between the two men. The one was a colossal human genius, and the other, extraordinary in the art of his profession, was entirely without the faculty of understanding or appreciating the distinguished man he flippantly raged at from his quarterdeck."[17]

Runciman, writing in 1917-1919, believed that the Allies' vendetta against Napoleon led directly to the inexorable rise of Prussia and to Kaiser Wilhelm's maniacal policies that resulted in World War One. Runciman also warned writers of history of the pitfalls that so many other British historians have fallen into: "The historian has a great deal to do with the manner in which the fame of a great man is handed down to posterity, and it should never be forgotten that historians have to depend on evidence which may be faulty, while their own judgment may not always be sound."[18]

When historians have imputed only infamy and evil to Napoleon, consciously ignoring his achievements and denigrating his actions, is it a wonder that the myth of the Corsican Ogre persists to this very day?

Runciman extols Nelson's bravery and seamanship yet he adds: "Nelson was a true descendant of a race of men who had never faltered in the traditional belief that the world should be governed and dominated by the British."[19]

Nelson's blinkered view of the world and his naivety when it came to politics had only one outcome: "Both he and many of his fellow-countrymen regarded the chosen chief on whom the French nation had democratically placed an imperial crown as the embodiment of a wild beast."[20]

Runciman draws another telling contrast: "He had a wholesome dislike of the French people and of Bonaparte, who was their idol at that time... Napoleon, on the other hand, had no real hatred of the British people, but during his wars with their government his avowed opinion was that "all the ills, and all the scourges that afflict mankind, came from London."'[21] Runciman thinks that they were both wrong and simply failed to understand each other's point of view. But then, all those assassination attempts *were* concocted in London.

He also says that: "The British were not only jealous and afraid of Napoleon's genius and amazing rise to eminence – which they attributed to his inordinate ambition to establish himself as the dominating factor in the affairs of the universe - but they determined that his power should not only not be acknowledged, but destroyed, and their policy after twenty years of bitter war was completely accomplished."[22]

Now we see why George III did not bother to reply to Napoleon's offer of peace in 1805. Napoleon was the phoenix borne aloft by the flames of Revolution, dazzling Paris with his brilliance. The British Government was terrified by his apparition, mortified by his greatness, yet determined to destroy him at all costs.

In London, the Prince of Wales was a bird of a very different feather: "He was known to be a cheat, a liar, and a faithless friend to men and to women, while in accordance with the splendid ethic of this type of person, he believed himself to be possessed of every saintly virtue."[23] While Napoleon commanded the Grand Army, the Prince Regent couldn't even command respect.

Runciman takes no prisoners when he compares the Emperor with other contemporary rulers: "His traducers proclaimed him an atheist, and we hear the same claptrap from people now who have not made themselves acquainted *with the real history of the man and his times.*" (My italics) He goes on: "We do not say he was a saint, but he was a better Christian, both in profession and action, than most of the kings that ruled prior to and during his period. In every way he excels the Louis of France, the Georges of Great Britain and Hanover, the Fredericks of Prussia, and the Alexanders of Russia. The latter two he puts far in the shade, both as a statesman, a warrior, and a wise, humane ruler..."[24]

After the Battle of Marengo in 1800, Napoleon wrote to the Emperor of Austria asking for peace – taking the first step again. He wrote: "The English threaten the balance far more than does France, for they have become the masters and tyrants of commerce, and are beyond the reach of resistance."[25] However, just two days before news of his victory, England concluded a new peace with Austria, lavish as ever with a loan bearing no interest whilst war continued.[26]
A separate peace was thus made impossible.

As Abbott remarks: "The consolidation of democratic power in France was dangerous to king and noble. William Pitt, the soul of the aristocratic government of England, determined still to prosecute the war. France could not harm England. But England, with her invincible fleet, could sweep the commerce of France from the sea." He continues: "Fox and his coadjutors with great eloquence opposed the war. Their efforts were, however, unavailing. The people of England, notwithstanding all the efforts of the government to defame the character of the First Consul, still cherished the conviction that, after all, Napoleon was their friend."[27]

Napoleon himself later remarked: "Pitt was the master of European policy. He held in his hands the moral fate of nations. But he made ill use of his power... But that for which posterity will, above all, execrate the memory of Pitt, is the hateful school, which he has left behind him; its insolent Machiavellism, its profound immorality, its cold egotism, and its utter disregard of justice and human happiness."[28]

If only Fox, despised by George III, had been the Prime Minister – Napoleon adds: "The death of Fox was one of the fatalities of my career. Had his life been prolonged, affairs would (have) taken a totally different turn. The cause of the people would have triumphed, and we should have established a new order of things in Europe."29

Finally, Napoleon was able to make peace with the Austrians at Luneville on February 9th 1801. England now rampaged alone. Sir Walter Scott stated that: "On every point, the English squadrons annihilated the commerce of France, crippled her revenues, and blockaded her forts."30 Like a spoilt brat, or the proverbial bull in a china shop, the British Government destroyed order in Europe.

Runciman speaks wisdom when he says: "We had no real grounds of quarrel with France nor with her rulers. The Revolution was their affair, and was no concern of ours, except in so far as it might harmfully reflect on us, and of this there was no likelihood if we left them alone."31 As he explains: "Had we approached Napoleon in a friendly spirit and on equal terms, without haughty condescension, he would have reciprocated our cordiality and put proper value on our friendship."32

When the preliminaries of peace between England and France were finally signed on October 1st 1801, the French Ambassador's carriage was pulled along by the London mob. This was too much for Nelson who fumed: "that our damned scoundrels dragged a Frenchman's carriage... The villains would have drawn Buonaparte if he had been able to get to London to cut the king's head off."33

This is England's 'hero' speaking, lamenting bitterly that the British people were tired of war and wanted peace with France. Those historians who castigate Napoleon for being a 'warmonger' please take note.

The most outrageous incident of British arrogance and callous disregard for human life came with the 1807 bombardment of the city of Copenhagen. Thomas Munch-Petersen in *Defying Napoleon* draws parallels with the invasion of Iraq in 2003: "Britain's operation against neutral Denmark was prompted by fear that her navy might fall into the hands of Napoleon and be turned against Britain."34

The operation was based on faulty 'intelligence'. Denmark had been scrupulously neutral before 1807 and, indeed, her neutrality was guaranteed by Tsar Alexander of Russia. This did not prevent the cowardly sneak attack by a combined English land and sea force. Some 2,000 innocent civilians were butchered, killed in their homes by 'shock and awe'. It was the first occasion that Congreve rockets were employed against civilian targets: "the first example in modern history of terror bombardment bring used against a major European city."[35]

When Canning learnt that he had been supplied with faulty information, he refused to clarify the matter in Parliament. Britain stole the Danish fleet of twenty ships of the line and rendered ALL her other vessels useless.

Canning had expected the Danes to give up their fleet instantly – the pride and soul of the Danish nation. If not: "her overseas trade would be destroyed, her colonies would be seized and her detained merchant shipping would be confiscated."[36]

The Danes refused, the British created a bloodbath in Copenhagen, and the result? They drove the Danish into an alliance with Napoleon, the very thing they had tried to prevent. Runciman is right to bewail the asinine political nous of Canning and his ilk.

Runciman came across a scrap of manuscript in Pitt's papers. Here is Pitt describing Napoleon: "I see various and opposite qualities... I see all the captious jealousy of conscious usurpation, dreaded, detested, and obeyed, the giddiness and intoxication of splendid but unmerited success, the arrogance, the presumption, the selfwill of unlimited and idolized power, and more dreadful than all in the plentitude of authority, the restless and incessant activity of guilt, but unsated ambition."[37]

Pitt must have been looking in a mirror. Here is a case of physician heal thyself, of the Greek 'know thyself', and perfidious Albion being described in the apparent ravings of a lunatic.

NOTES

1. John Abbott *The History of Napoleon Bonaparte* (1851) From *Harper's New Monthly Magazine*. See Preface. This history came out in instalments and was later published as a book in 1855.
2. Ibid. See Preface
3. Ibid. See Preface
4. Elting 59
5. Ibid. 119
6. Ibid. 119
7. Ibid. 59
8. Ibid. 63
9. Ibid. 118
10. Ibid. 236
11. Ibid. 189
12. Christopher Lee *Nelson and Napoleon* (London: Headline, 2005) Quoted on 160-161.
13. Ibid. 161.
14. William Napier *History of the War in the Peninsula* (1828) Chapter One, 1
15. Ibid. 1
16. Ibid. 1
17. Runciman See Preface, 3 (when printed off) From http://www.gutenberg.org/etext/15299
18. Ibid. 11 (when printed – there are no page numbers on the screen)
19. Ibid. 26
20. Ibid. 26
21. Ibid. 27
22. Ibid. 27
23. Ibid. 38
24. Ibid. 53-54
25. Abbott 16-17 of Part One (when printed off) See: www.fullbooks.com/Napoleon-Bonaparte1.html
26. Ibid. 21
27. Ibid. 22
28. Ibid. 22
29. Ibid. 23
30. Ibid. 26   Sir Walter Scott is quoted here by Abbott himself.
31. Runciman 67
32. Ibid. 67
33. Ibid. 70-71
34. Thomas Munch-Peterson *Defying Napoleon* (Stroud, England: Sutton Publishing, 2007) on dust jacket
35. Ibid. on dust jacket
36. Ibid. 218
37. Runciman 127

ENGLAND'S UNLIKELY HERO – NAPOLEON

"He is a fine fellow, who does not deserve his fate."
(Crew of the *HMS Northumberland* on the way to Saint Helena)

When it comes to their historians, the nation that spawned Shakespeare needs to be treated with caution. The first principle when reading an English history in relation to Napoleonic France should be: "Is this a swagger I see before me?"

They take as given, almost by definition, that the English cause was ever just and righteous and that Napoleon, a Frenchman, nay, not even that, a mere Corsican, was an inveterate warmonger and a loser to boot, unfit to buckle the Duke of Wellington's shoes. Because Wellington defeated him at Waterloo, the chap must have been a very bad sort from the start. Many of the following accounts come from hostile English historians and observers. Nevertheless, they often say much more than they themselves realized.

In 1900 Lord Rosebery wrote: "In England his name was a synonym for the author of all evil. He was, indeed, in our national judgment, a devil seven times worse than the others. *But then we knew nothing at all about him.*" (My italics)[1] That, in a nutshell, is why there are so many waspish comments about Napoleon even to this day.

The Appendix in Rosebery's *The Last Phase* is much more revealing and includes comments from people who actually met the Emperor. Captain Maitland wrote: "Napoleon Buonaparte, when he came on board the Bellerophon on the 15th July 1815... was then a remarkably strong, well-built man, about five feet seven inches high..."[2]

Five feet seven? But everyone knows Napoleon was 'small'. Actually, he wasn't, he was the average height for his day. The reason he got his nickname of The Little Corporal was because only the tallest men were allowed to become grenadiers and Guardsmen. And French measurements were not the same as British ones, a French 'foot' was bigger.

Maitland continues: "His manners were extremely pleasing and affable; he joined in every conversation, related numerous anecdotes, and endeavoured in every way, to promote good humour: he even admitted his attendants to great familiarity; and I saw one or two instances of their contradicting him in the most direct terms, though they generally treated him with much respect."3

Yet Rosebery states: "He had no checks or assistance from advice, for his ministers were cyphers."4 Napoleon certainly listened to Talleyrand early on, perhaps too much – as the Duke of Enghien Affair was set in motion at the behest of that defrocked priest.5 Fouché and Talleyrand gave 'advice' to everybody. Not just Napoleon, but the Tsar, the Bourbons and the British. They continued with plots and treacheries throughout Napoleon's rule. Had he been the evil dictator he is often supposed to be, he would have had both of them shot. At Saint Helena he was to rue the fact he hadn't. Mere cyphers those two were not. Rosebery himself concedes: "To use a common vulgarism, he was not, we think, as black as he is painted."6

Maitland illuminates Napoleon even further when he says: "He possessed to a wonderful degree, a faculty in making a favourable impression upon those with whom he entered into conversation: this appeared to me to be accomplished by turning the subject to matters he supposed the person he was addressing was well acquainted with, and on which he could show himself to advantage."7

Rosebery says: "He was it may be fairly alleged, indulgent and affectionate to his family, particularly in his first, better years; dutiful to his mother; kind to his early friends."8

In *Swords Around a Throne*, John Elting wrote that Napoleon never forgot someone who had been kind or helpful to him. *That* is why Talleyrand lived to see old age. Despite his many treacheries, and the Emperor railing at him and calling him "Shit in a silk stocking"9 – Napoleon never forgot their earlier friendship.10

Even Rosebery has to admit: "Napoleon was assuredly great. Besides that indefinable spark which we call genius, he represents a combination of intellect and energy which has never been equalled, never certainly, surpassed."[11] And the noble Lord goes further and quotes another of his station, Lord Dudley: "He has thrown doubt on all past glory; he has made all future renown impossible."[12] Praise indeed from the land of his supposedly inveterate enemies.

The Appendix also shows the stark reality of Napoleon's imprisonment on Saint Helena and his subsequent rapid physical decline. On July 31st 1815, Bunbury describes him: "Napoleon appears to be about five feet six inches high... The general character of his countenance was grave and almost melancholy; but no trace of severity or violent passion was allowed to appear. I have seldom seen a man of stronger make, or better fitted to endure fatigue."[13]

On June 25th 1816, Lady Malcolm states that: "She was struck by the kindness of his expression so contrary to the fierceness she had expected. She saw no trace of great ability; his countenance seemed rather to indicate gentleness..."[14]
A very interesting observation. No doubt, having heard so much about the Corsican Ogre, she was surprised to find that he was human after all.

On September 1st 1817, Henry paints a sad picture of the former Emperor's decline: "The features instantly reminded me of the prints of him which we had seen. On the whole, his general look was more that of an obese Spanish or Portuguese friar, *than the hero of modern times...* A fascinated prestige, which we had cherished all our lives, then vanished like gossamer in the sun. *The great Napoleon* had merged in an unsightly and obese individual; and we looked in vain for that overwhelming power of eye and force of expression, which we had been taught to expect by a delusive imagination." (My italics)[15]

We now know, thanks to the work of Ben Weider and Sten Forshufvud, that Napoleon was being poisoned with arsenic by Montholon. Perhaps its insidious progress is already evident here as obeseness is one of its symptoms.[16]

John Bowle (1973)[17] who says Napoleon was the first of the modern dictators, quotes Nelson in 1805: "Never was the probability of universal monarchy more nearly realized than in the person of the Corsican."[18] To Nelson, responsible for the massacre of republicans in Naples, only universal *British* monarchy would do.[19]

Bowle, another hostile critic, comments on Napoleon's personal affability: "His charm, when he switched it on, was apparently irresistible; as when he got round his insular British captors on *HMS Bellerophon*, and the British oligarchy had to take care that he should not meet and hypnotise the Prince Regent. This fascination briefly won over the neurotic Tsar Alexander..."[20]

Another view from the sanguinary heights of British arrogance comes from Elizabeth Longford who wrote the introduction to his book – it is an exercise in nationalistic chauvinism. She recounts that: "His passion for the actress Mademoiselle Georges had been so tumultuous that once during a rendezvous in his palace he collapsed in her arms at dead of night in a faint. It was she who was blamed and banned from the Tuileries. No wonder she called Wellington 'much stronger'."[21]

Longford goes on: "There can be nothing but thankfulness for Waterloo."[22] A slightly insouciant remark to say the least. If the Allies had accepted the peace terms offered by Napoleon on his return from Elba, to rapturous popular acclaim in France, there would have been no need for war. After it, the White Terror launched on the direct orders of Lord Liverpool, the British Prime Minister, led to the judicial murders of dozens of French soldiers and former supporters of Napoleon. That is nothing to crow about.[23]

Neither is the effect that Louis XVIII, dumped on France by her hero, the illustrious Duke of Wellington himself, had on the country, leave alone that of his hideous brother d'Artois, the future Charles X. Hundreds of people were killed in France after Waterloo and Wellington, who as Commander-in Chief of the Allied armies until 1818, could have done a lot to prevent it, did absolutely nothing.[24]

The great lady continues – after the abasement of Napoleonic France she can afford to be 'generous': "Nevertheless, so compelling was the Emperor's magnetism that English Whigs considered Europe fortunate to be in such rapacious hands and under such heavy boots. They wept when he abdicated, sent him presents and beautified their houses with his bust."[25] Longford says nothing about the British citizens kicked out of their own country by aristocratic boots and sent to Australia, merely for questioning the rule of their benighted, selfish masters.[26]

When Prime Minister, Wellington held out against reform and was indifferent to the plight of those caught up in economic depression. As a result, people rioted outside Apsley House, his London residence and smashed his windows. The public wanted to give Wellington – the boot. The Downing Street website says: "He defended rule by the elite and refused to expand the franchise."[27] Wellington held the common man in contempt throughout his life.

Christopher Lee gets his fangs into Napoleon in *Nelson and Napoleon.* The dust jacket of his book speaks of "the megalomania of Napoleon to invade England," which pretty much sets the tone.[28] There is no mention of the numerous assassination attempts on his life financed by London nor the help given by the British Cabinet to d'Artois in fomenting his plots. Napoleon had a right to consider the Cabinet little more than Brittunculi – wretched little Brits in a Roman phrase – because even during the Treaty of Amiens, these conspiracies continued.[29]

Lee states that: "Nelson was a perfect hero: brilliant, anti-establishment, romantic and – above all – victorious, especially in death."[30] In terms of historical fact, Nelson was a consummately arrogant man – even for the British at that time. Despite having another man's wife on his arm – Emma Hamilton – he was angered when the couple were not accepted by polite society. Over zealous in the pursuit of prize money from captured vessels, Nelson had a chip on both shoulders – he could have played all night at Las Vegas with no trouble at all.[31]

Yet even Lee has to admit that: "The fighting started because the rest of Europe, Britain included, believed that Bonaparte

could – and probably would – export the French Revolution."
And he speaks of "the eighteenth-century arrogance of the
eighteenth-century British, who believed above all in the
divine gift of Protestantism. All those who were not Protestants
were, by simple definition, second rate. Bonaparte's idea of a
secular society fitted easily into this British conceit."[32]

As for England's elite, here is Lee's own assessment: "The
ruling class was a small society of relatives mostly drawn from
the aristocracy at a time when parliamentary seats were
brought, sold and owned by that same aristocracy." (My
italics)[33] Here, he is undoubtedly right.

He also comments on Napoleon's peace offering to the
British: "Some have regarded the letter he wrote on 2 Jan 1805
as an offer of peace. But was it really that?"[34] Napoleon wrote:
"If your Majesty will but consider the matter personally, you
will see that war is purposeless, and can lead to no definite
result. And it is a miserable prospect for two peoples to fight
merely for the sake of fighting. The world is big enough for
both our peoples to live on."[35]

Isn't that just too reasonable by half? Here is strong support
for Franceschi and Weiders' thesis in *The Wars Against
Napoleon*, that no matter how hard he tried, the British would
not accept peace.[36] It was their refusal to leave Malta, as agreed
in the Treaty of Amiens, that led to renewed war. Why should
we be so cynical about Napoleon's offer?[37]

The Treaty of Amiens was welcomed by the British *and* the
French public. Tourists flocked across the Channel in both
directions. Frank McLynn tells us: "British public opinion
demanded peace."[38] This was despite the official campaign in
the British media against Napoleon. McLynn adds: "Napoleon
also raised the question of the vile propaganda cartoons about
him being printed in the English newspapers, portraying him
as a tyrant and ogre. The *Morning Post* had just described him
as 'an unclassifiable being, half African, half European, a
Mediterranean mulatto'. In cartoons he was usually portrayed
as a pygmy with an enormous nose."[39] It was only the so-called
British elite who wanted to continue with war against

Napoleon and they tried to get the public on board by means of such pathetic and racist diatribes.

John Strawson's book *The Duke and the Emperor* is a tour de force in character assassination: Wellington walks on water, while Napoleon is a creature from the abyss.[40] Strawson opines: "The fact is that, as Wellington is alleged to have said of the Emperor, 'the feller wasn't quite a gentleman.' Wellington most assuredly was. This contrast in character was absolute. Napoleon was treacherous, disloyal, amoral, a cheat, a liar and a bully – fit for treasons strategems and spoils. His only limits were his own will-power, egotism and ambition."[41]

Considering, after such objectivity, that the writer 'isn't quite an historian', one can compare Napoleon's return from Elba, to overwhelming popular acclaim, to Wellington's hiding in Apsley House as his windows were being broken by those angry crowds.

Strawson goes on with overweening partiality: "This difference in breeding was to some extent reflected in the armies that the two men commanded. The Grand Armee was full of first-class soldiers, but not many of them were gentlemen... the British Army on the other hand was largely officered by gentlemen and many of them were excellent soldiers."[42]

Was that why the English abandoned their women and children during Moore's retreat to Corunna?[43] To Strawson, being a 'gentleman' is the touchstone to everything. He seems not just to be writing of the C19th but living in it.

Strawson then undermines his own case completely. How do his British captors view the Corsican usurper? : "Captain Maitland under whose protection Napoleon sailed from Rochefort to England in July 1815, recorded their feeling that 'if the people of England knew him as well as we do, they would not touch a hair on his head'. These sentiments were echoed again by the men of the Northumberland who, during the voyage to Saint Helena, had every opportunity to study their celebrated passenger: 'He is a fine fellow, who does not deserve his fate'."[44]

Those men met and talked with Napoleon thus Strawson's own ranting at the opening of his book is even more inexcusable. In fact, when Napoleon got to Torbay and later, Plymouth, the British public came to snatch a glimpse of him in their droves. McLynn says he was "the sensation of the hour... His one card was public opinion and the legal skill of his British supporters."45 But the corrupt Establishment instructed the Admiralty to order Maitland to sail for Saint Helena before Napoleon got the chance to step ashore. His fate was sealed.46

Meanwhile, Byron sung his praises and castigated the Duke: "Wellington is the Cub of Fortune but she will never lick him into shape... Victory was never before wasted on such an unprofitable soil, as this dunghill of Tyranny..."47 Strawson's view, that Wellington was a better man than Napoleon is utterly destroyed in his own book, at the very end of which he states: "For Napoleon, the great player, the gigantic gambler, the soaring eagle, there is a shorter tribute. He was a modern Caesar, and bestrode the world like a Colossus. When we read or write of him today, he still does."48

In England, when Napoleon died, Sir James Mackintosh remarked: "What a sensation this event would have had nine years ago and what a sensation it will make in nine hundred years." And he added: "Of all great conquerors Napoleon is the most remarkable."49

Sir Robert Wilson, formerly one of the Emperor's bitterest enemies, went into mourning when he saw a placard on London walls appealing to all those who admired talent and courage in adversity to honour 'this premature death.'50

Who then, as now, is the measure of all things? Napoleon. Even his detractors, Bowle, Lee, Longford, Strawson et al, pitch Wellington and Nelson against him as if, like Native Americans of the C19th, they believe that the greater their enemy, the greater their own heroes are themselves. Napoleon was the man of the century. He was not just a soldier, he was the ruler of an empire, a legislator, a writer, a visionary, an adventurer and romantic who personally instituted the whole field of Egyptology. We shall not see his like again.

NOTES

1. Rosebery 247
2. Ibid. 253
3. Ibid. 253
4. Ibid. 241
5. General Michel Franceschi in *The Duke of Enghien Affair: A Plot Against Napoleon* (2005) quotes Napoleon's secretary Meneval on page 28: "I am convinced," he wrote, "that Napoleon, sufficiently comforted by the humiliation he had inflicted on his enemies by foiling their plot, would have leaned towards mercy and sparing the prince's life."
6. Rosebery 248
7. Ibid. 253
8. Ibid. 249
9. J.F. Bernard *Talleyrand: A Biography* (London: History Book Club, 1973) 13
10. Rosebery 249 says: "M. de Remusat witnessed in 1806 a scene of almost hysterical and insurmountable emotion when Napoleon embraced Talleyrand and Josephine, declaring that it was hard to part from the two people that one loved the most; and, utterly unable to control himself, fell into strong convulsions." Her memoirs are, however, not very reliable, having been written for a Royalist audience.
11. Ibid. 252
12. Ibid. 252
13. Ibid. 254-255
14. Ibid. 255
15. Ibid. 256
16. See Ben Weider and David Hapgoods' *The Murder of Napoleon* (New York: Congdon & Lattès, 1982)
17. John Bowle *Napoleon* (London: Weidenfeld and Nicolson, 1973)
18. Ibid. 12
19. See Roger Knight's review *An Admiral with a Star Quality* by Matthew Nicholls (2005) at www.oxonianreview.org/issues/5-1/5-1nicholls.html : "his over-hasty execution of Neopolitan rebels in 1799, and especially the hanging of Caracciolo, cast a long shadow over his career, 'paralysing' as one contemporary put it, 'all the energy and zeal which distinguished him in every other situation.' "
20. Bowle 17
21. Ibid. 7
22. Ibid. 7 Longford also criticizes here Napoleon's "loathing for the masses" – a trait Wellington shared of course. Yet, Napoleon had the 'common touch' with his soldiers whereas Wellington was haughty and distant to his men.
23. David Hamilton-Williams' *The Fall of Napoleon* (London: Arms and Armour, 1994) 261-262, quotes a letter from Lord Liverpool to Louis XVIII:

"The forbearance manifested at the present moment can be considered in no other light than weakness, and NOT mercy... what dangers might not be apprehended from forty thousand officers unemployed – men of desperate fortunes, and possessing a large proportion of talent and energy of the country! A severe example made of the conspirators who brought back Buonaparte could alone have any effect in countering these dangers." Hamilton-Williams adds on 262: "It will be seen clearly from these letters that in Liverpool's opinion, only a spate of terror, executions and imprisonment would subdue the republicans and imperialists."

24. John Strawson in *The Duke and the Emperor* (London: Constable, 1994) 241 states, for example: "During Ney's trial many appeals were made to the Duke of Wellington to intervene. But he did not." And he adds on 242: "still we know that *had* he intervened, Ney would not have been executed."
25. Bowle 8
26. David Hamilton-Williams op.cit. 330: "During the nine years from 1816 to 1825, 78,400 men and women were transported."
27. See www.number-10.gov.uk/ and see entry for The Duke of Wellington.
28. Christopher Lee *Nelson and Napoleon* (London: Headline, 2005)
29. David Hamilton-Williams op. cit. 304: "On 27 March Napoleon had concluded the Peace of Amiens with Britain, but the British Cabinet, unknown to Parliament, had neither asked the Bourbons to quit England nor closed down d'Artois' underground activities in Jersey."
30. Lee 3-4
31. www.historyofwar.org/articles/people_nelson_mid.html Nelson Horatio, Admiral (1759-1805): 1798-1803 states under *Napoleonic Wars – Naples and Emma*: "Nelson had not been impressed during his previous dealings with Naples, describing it as a 'country of fiddlers and poets, whores and scoundrels."
32. Lee 21 and 40-41
33. Ibid. 113
34. Ibid. 160
35. Ibid. 161
36. General Michel Franceschi and Ben Weider *The Wars Against Napoleon* (New York: Savas Beatie, 2008)
37. Hamilton-Williams op. cit. 287 says: "it should be remembered that in almost none of the wars of the period had Napoleon been the aggressor or the first to declare war."
38. Frank McLynn *Napoleon* (London: Pimlico, 1998) 235
39. Ibid. 265
40. John Strawson *The Duke and The Emperor* (London: Constable, 1994) This book is based on a false premise. This is hardly a comparison of equals. Napoleon ruled an empire and was in a league of his own.
41. Ibid. 17
42. Ibid. 18
43. Franceschi and Weider 134: "the British general abandoned to this "henchman of the devil," Napoleon, a thousand British women and children,

found on January 2, 1809, in a large shed at Astorga. They were starving, shivering with cold, and trembling with fear. The mothers threw themselves at the emperor's feet and begged him to preserve the lives of their children. He made all arrangements to reassure, lodge, warm, and feed these unfortunates before returning them in good health to the British army several days later."

44. Strawson 232-233. He also says on 232 "the ships company of HMS Undaunted, which took the Emperor to Elba, had wished him 'long life and prosperity' and 'better luck another time'..."
45. McLynn 635
46. Ibid. 636. After three days Napoleon was transferred to the Northumberland under Admiral Cockburn, which actually went to Saint Helena.
47. Strawson 287-288
48. Ibid. 303-304
49. Gilbert Martineau *Napoleon's Last Journey* (London: John Murray. 1976) 2
50. Ibid. 3

COIGNET OF THE GUARD: PART ONE
A WRETCHED BEGINNING

"My motto has always been: A career open to all
talents, without distinction of birth... Be successful!"
(Napoleon)

Jean-Roch Coignet was born at Druyes-les-Belles-Fontaines in
Yonne in 1776. He very nearly shared the same day of birth as
the seven year old future Emperor, for Coignet's birthday was
August 16th, a day later than his more famous counterpart. He
lived a very full life at an epoch making period in history and
was destined to play a part at the epicentre of the Empire in
the very presence of Napoleon. But all this was far-off in the
future. Coignet's beginnings could not have been humbler,
while his early life was dire in the extreme.

Coignet's initial years could have been a horror story penned
by the Brothers Grimm or a dark tale told by Hans Christian
Andersen. He was virtually abandoned by his wastrel father,
nicknamed The Lover, for his siring of more than thirty
illegitimate offspring as well as his issue by his three wives.
Coignet's mother was the second of these and when she died
the orphaned Jean-Roch and his three siblings were plunged
into a veritable nightmare of pain and want. His eighteen-year-
old stepmother, formerly the family servant and now his
father's third wife, was called The Beauty on account of her
looks, but she had a heart as cold and black as obsidian glass.
She resolved to get rid of her unwanted charges as soon as
possible. There is an old English saying that: 'Many of the
fairest without are the foulest within.' And The Beauty was a
wicked stepmother of proverbial proportions.

She so starved young Coignet and Pierre, his elder brother by
a year, the two of them decided to run away from home. As
Coignet put it: "We poor little orphans were beaten night and
day. She choked us to give us a good colour."[1] They headed for
Étais, an hour's walk away and arrived the day of a fair: "My

brother put a bunch of oak leaves in my little hat, and hired me out as a shepherd."2 Years later, Coignet would find himself shepherding the Imperial baggage wagons in the heart of Russia.

Coignet at eight years old, found himself guarding a flock of sheep next to a forest by the village of Chamois. His job was to prevent the sheep from straying into the dark wood. Suddenly a huge wolf ran out of the trees and tried to pull down one of the finest specimens in the flock. Young Coignet was soon holding the sheep by its hind legs while the wolf was pulling at the other end in a bizarre life and death struggle. Fortunately, two trained dogs took the wolf down, but here is an early indication of the pluckiness and toughness of this peasant boy.3

Later, at the fair at Entrains, he hired himself out for thirty francs a year to two farmers of Les Bardins. His job was to gather wood and take it to the wharves in three ox-drawn wagons: "I became covered with vermin, and was perfectly wretched."4 Every night, he slept alongside his oxen in a wood beneath the stars. Once, his charges wandered off whilst he slept and he had to look for them amidst the gloom. Soon his legs were torn to shreds by briers and blood was running into his wooden sabots: "Often, on my way, I used to encounter wolves, with eyes shining like sparks, but my courage never abandoned me."5 He was relieved to find his wayward teams. For three years the child who had once danced with a wolf, saw more of these predators than he did of other human beings. Verminous and dejected, he endured his torment with admirable fortitude and resolve.

At the age of twelve, Coignet returned to his home village, where even his father no longer knew him. At Sunday Mass: "I had at once recognized my father who sung among the choristers; little did he know that one of his children whom he had abandoned was so near him."6 Only now, did Coignet learn the fate of Alexander and Marianne, his little brother and sister. The Beauty had taken them to the forest of Druyes and left them there to die. Fortunately, after three days of tearful wandering they were found by Father Thibault a miller who took them into his care. Not surprisingly, Coignet could not stand the sight of his stepmother and he did his best to avoid her.

Hiring himself out to his half-sister, who had no idea they were related, he became a stableboy at an inn and a go-for – 'go for this... go for that'. Red-headed Coignet felt bitter and must have cried himself to sleep on many an occasion: "so great was my mortification at the idea of being a servant in my sister's house and that at my father's door."[7] But life for young Coignet was about to change.

"Chance makes a plaything of a man's life," Seneca wrote.[8] And so it was that by sheer chance, two gentlemen horse-traders stopped at the inn on their way to the fair at Entrains. Asked by them to be their guide, Coignet made the acquaintance of Monsieur Potier and Monsieur Huzé. Potier proved to be his saviour. Although short and ugly in Coignet's eyes, Potier had a heart of gold. When he heard of the terrible treatment Coignet had received at the hands of his own family, he decided to take the intelligent twelve-year-old boy under his wing. At a tearful denouement with his father, stepmother and half-sister, the whole village turned out to wish Coignet a safe journey.[9]

His new home was at Coulommiers, only fifteen leagues (45 miles) from Paris. Coignet was full of praise for his new employer: "He did not seem like a master, he was a father to everyone. A disagreeable word never fell from his lips."[10] After saving Potier's prized pigs during a flood, Coignet became his acting 'secretary'. For this bright but illiterate peasant boy this was like a dream come true.

Eventually, he accompanied Potier to the Reims fair to buy horses to sell to the new peers of the Republic. Suddenly, he found himself with fifty-five horses to train. It took him two months: "At the end of that time I was worn out; my lungs were affected, I spat blood, but I had acquitted myself with honour."[11] Then the peers came to inspect the new horses in person. Coignet rode all the horses and was praised for his skill. One very special animal was reserved for the *procureur* of the Republic. He decided to present it to the president of the Assembly and so pleased was the *procureur* that he offered

Coignet a job. Loyal to Potier, he refused, but what social circles young Coignet was now moving in![12]

Accompanying Potier to the École Militaire in Paris, he again demonstrated his talents as a trainer and rider. As a result of Potier's fair dealing there was a further order for 200 artillery horses with tight specifications as to the type of animals accepted by the Military. Potier found 300 and all were accepted. A decade later, it was the lack of such fine animals that cost Napoleon his Empire, after thousands of artillery and cavalry horses were lost in Russia.[13]

Despite his abilities, the École Militaire did not give Coignet the customary personal fee and he was most disappointed. Potier, however, gave him a watch, two hundred francs for training the peers' horses and two louis (forty francs), for the special mount: "What a fortune it was for me!"[14] Coignet wrote. Potier made 30,000 francs from the two deals. The quality of French cavalry depended upon such men.

Coignet could put his hand to anything. He learnt how to plough and to mill flour: "At sixteen I could lift a bag like a man. At eighteen I could lift a bag weighing three hundred and twenty-five pounds."[15] Young Coignet was one of the very few Frenchmen who could have 'lifted' the future Louis XVIII – who spent most of his exile happily, if somewhat lessé majesté, in England. However, by now, "the position of being a servant began to be exceedingly distasteful to me. My thoughts turned towards a soldier's life."[16]

His trips to the École Militaire, the sight of fine uniforms and the camaraderie of military men, had stirred his imagination. Nevertheless, knowing which side his bread was buttered on, he remained with Potier until he was conscripted. Even then, he was so prized that his master would have bought him a substitute if necessary.[17] However, Jean-Roch Coignet sensed that he had another destiny.

Coignet joined the Army shortly before Napoleon returned from Egypt in 1799. He had once told Potier: "If ever I am a soldier, I will do my best to get into the hussars; they are so splendid."[18] In fact, he began his career as a grenadier. Sent to wretched barracks at Fontainebleau, he became part of a battalion of 1,800 men under General Lefebvre. After two months, they heard that Napoleon was on his way to Paris. This electrified them all: "Our officers were full of excitement, because the chief of our battalion knew him, and the whole battalion was delighted by the news."[19]

Soon, they heard that Napoleon was coming to Fontainebleau. Impressed by the battalion's turn out, he gave orders for a march to Courbevoie as cries of "Vive Bonaparte" filled the air. Sent on to the École Militaire, which Coignet knew from his days as a horse-trader, a distribution of cartridges was made to the soldiers. Finally, they reached St. Cloud. Napoleon had decided on a little bill and coup with the discredited, corrupt representatives of the people – the Directory.[20]

Coignet sets the scene: "The grenadiers of the Directory and the Five Hundred were in line in the front court; a half-brigade of infantry was stationed near the great gate, and four companies of grenadiers behind the guard of the Directory. Cries of "Vive Bonaparte" were heard on all sides..."[21]

Napoleon saluted them all and spoke to their officers. Coignet saw him go up the steps alone. Then there were cries and Napoleon came out and climbed the steps again with a platoon of grenadiers: "Then the noise increased... We saw stout gentlemen jumping out of the windows..."[22]

A new broom had swept the fetid hall of stale politicians. The coup of Brumaire had changed the destiny of France.

Frank McLynn states that: "the Guardsmen, who guarded the Chateau and officially owed their loyalty to the Assembly... had been considering their position. The deciding factor had been their conviction that if they did not obey Napoleon and his allies, he would unleash on them Murat's irate troops slavering outside the Chateau and they would suffer the same fate as the unfortunate Swiss Guardsmen in the Tuileries on 10 August 1792."[23]

This rather emotional and sensational passage does not accord with what Coignet saw, an eyewitness to the events in question. The cries of "Vive Bonaparte" Coignet heard "on all sides" and Napoleon's enthusiastic welcome generally by the soldiers, probably had far more to do with their compliance. It is worth adding, that Napoleon saved the life of one of those very Swiss Guards. As a young man, he himself had been an eyewitness to that catastrophe and had been traumatised by the callous bloodshed going on all around him. So McLynn must not be allowed to get away with this crass attempt at guilt by association.24

Coignet was soon 'adopted' by two old sweats when they discovered just how much money Potier had given him when he left Coulommiers. For the odd dozen drams, they trained him in drill for four hours a day and two hours a day of fencing during a winter spent in Paris.25

In 1800 Napoleon returned to Italy and Coignet found himself at St. Pierre at the foot of the formidable St. Bernard pass. Cannons had to be placed in hollowed-out tree trunks and dragged up the slopes. Coignet was placed at the front of ten men on the right side of one cannon, next to the precipices. Slipping and sliding, they eventually reached the snow where the going was smoother.26

Arriving at the famous monastery at the top, the monks gave the soldiers bread and cheese and a bucket of wine for every twelve men. Coignet wrote: "I cannot find words to express the veneration I feel for those men."27 The Army then had to by-pass the impregnable fort at Bard and they did so, at the dead of night, with shoes and wheels padded with straw. Then they descended into another world, a paradise with beautiful cities like Milan.

At Montebello, Coignet had his baptism of fire. After initial progress had been made, the Austrians retaliated. At the entrance to the village the French were met by grapeshot. His Captain, Merle, told the men to dive into trenches but Coignet did not hear him: "I rushed past our drummers, towards the gun, and fell upon the gunners... I bayoneted all five of them, then leaped upon the piece and my captain embraced me as he went by. He told me to guard my cannon..."28

Shortly after, General Berthier galloped up and in his nasal tone he asked him what he was doing. Upon hearing of Coignet's bravery, he took note of his name and told him to visit the First Consul with his Captain at ten o'clock. He rejoined Merle just in time to save his life by shooting a Hungarian grenadier who had him in his sights. Seeing a French sergeant surrounded by three enemy grenadiers, Coignet killed two of them with his bayonet while the sergeant dealt with the third. So it was, that on his very first day of battle Jean-Roch Coignet accounted for no less than eight enemy soldiers.[29]

Napoleon arrived in time to see the battle won. Later, a nervous Coignet was presented to him. He "took me by the ear. I thought he was going to scold me, but, on the contrary, he was very kind..." Napoleon said: "it is a good beginning,"[30] and instructed Berthier to put Coignet down for a musket of honour. He also promised him a place in the Guard when he had served in four campaigns. Coignet was then embraced by the sergeant whose life he had saved and the whole Company cheered him.

As well as being brave, Coignet was generous and he made friends easily. Despite the way he had been treated himself as a boy, he was always kind to friends and strangers alike. That day he had saved the lives of two of his comrades, later, in the freezing snows of Poland, he would save the lives of his starving regiment. It is no wonder that he was popular.

The Battle of Marengo that followed was as closely fought as Waterloo. Following the retreating Austrians, the French found nothing to eat as all the villages had been pillaged. After a night march the men were hungry and exhausted. A couple of days later on June 13th, they were placed in line of battle. All night they stood to arms until attacked the following morning. Coignet was led into battle with a company of grenadiers only to find a column of Austrians deploying in front of him: "The balls came from every direction, and I was obliged to lie down... I believed myself lost."[31] When his division advanced he was able to extricate himself, one of only 14 survivors out of a company of 170. All the rest had either been killed or wounded.

Blasted by Austrian artillery, the French had to give way: "no one came to our support. Our musket-barrels were so hot that it became impossible to load for fear of igniting the cartridges.

There was nothing for it but to piss into the barrels to cool them…"32 Austrian cavalry then drove in the platoons of Coignet's half-brigade, sabring everyone within reach. Coignet took a savage blow that almost cut his queue off, causing him to tumble into a ditch.33 Kellerman's French dragoons retaliated and, on his back in the ditch, Coignet saw the huge horses jumping over it, first in one direction then the other as they pounded the ground within inches of him. Desperate now, he grabbed the tail of a retreating dragoon's horse and was catapulted away, only to fall senseless soon after. Staggering back to his own lines he was ordered to the rear because of his wound but he insisted on remaining to fight on. But all the French had to withdraw for the enemy was far too strong.34

Napoleon appeared: "Courage soldiers… the reserves are coming. Stand firm!" The men shouted "Vive Bonaparte!"35

By two o'clock even the officers were saying that the battle was lost. Finally, the reserves arrived. They got into position behind a very tall hedge, which concealed even the cavalry. When the Austrians approached, thinking the battle won, they received a rude awakening. General Desaix's division routed them. Four thousand prisoners were taken. Coignet got a scratch on his right eyelid parrying a bayonet thrust. His opponent was not so lucky - he became Coignet's ninth victim.36

That evening Merle invited Coignet to supper. Coignet used the opportunity to ask to go the headquarters to see some acquaintances in the Guard. With a companion he went to the chateau of Marengo and asked for a certain cavalry sergeant who had been in the guard of the Directory for nine years. When the man appeared, Coignet reminded him that he had trained his cavalry mounts. Presented to his captain, he was given bread and five francs to drink the health of the captain whose cavalry charges had saved the day at Marengo. A bottle of brandy was given to Coignet to present to Merle.37

On the way back: "We saw the battlefield covered with Austrian and French soldiers who were picking up the dead and placing them in piles and dragging them along with their musket straps. Men and horse were laid pell-mell in the same heap, and set on fire in order to preserve us from pestilence."38 When he gave Merle the gift, his Captain said that Coignet must have been born under a lucky star. As if to make up for his hideous childhood, he did seem to have a charmed life as a soldier. He survived both Russia in 1812 and the Battle of Waterloo.

There was a closeness between officers and men in the French Army that did not exist in other countries at that time. There were many genuine friendships as epitomised by that between Coignet and Merle. The revolutionary spirit of equality had permeated all ranks. The common soldier was even allowed to approach his Emperor with a petition or request. Napoleon himself lived amongst his Guard when on campaign, sharing their food and chuckling at their antics. Coignet had a good sense of humour, like many of his comrades, and sometimes they even had their Emperor howling with laughter.

On June 26th, the defeated Austrians filed by as they began their retreat. They greatly outnumbered the surviving French. It took three days for their columns to pass by. Half of their stores were left to the ravenous French and forty leagues of countryside were ceded as they retired behind the Mincio. Coignet and his comrades followed on behind the rear of the Austrian columns: "they marched on the left and we on the right side of the road. No one quarrelled, and we were the best friends in the world."39

The wars that Austria launched against Napoleon were usually fought in a 'gentlemanly' style and, aside from the heat of battle, the common soldiers of each army respected their opponents as fellow professionals. It was very different from the wars to the knife that the French faced in Spain and Russia – as Coignet was soon to discover.

During the three months of truce that followed, Coignet was based at Cremona, a pesthole where he faced extreme want. He wrote to his father and uncle hoping for a little money. They both responded with excuses, neither sent him a sou. He even had to find the three francs to pay for their replies! His comrades both wrote on his behalf and read their words to him. He would never write to his father again.40

On September 15th the truce ended and Coignet was very glad to get back into the field. After 25,000 men crossed the Mincio river: "There was a terrible battle; our troops, thoroughly beaten, were obliged to fall back..."41 At another bridge three miles away, the French tried again. The *hussars de la mort*, wishing to avenge themselves for losses at Montebello: "fell upon the head of the Austrian column... sabred them and carried off six thousand prisoners and four colours. Our three battalions of grenadiers crossed immediately, under General Lebrun, a good soldier."42

The whole Army followed. After more carnage, the Austrians were forced to take the road to Verona. By-passing a fort where Austrian troops were bottled up, the French camped two miles beyond it. Coignet found himself on sentry duty a little after midnight in pitch-blackness. He was ordered to fire without warning at anything that moved. When the moon came out he saw a Hungarian in a fur cap approaching. He fired, alerting the whole Army and flashes of light stabbed from the mouths of many muskets into the darkness along the whole French line. There being no reply from the Austrians, when some of his comrades joined him, they went forward together. Coignet discovered that he had 'killed' a willow tree with a bushy top. His major said he had done his duty and that anyone could have been deceived.43

Coignet was sent via Viacenza to the marshes on the Venetian coast. When Mantua surrendered he was ordered to Verona to celebrate peace. Learning that his half-brigade was going back to Paris he was ecstatic, but when he arrived at Lyon, orders were changed – his new destination was Portugal.44

In tattered clothing, he started for Bayonne. Some French soldiers bought Malaga wine at three sous a bottle and became so drunk on account of its potency that they had to continue the journey on carts. After a week they had still not recovered: "Not a soldier could eat his ration, the wine had been so strong."45 They had to be spoon-fed. From Vittoria they went via Burgos to Valladolid. The straw they slept in was crawling with lice.

Coignet was delighted to be made a sapper on account of his, by now, impressive beard. At night all Frenchmen were confined to their billets because isolated soldiers were likely to be murdered by the Spaniards. While in Salamanca, where he spent his time at reviews, Coignet heard that peace had been made without a battle. When his quarter-master-sergeant was beaten to death with clubs by the local inhabitants the grenadiers caught up with the killers and bayoneted them. This was but a foretaste of the horrors the French would later meet with in Spain.46

Back in Bordeaux, Coignet was billeted upon a nervous old lady who did not like soldiers. It was not simply because his foot-long beard was intimidating. She told him what had happened to her during the Revolution:
"I have had terrible experiences. Robespierre sent fourteen members of my family to the guillotine, and the monster only spared me myself because I gave him thirty thousand francs' worth of plate and jewels. Yes, and he made me lie with him to save my husband's life, and then had him beheaded next morning. Such, sir, have been my family's sufferings. The scoundrel was punished in the end, but it was too late."47

If Robespierre was a child of the Revolution, he was illegitimate in every sense of the word. So much for liberty, equality and fraternity. Compared to him, Napoleon was reason incarnate. Well did Napoleon, the disparaged 'Corsican Ogre', rescue France from such Frenchmen. The Emperor even refused to execute his own worst enemies, Talleyrand, Fouché and Bernadotte, who were traitors to their country.

At Tours, Coignet met an old soldier of 102 who had served 84 years as a private in his half-brigade. Napoleon had given him the honour of eating at the general's table. When he was posted to Le Mans, Coignet got a letter from Paris from his long lost sister, Marianne. For years he had been tormented by not knowing what had happened to her and his brothers. A very sensitive man, Coignet had kept all this worries to himself. Soon he was nominated for the cross of honour by Merle and his Colonel. Better still, they made sure he was appointed to the Guard, as Napoleon had promised him after Montebello. Things were looking up for the peasant boy from Druyes.48

Everyone came to see him off and he carried 200 francs in back pay in his pocket. But most importantly: "I was glad to set out for Paris, and to be able to go and embrace my good sister whom I had not seen since she was seven years old."49

When he got to the Capuchin barracks near the Place Vendome, he was messed with the third company of the First Battalion. Renard, his Captain, was a short man with a big voice. Ironically, he told Coignet that he was too small to be in the Guard. Pointing out that he had a musket of honour and a letter from General Hulin for the Colonel, Renard decided to keep him in the company – but first he had to get permission from the War Office. Coignet told him that it was Berthier himself who had found him on the captured cannon.50

The next day, Berthier told Renard: "you will receive a letter for him tomorrow at ten o'clock; he is a soldier worth having, be sure to keep him in your company."51 From Berthier, Coignet was taken to the Iron Marshal, Davout. Despite his fearsome reputation, he greeted Coignet pleasantly: "You bring me a sapper with a fine beard," he told Renard. The Captain repeated that Coignet was too small to be in the Guard. Davout stated: "We must cheat the measure,"52 and personally advised them to place two packs of cards in his socks when Coignet was officially measured. So it was, with Berthier's blessing and Davout's connivance, Jean-Roch Coignet became the smallest ever member of Napoleon's Imperial Guard.

Coignet shared a cot with the tallest man in the regiment, at six feet four inches. He was a cheerful soul and dubbed Jean-Roch his 'dwarf'. He had burst out laughing as soon as he saw him. Coignet got off to a good start by giving ten francs to the Corporal of the mess – generous as always.53 As soon as possible, he arranged to meet his sister in the Place du Pont-Neuf: "She came to me crying with joy."54 He felt even more elated when he heard the news that his elder brother Pierre was also in Paris.

Soon after, the three of them met, however, Pierre was sceptical until Jean-Roch reminded him how he had hired him out as a shepherd: "At this he rushed to me, and we were all three locked in one another's arms, weeping with joy so loudly that every one in the house hastened to see the poor creatures who were now restored to one another after seventeen years of separation."[55]

Fate can be extremely cruel. The shock of the reunion was so great that Marianne took ill and died six weeks later. Pierre was utterly devastated and could not live without her. He was dead within three months: "I have never recovered from that trouble," Coignet wrote.[56] It is impossible to imagine the anguish he must have suffered. He had gone through so much heartache before he found them, only to lose them both almost immediately. And he still had no idea of what had happened to his other brother, Alexander.

NOTES

N.B. Coignet uses lower case for officers in his book. I have used Captain, Corporal etc. for *his* own officers to make things clearer.
1. *Captain Coignet* by Jean-Roch Coignet (1850) (www.Leonaur.com 2007) 7
2. Ibid. 8
3. Ibid. 8-9
4. Ibid. 9
5. Ibid. 9
6. Ibid. 10
7. Ibid. 12
8. Seneca Roman writer of the first Century AD. Quotation from title sequence of the film *Fire in the Sky*.
9. *Captain Coignet* op.cit. 21
10. Ibid. 25
11. Ibid. 35
12. Ibid. 38
13. Ibid. 39-40
14. Ibid. 41
15. Ibid. 41
16. Ibid. 41

17. Ibid. 55
18. Ibid. 55
19. Ibid 58
20. Ibid. 59-60
21. Ibid. 59
22. Ibid. 60
23. *Napoleon* by Frank McLynn (London: Pimlico, 1998) 218
24. See *Napoleon Immortal* by James Kemble (London: John Murray, 1959) 63 and *Napoleon* by Vincent Cronin (Harmondsworth, England: Penguin, 1971) 74
25. *Captain Coignet* op.cit. 62
26. Ibid. 63-66
27. Ibid. 66
28. Ibid. 71
29. Ibid. 73
30. Ibid. 74
31. Ibid. 77
32. Ibid. 78-79
33. A queue was the ponytail customarily worn by grenadiers. This, with a moustache and a couple of gold earrings, was de rigueur for later Imperial Guardsmen. Coignet had a thick head of hair even at the age of 72.
34. Ibid. 80
35. Ibid. 80
36. Ibid. 82
37. Ibid. 83-84
38. Ibid. 84
39. Ibid. 86
40. Ibid. 86
41. Ibid. 88
42. Ibid. 88-89
43. Ibid. 89-90
44. Ibid. 91
45. Ibid. 92
46. Ibid. 93
47. Ibid. 93
48. Ibid. 94
49. Ibid. 95
50. Ibid, 95-97
51. Ibid. 95
52. Ibid. 97
53. Ibid. 98
54. Ibid. 99
55. Ibid. 99
56. Ibid. 100

COIGNET OF THE GUARD: PART TWO
A BAND OF BROTHERS

"If there is one fact in history capable of incontestable proof, it is that from the assumption of power by Napoleon to his downfall, England lay at the bottom of nearly every war that desolated Europe; and it is equally clear that at the outset she had not a wrong to redress or a right to secure."[1]

Napoleon took every care of his 'children' – the Guard. Coignet describes a surprise visit to the barracks by him and General Lannes, his favourite. When the Consul saw that Coignet's bedmate was too big for his cot, he ordered new beds for everyone in the Guard. Napoleon walked through all the rooms, lectured the officers and even inspected the bread ration: "That is not the right kind. I pay for white bread. I wish to have it every day... order the quartermaster to come to me."[2] Nothing escaped his eagle eye. Aware that there was dissatisfaction amongst the men, he ordered a review and said he would listen to complaints.

At noon on the following Sunday, Napoleon appeared at the Tuileries on a magnificent white horse that had once belonged to Louis XVI. Walking amongst the soldiers, he received petitions and listened to the concerns of the rank and file. Coignet adds: "The petitions were almost all granted, and the contentment was general."[3] Napoleon was an expert at man-management and an incomparable leader of men.

English troopers were disciplined with the whip, Russians with the knout, but there was no corporal punishment in the French Army. Napoleon had been struck by an older boy during drill practice while a student at Brienne. He threw down his arms in protest. Subsequently, Alexandre des Mazis was assigned to instruct him and the two became great friends.[4] So, the First Consul had had first-hand experience of being beaten and the indignity of it was spared his own soldiers.

Even the officers had to address members of the Guard as 'Monsieur'. Wellington may have called his soldiers 'the scum of the earth', but Napoleon knew better. Guardsmen also outranked their fellows in the Line, a Corporal in the Guard being the equivalent of a Sergeant in the Line. It was jokingly said that even a donkey became a mule if it was assigned to the Guard. With such dutiful care, good pay, their first call upon the rations, and generous rewards for bravery and ability in the field, Napoleon won the loyalty, admiration, adulation and even love of his personal bodyguard. His own bearing in the face of the enemy was legendary.5

Unlike Tsar Alexander or Emperor Francis of Austria, Napoleon was often to be found where the action and fighting was at its hottest. At Wagram in 1809, as he directed his men under a veritable canopy of Austrian cannonballs, the Guard cried 'Emperor to the rear' and threatened to lay down their arms unless he complied. Reluctantly, he retired to the island of Lobau and watched the proceedings from high up in a tree! Coignet was a witness to this.6

On June 14th 1804 at the Invalides, Jean-Roch Coignet was awarded the Legion of Honour for his bravery. Before Napoleon, resplendent upon a throne with Josephine nearby, Prince Eugene Beauharnais holding the pins and Murat clutching the crosses, he heard his name announced to the august throng – the very first of 1,800 Guardsmen to be so honoured. But when he approached the foot of the throne, Eugene stopped him. Here, Murat interceded for him: "Prince, the candidates for the cross of the Legion of Honour are equals; he has been called, he can pass up."7

Those few words, in a nutshell, summarize the best aspects of the French Revolution. And through his greatness, Napoleon spread equality to the humblest men in his realm, even to a former peasant boy from Druyes.

Coignet became an instant celebrity, with beautiful women asking *him* for kisses and everyone wanting to see his cross. Back at the barracks, a sentry presented arms to him and he looked back over his shoulder in surprise – there had been an order to salute all recipients of the Legion of Honour. Coignet was so pleased he forced the soldier to accept five francs and invited him to breakfast. Later, his Lieutenant insisted Coignet accompany him to the Palais Royal where everything was free to him: "How delightful that evening had been to me. I had never known anything like it before."[8] Such were brave men, even common soldiers, treated in Napoleonic France.

However, as so often in life, behind every silver lining there lurked a dark cloud.

A few days later, again at the Palais Royal, a stranger begged him to accept a cup of coffee in celebration. At first he refused, but the man was dogged. Relenting, Coignet followed him to the Café de la Régence. There he drank a cup of black coffee – very black coffee, for it had been laced with poison. Suddenly, the stranger disappeared and almost immediately, Coignet collapsed in agony. Taken to the hospital at Gros-Caillou, he spent eight days and nights in acute discomfort. Massages, stomach pumps, nothing seemed to help him.[9]

Fortunately: "My condition was reported to the First Consul, who ordered two physicians to attend me during the night, and attendants day and night. Every possible care was lavished on me."[10] For forty days, Coignet suffered. Finally, Baron Larrey, Chief Surgeon to the Guard and esteemed by Napoleon as the best man he ever met, was called in and his remedies saved Coignet's life.

Slowly, he recovered, and he had no doubt as to what had happened. It was: "revenge which had been attempted upon me by one who could not wreak it upon the First Consul himself; for it was one of the spies of Cadoudal who had watched his opportunity to kill me."[11]

This episode demonstrates the depths to which royalist assassins would stoop. They did not care if innocent people suffered, just so long as they could vent their spleen with another atrocity in the name of the 'divine right' principal. It is abundantly clear that they had no principles and all their murderous exploits were paid for with English gold, secretly supplied without the knowledge of Parliament by a criminal cabal in the Cabinet.[12]

In contrast, we see the care and attention Napoleon was prepared to give in order to save the life of just one of *his* soldiers. This says everything about Napoleon's view of equality and fraternity – his actions speak louder than mere words. Years later in Russia, Coignet was horrified when the Russians allowed their wounded men to be burnt to death by their own side in order to deny French soldiers shelter. Similarly, Tsar Alexander and Emperor Francis fled the field after Austerlitz without a thought for their wounded. Coignet describes time after time how Napoleon always camped on the battlefield so as to give succour to the wounded of *both* sides.

In his book *The Eagle in Splendour*[13] the English 'historian' Philip Mansel talks of "the Emperor's endless wars"[14] and he states that: "By 1809, or earlier, the army and its leaders were beginning to tire of fighting."[15] He does not say here that the war of 1809 was started by an Austrian invasion of Bavaria, Napoleon's ally, without even a declaration of war. Nor does he mention the generous dollop of gold the English Cabinet gave the Austrians to encourage them in yet another fatal miscalculation – Napoleon defeated them yet again. As he had done in 1805 when English gold brought both them and the Russians into the field against France.

After talking of *Napoleon's* wars, on Page 163, Mansel then completely contradicts himself by adding that: "Although some wars were started by other powers (for example, those of 1806 with Prussia and of 1809 with Austria), their real cause was the Emperor's disregard of neutrality combined with his apparently limitless appetite for territorial expansion."[16] As we have seen, this is utter nonsense.

He then makes the astonishing assertion on Page 178, that: "Francis I of Austria was a simple, peaceful monarch..."[17] This is risible. What then was he doing in 1805, 1809, 1813 and 1814, when Austria attacked France? Did he simply have his back turned or was he asleep? Austria played its unsavoury part in the dismemberment of Poland in the C18th. The leopard had not changed its spots in the early C19th.

Furthermore, Francis I helped to disinherit his own grandson in 1814. He denied Marie Louise access to Napoleon when the

Emperor was in Elba and he set her up with a one-eyed lover Neipperg, to distract her from her marriage vows. The misery endured by Napoleon's son at the Austrian Court is well known. Yes, Francis was a real charmer.

Mansel's book is a collection of beautiful pictures threaded together with malicious invective. His pompous, one-sided fiction reads like a belated apologia by Cecil Rhodes for the British Empire in Africa, as if the English were empowered with a divine right to conquer races and peoples less fit for domination than themselves. The Oxford man writes with such arrogance himself that he could have been at the Oxford Court of Charles Ist during the *English* Revolution, not a dispassionate historian reflecting upon the history of two competing powers that had been in conflict for over fifty years. The dust jacket of his book says of Napoleon: "His policy of territorial expansionism was pursued with an arrogance and inhumanity which turned all Europe against him."[18]

Why was it then, that in Europe the running joke was that 'England will fight to the last drop of Prussian, Austrian and Russian blood.'[19] Or, that the Emperor Francis, in a rare moment of enlightenment, stated that 'the English trade in human flesh.'[20] Rather than talking of the Eagle in splendour, he tries to make Napoleon out as little more than a plucked chicken. He fails abysmally. *England* really started the war after the Treaty of Amiens, the war of 1805, the war of 1809 – and the war of 1812 against the Americans.

Mansel either betrays his ignorance or else he consciously deploys misinformation in his campaign of vilification. Either way, he defeats his object. It may be his story but it isn't history. Mansel's Napoleon always has a glass half empty, never half full. We need not dwell any longer upon his mischievous revisionism.

Coignet's Napoleon of 1850 is very different, as is Abbott's of 1855, Runciman's of 1919, Markham's of 1963, Cronin's of 1971, and Elting's of 1988.[21] Heine, Goethe and Nietzsche speak highly of him. Churchill thought that Napoleon was: "The greatest man of action born in Europe since Julius Caesar."[22] Chateaubriand, who was a Breton royalist and political enemy said he possessed: "The mightiest breath of life that ever animated human clay."23 Charles Whiting, the English historian calls him "Napoleon the Great".24

When Napoleon died in 1821, even former enemies were moved. Napier, the great historian of the Peninsular War was devastated, and even though he was suffering himself from an old wound sustained in England's wars against France, he wept bitterly. Wilson, the English attaché to Kutuzov's Russian army in 1812 was deeply saddened. While Hazlitt, the great essayist and biographer of Napoleon was utterly inconsolable.25 Such men put the 'great' into Great Britain, yet they willingly acknowledged someone even more *fantastique* on the other side of the Channel.

Napoleon was a Titan, born into a world were men were no longer like gods. His great powers were feared and envied: his brilliance ensured his own eclipse. His monumental stature was insufferable to the petty tyrants that ruled the Europe of his day. Like Lilliputians they conspired to bring him down.

So why do people write books about a person they so clearly hate? Perhaps jealousy and envy are part of it – and the fact that they themselves are obviously captivated by the man they seek to impugn. On average, three books a day are written about Napoleon, a thousand a year. Now, they are over 300,000 of them.26 If Napoleon was so inconsequential, hateful and incompetent as many insist, why do they bother?

More books have been written about Napoleon than any other human being who has ever graced the face of the Earth. Thomas J. Vance hits the nail on the head when he says of Americans: "they were captivated by Napoleon's achievements through talent as opposed to birthright like many other European heads of state. Napoleon was celebrated as a self-made man."27 Plays were produced about him as early as 1820 in the States and by 1859 fifteen towns were named after him.28

Furthermore, the long-suffering English taxpayer saw the National Debt of his country soar because of the bellicose policies of Pitt and his ilk. And it was the poorest members of society that suffered, the so-called 'lower orders', not the 'great and the good' that had got the country into such horrendous debt. There was always plenty of money to pay for the Prime Minister's port, while even Charles James Fox of the peace party could squander hundreds in a night's gambling. If we British need heroes, we can find them in Churchill, or Churchill's own hero, Alfred the Great – we do not need to search for them amidst the dregs of the aristocracy that crushed all dissent in Britain in the early decades of the C19th.[29]

Long after Napoleon had been exiled to Saint Helena and could no longer be used as an excuse for internal repression, the British authorities were massacring their own people – as at Peterloo in 1819 – where innocent men, women and children were charged by mounted militia in Manchester and many were killed, simply for debating how the country was being run. When he became Prime Minister, Wellington was dead set against an extension of the franchise.

Well might George Bernard Shaw say of Napoleon in the preamble to his play *The Man of Destiny* (1897) that: "it is even now impossible to live in England without sometimes feeling how much that country lost in not being conquered by him..."[30]

How many 'English' Coignets never got their chance to shine and raise themselves out of the mire because of the aristocratic stranglehold on power? Privilege prevented progress in the benighted realm of George III – and it wasn't just the King that was insane. Britain at that time had a virtual caste system.

After his brush with death, Coignet was allowed to return home to recuperate. As if in compensation for his recent ordeal, he heard that his brother Alexander was still living with Thibault the miller and they were soon reunited. At Druyes a crowd was waiting for him: "There he is, good M. Coignet; he has not wasted his time, he has won that fine cross! The good God has blessed him on account of all the suffering his stepmother made him endure!"[31] Embracing his father, they made up, but he still refused to have anything to do with The Beauty.

Coignet was soon inundated with invitations. He even received a letter from the prefect of the Yonne written at the command of Davout, inviting him to take part in a wolf hunt. Once again, Davout belies the cold character attributed to him by many writers. He personally requested Coignet's company, demonstrating the 'band of brothers' mentality that was so pervasive amongst the Guard: "The marshal recognized me immediately. 'Here is my grenadier,' said he to the prefect... 'This is the smallest of my grenadiers. Now make yourself thoroughly happy in your native place.' "32

When he got back to Paris, he placed Alexander with a wine-merchant. At the barracks he heard about the preparations for an invasion of England and soon he was taking part in manoeuvres by land and upon the water. Coignet describes how two hundred pinnaces went out to sea in line, "commanded by a good admiral, who was on a fine frigate in the middle."33 And day after day, the men drilled onshore.

At the camp of Ambleteuse he got a visit from his old bedmate. His giant friend had left the Guard under unusual circumstances. One night, on the way to bed, the First Consul saw him on guard outside his chamber and he paused in amazement: "There was more than sufficient cause for his astonishment. Imagine a man six feet four inches tall, wearing a bearskin cap eighteen inches high and a plume at least a foot higher than the cap."34 Napoleon decided he would make a good drum major and sent him to find his officer.

In confusion, the man left his musket on the floor and came back for it. Napoleon said: "Never mind, I will watch it, and wait for you."35 When the Guardsman told his officer the 'little corporal' was on duty in his place he was not believed. However, when the two of them returned they saw him pacing up and down beside the musket. Soldiers often spoke of Le Tondu standing in for their exhausted comrades on guard duty and they were never believed. Here, is one occasion when it definitely happened.

Coignet gives an interesting account of a tussle with the Royal Navy. A 74 gun vessel sailed close to shore and unleashed a broadside into the French camp. A man called Despienne begged Napoleon to be allowed to fire back with a mortar, claiming he could hit the ship in two shots. The first flew over the rigging but the second fell directly amidships: "There was a shout of joy. 'I will make you lieutenant in my artillery,' said he to Despienne."[36]

Small French boats then pursued the stricken vessel and others that came to its rescue: "It was a sight to see our little terriers after their great hounds. The English tried to return to the charge, but they were roughly received... Our little boats made havoc of them."[37] The Admiralty had unleashed the dogs of war, only for the French to shoot their fox. Not every naval engagement was a foregone British victory, despite the received wisdom amongst many English historians.

On the eve of embarkation for his Channel crossing, Coignet and his comrades were given new marching orders. The Austrian lust for the gold languishing in the vaults of the Bank of England had worked its black magic, so Emperor Francis and Napoleon were at war. Coignet had to march day and night with men tumbling into ditches all around him, fast asleep. Eventually, it was his turn. Napoleon had his 'long boots on' and the Grand Army was striding towards a masterful encirclement of the Austrian forces at Ulm, with Ney and Murat in the vanguard.[38]

At Ulm the dwelling of a citizen went up in flames. Napoleon blamed his Guard who had lit fires in order to dry themselves after a river crossing. He was furious: " 'You shall pay for it,' said the Emperor angrily. 'I will give six hundred francs and you shall give a day's pay. Let that sum be immediately paid over to the owner of the house.' "[39] As a consequence, the 'victim' became very rich. Later, at Moscow in 1812, Napoleon did his best to save the houses and palaces in the city from the fires started on the orders of the Russian governor, Count Rostopchin. He was always adamant that ordinary citizens and noncombatants should not suffer unduly from the ravages of war.

On October 19th 1805, General Mack surrendered. How did Napoleon treat this defeated army? Coignet states that: "General Mack came at their head to surrender his sword to the Emperor. This the Emperor refused to accept (all the officers and generals retained their swords and knapsacks), and he talked a long time with the superior officers."40 This was strange behaviour for a 'Corsican Ogre'.

The Grand Army then made forced marches to Vienna. The soldiers joked: "Our Emperor makes war not with our arms but with our legs."41 They covered up to sixty miles a day. Coignet saw Schoenbrunn, the palace of the Austrian Emperor and, before long, after marches through villages covered in snow, the Army arrived at Brunn in Moravia, where Napoleon established his headquarters.42

In a small place nearby called Austerlitz, history was about to be made.

"The Emperor went our every day to make reconnaissances along the line, and returned satisfied. He seemed delighted; his pinches of snuff took effect (this was always a proof of his contentment), and with his hands behind his back he went about talking to everyone."43 No one would have guessed that the French supply lines were stretched to breaking point, that many of the soldiers were on the brink of exhaustion, or that the Russians and Austrian armies under the joint command of Tsar Alexander and Emperor Francis greatly outnumbered the French. In the deathly ballet that was soon to follow, it was as if Napoleon had choreographed every move the enemy was about to make and had told them exactly when to make them. He was on the eve of one of the greatest military victories ever – only a few battles like Cannae come anywhere near it in military perfection.44

On the evening of December 1st 1805, Napoleon began a visit to the outposts. His horse-grenadiers carried lighted torches which encouraged the Guard to set fire to brands of straw. A resounding cry of "Vive l'Empereur!' rent the air. Drums thundered and the bands played. Above them, on the soon to be famous Pratzen Heights, bemused Russians gazed down upon the spectacle.45

On the morning of December 2nd, 25,000 men of the Guard waited with baited breath alongside the rest of the Army. Then: "The drums and music mingled together. It was enough to make a paralytic move forward."46 Like a fast-forward video the battle whirled in a tumult of sound, fury, blood and gore. At first the Russians seemed to have the upper hand, but Napoleon's masterplan proceeded with robotic logic, his soldiers drilled to perfection in the sea breezes of Boulogne.

Coignet describes how one of Napoleon's Mamelukes brought three different standards to the Emperor's feet. Napoleon tried to stop him from descending into the melee yet again but the unknown hero died soon after. The Russian imperial guard fought magnificently but Bessières 'black horses', the French mounted grenadiers, responded to the challenge.[47] Coignet's turn came and the Guard charged forward to attack the Russian infantry and for several terrible minutes no one knew who had the upper hand. Then, as Napoleon used to say, the 'moment of decision' came – and the enemy retreated into a valley of frozen ponds. French cannon balls smashed into the ice sheets and added to the panic of the enemy: "All the troops clapped their hands, and our Napoleon wreaked vengeance on his snuff-box; it was a total rout."[48]

Coignet and his friends liked a good laugh. After the high tension of battle, they were obviously in the mood. When a confused hare hopped toward them Captain Renard tried to skewer it with his sabre and he ran after it until it disappeared down a hole. All the while the soldiers cried: "The fox won't catch the hare..."[49] Coignet reveals the bonds that united the men of all ranks when he adds: "so we laughed at him, and we laughed so much the harder, because the captain was the best man in the world, esteemed and loved by all his soldiers."[50] As for Napoleon: "the Emperor occupied himself in seeing that the wounded were picked up."[51]

That night, the temperature plummeted. In a nearby village Coignet discovered a huge pine cask like a giant coffin and he manhandled it back to the bivouac. Captain Renard asked if he could share this novel sleeping arrangement. Packed with straw and topped by a feather bed, it made a comfortable roost for the pair. Renard told him: "I shall remember you all my life."[52]

After Francis of Austria came to make peace – the Tsar had fled weeping like a baby – the Guard was eventually sent back to France. On the way, the Bavarians welcomed them.[53] Like

Bourgogne, Coignet found that the Germans, especially the women, often preferred the French soldiers to their own. Perhaps they had a little more je ne sais quoi.

At Meaux, in Brie, Coignet was billeted on a rich woman who always sent such inconvenient travellers to an inn. When she told him she did not take lodgers, Coignet said that, as he was tired, if she would go and buy him a bottle of wine with the fifteen sous he offered her, he would leave. When she returned, she found him in her bed, rolling around as if seriously ill. The shrew had to spend the night on the sofa: "The neighbours were delighted with the joke I had played."[54]

In 1806 Jean-Roch took part in the Jena campaign. On October 13th, the soldiers had to haul their cannon up a steep incline to a high plateau in the dead of night, Napoleon directing everything. Scrounging for supplies from deserted houses nearby, the men returned with plenty of wine and sugar and made merry. Coignet adds that they drank the health of the King of Prussia all night long. As for Napoleon: "Seeing us all so happy, put the Emperor in good spirits."[55] When he did his rounds, guided by a single light, the Prussians fired upon him, but he was unscathed.

In the early hours of October 14th, Prussian cannon announced the opening of battle. Darkness, then fog, caused the French to stumble and bump into each other. A halt was called so that the lines could be dressed. Marshal Lannes attacked on the left, the Guard advanced in the centre, and the Prussian line was broken. When the sun came out at ten o'clock, Coignet saw the carriage of the Queen of Prussia with its fairy tale team of white horses trying to make its escape.[56]

Renewed fighting on the left wing caused an angry Napoleon to send an officer to see what was happening - Ney's men were under attack from enemy cavalry. French horsemen were sent to counter the threat and the whole Army then advanced. Ney and Lannes in concert turned the tide and restored the Emperor's good humour.[57]

Murat brought a whole division of Saxons back, escorted by his dragoons and cuirassiers. The prisoners were covered in blood: "The Emperor reviewed them, and we gave them all wine... We had at least a thousand bottles of sealed wine left, and we saved their lives."58 They were given the choice of joining the French or remaining prisoners, as their ruler was not an enemy of France. He was, in fact, to become one of Napoleon's staunchest allies, loyal and steadfast, even when his troops deserted their post at a critical moment at Leipzig and notoriously changed sides, precipitating Napoleon's defeat at the Battle of the Nations.

Davout had an even more dramatic victory at Auerstädt where, with his single corps, he destroyed the main body of the Prussian army. Following this double hammerblow, Napoleon marched to Erfurt, Potsdam, then on to Berlin. He entered the Charlottenburg gate on his way to the King of Prussia's palace at the head of 20,000 grenadiers – Coignet somewhere amongst them.59

Coignet gives a little vignette of Napoleon: "the Emperor moved proudly along in his plain dress, with his small hat and his one-sou cockade. His staff was in full uniform, and it was a curious sight to see the worst-dressed man the master of such a splendid army."60 The locals crowded forward in an effort to see their conqueror, as eager as the Parisians after Austerlitz, a year before.

Coignet's adventures were just beginning and the two glorious victories would soon be forgotten in the desolate hungry wastes of a frozen Poland. In the distance lay the campaigns of Moscow and Waterloo. But Jean-Roch Coignet would rise to every challenge.

NOTES

1. Extract from an anonymous letter to the New York Daily Times, August 23rd 1853 supporting John Abbott whose Life of Napoleon was appearing in serial form in Harper's Magazine. Bishop Potter had castigated Abbott at the "Education Convention" in Pittsburg. Abbott's book *The History of Napoleon Bonaparte* was published in 1855.

2. Jean-Roch Coignet *Captain Coignet* (1850) (www.Leonaur.com 2007) 101

3. Ibid. 102

4. Vincent Cronin *Napoleon* (1971) 43 A senior cadet ignored regulations and rapped him over the knuckles, so Napoleon threw his musket at his instructor's head!

5. John R. Elting *Swords Around A Throne* (London: Weidenfeld and Nicolson, 1989) See this book for a host of fascinating details about Napoleon's Grand Army.

6. Coignet op. cit. 172. The actual words were: "We will lay down our arms, if the Emperor does not go to the rear instantly."

7. Ibid. 104

8. Ibid. 105

9. Ibid. 107   "I met a superb looking man..." Coignet states. Blue blood, black heart?

10. Ibid. 108

11. Ibid. 109   See also Cronin op. cit., 292-293. Georges Cadoudal was a Breton terrorist. In 1800 he was part of "the underground army working on orders from London for the restoration of Louis XVIII to the throne of France."

12. i.   See David Hamilton-Williams *The Fall of Napoleon* (London: Arms And Armour Press, 1994) Appendix II The Royalist Underground and the Chevaliers de la Foi 302-308. On 303-304 he states: "One of the leaders of the *Chouannerie* (a band of royalist guerrillas who had operated in Brittany and Normandy, and known as Chouans...), Georges Cadoudal, had been offered a commission in the army by Napoleon, after their resistance had ceased, but he declined and escaped to Jersey. There he formulated a plot to assassinate Napoleon with a bomb. *D'ARTOIS* was in agreement as was *WILLIAM PITT,* who authorized d'Auvergne to provide the half-ton of gunpowder, expenses, and to land Cadoudal on the French coast." (My capitals and italics) D'Artois was Louis XVIII's younger brother and heir, a truly obnoxious man.

ii.   Felix Markham *Napoleon* (New York: New American Library, 1963) 112-113 says "The English historian, Holland Rose, writing at the beginning of the twentieth century, comments, 'But when all is said the British Government must stand accused of one of the most heinous of crimes.' " In England, Pitt is often seen as a 'hero' – it is almost unbelievable. State sponsored terrorism was fine when *England* practised it.

iii. See http://napoleonistyka.atspace.com go to the section on the *British Army* then *Great Britain during the Napoleonic Wars* sub-heading *Britain and the coalitions against France*. This is an excellent website with information from many sources. It says: "British prime minister Pitt announced on 31 Jan 1793 that Britain was involved in a 'war of extermination' with France." No hostile intentions there then! At the time, Napoleon was 23 and virtually unknown outside Corsica. His Toulon exploits occurred later that year. It is *ridiculous* to call England's war against France and later, Napoleon, the *Napoleonic Wars.*

13. Philip Mansel *The Eagle In Splendour* (London: George Philip, 1987)

14. Ibid. 163

15. Ibid. 166

16. Ibid. 163

17. Ibid. 178

18. Ibid. As with all books of this kind, they blacken Napoleon's character *before* page 1. The dust jacket and the rest of the book belong in the dustbin of history – although I would save the pictures.

19. See http://napoleonistyka.atspace.com Article: *British Army* then under *Great Britain and the Napoleonic Wars* sub-heading *Britain and the coalitions against France* there is a quote from Mr. Nicholls in a speech to Parliament in July 1800: " 'even our allies had said that the English covered Germany with blood and gold.' In Europe was born (the) saying: "England will fight against Napoleon to the last drop of Prussian, Austrian and Russian blood'."

20. General Michel Franceschi and Ben Weider *The Wars Against Napoleon* (New York: Savas Beatie, 2008) 109 'On Dec 4, he (Napoleon) received the Austrian emperor in an improvised bivouac near Austerlitz, in order to discuss the basis for a peace treaty. Put at ease by the courtesy and good humor of his conqueror, the Emperor Francis let fall several confidences. He admitted to having been duped by the British: "The English trade in human flesh. There is no doubt that France was correct in its quarrel with England." '

21. Abbott and Elting were American, Cronin, Markham and Runciman, English historians.

22. http://www.boneybooks.com/

23. Ibid.

24. Charles Whiting *'45* (London: Guild Publishing, 1985) 139 Whiting is an excellent historian who actually fought in the war he writes about – WWII. He is scrupulously fair to Canadians, Americans, British and Germans alike.

25. http://www.freebookstoread.com/chrsh10_13.htm Characters of Shakespeare's Plays Wm. Hazlitt 13-14 (of 506) mentions both Napier and Hazlitt. For Wilson see Chapter Four *England's Unlikely Hero - Napoleon*.

26. Podcast 1 David Markham and Cameron Reilly 7/2/06 "An Introduction to Napoleon Bonaparte"

27. Article: Thomas J. Vance *The Faint Echo Of C19th American Napoleonic Biography* 1. at:

http://www.napoleonic-literature.com/Articles/Faint_Echo.htm

28. Ibid. 1

29. Alfred the Great held the last English enclave of Wessex against the Danish hordes, and saved the essential Englishness of the British nation. His grandson Athelstan destroyed the Northern Coalition of Scots, Norse Vikings and Northumbrians in AD 937 and extended the English realm. Both these men are far more important to English history than the likes of Pitt, Wellington, Canning, Nelson and Castlereagh.

30. Play: George Bernard Shaw *The Man Of Destiny* (1897) 1

31. Coignet op.cit. 111

32. Ibid. 113

33. Ibid. 114

34. Ibid. 115

35. Ibid. 116

36. Ibid. 117

37. Ibid. 117

38. Ibid. 118-119

39. Ibid. 119-120

40. Ibid. 120

41. Ibid. 120

42. Ibid.,121-122

43. Ibid. 122

44. At Cannae, Hannibal surrounded a much larger Roman army and utterly crushed it. An estimated 60,000 Romans died. To the Romans, 'might was right' – as it was with the divine right monarchies of Napoleon's day. When Napoleon left France in 1815, massive internal repression began at the insistence of Lord Liverpool, the British Prime Minister. Napoleon's former allies were hunted down and mercilessly executed.

45. Coignet op.cit.123

46. Ibid. 124

47. Ibid. 125

48. Ibid. 125

49. Ibid. 126

50. Ibid. 126

51. Ibid. 126

52. Ibid. 127

53. Ibid. 127

54. Ibid. 128-129

55. Ibid. 131

56. Ibid. 132

57. Ibid. 132

58. Ibid. 132

59. Ibid. 133

60. Ibid. 133

COIGNET OF THE GUARD: PART THREE
STARING DEATH IN THE FACE

"After victory, there are no longer enemies, only men."
(Napoleon)[1]

From Berlin, Coignet marched to the Polish frontier and on to
Posen and Warsaw. There was a foretaste of 1812 about it all:
"The Russians were good enough to give their beautiful cities
up to us, but they were not so generous about provisions; they
ravaged the whole country, and carried off everything to the
other side..."[2] The Russians were waiting on the far side of the
Vistula, the largest river in Poland.[3] At midnight, 500 French
swimmers stole across the water, carrying their muskets on
their heads. When Ney found boats to make a bridge, Napoleon
said: "That man is a lion."[4]

In Warsaw, Jewish businessmen secured the necessary
supplies for the Army: "the Jews saved the army as well as
made their fortunes."[5] The Emperor was doing his best to pay
his way in a foreign land. The general lack of provisions was a
harbinger of cruel deprivation to come. And the cold and frost
was setting in.

Reviews were held in preparation for a renewal of the
conflict. At one, the oldest man in Poland, supposedly 117,
presented himself to Napoleon.[6] When the roads were frozen
enough to facilitate travel, Coignet got his biscuit ration for
fourteen days. Deciding to supplement this meagre fare, he
spent twenty francs on meat – all his got for it was a pound of
ham.[7] When we recall that, back in France, 300 francs could
buy a decent horse, or in Spain, 3 *sous* bought a bottle of that
rot-gut Malaga wine, it can be appreciated that food prices had
risen astronomically. This would have made the men fearful for
their futures. When food simply could not be found, starvation
was bound to follow.

Coignet and his comrades, trudging along sandy roads, were
soon lost in the woods and forests. When they arrived at

villages they found them all deserted. Meanwhile, winter stalked them like an unseen predator and morale plummeted. What might be called 'Coignet's luck' came to the rescue. In a bivouac left by the Russians, he found two loaves secreted amidst some straw. In the dark, he carefully handed a piece of bread to Captain Renard. They later hid themselves in order to eat it.8 Again, this is so redolent of the 1812 campaign.

Snow gave way to thaws, soldiers sinking up to their knees in the boggy sand. Conditions got so bad that there were sixty suicides in the two days before the Army arrived at Pultusk: "Here we reached the depths of our misery, it could not possibly have been worse."9 Even Napoleon's carriage got stuck in the mud and he had to abandon it.

It was at Pultusk that the Emperor christened his Guard *grognards* or grousers.10 Indeed, they had plenty to bitch about. Coignet, true to his generous nature, decided to share two eggs he had bought with his Colonel. The officer insisted he take a gold napoleon in return. Food had truly reached the same sort of Klondike prices written of by Jack London during the Alaskan Goldrush.11 Coignet had worked for thirty francs a *year* as a boy.12

Some horse grenadiers saw a huge pig and they chased it back to camp. Coignet ambushed the beast and killed it with his sabre. Receiving his share of the spoils, he went to headquarters in search of salt. Only then did he discover that he and his comrades had taken their food from Napoleon's table. The Lieutenant on duty told him: "The Emperor was furious at losing his dinner... his stomach was as empty as anyone's."13

The next day there were only twenty potatoes for every eighteen men. It could not go on. Napoleon ordered Count Dorsenne to take the Guard back to Warsaw. Coignet describes France's elite soldiers at this time: "we were in a perfect state of starvation; hollow-eyed, sunken-cheeked, and unshaved. We looked like dead men rising from the tomb."14 He reckoned they had aged ten years in a fortnight. Fortunately, on New Year's Day 1807, they arrived at Warsaw and were treated like heroes by the Poles, the most loyal of Napoleon's allies.15

Then the Russians struck, moving towards the city. Napoleon responded and by early February the Army was marching towards Eylau. In the grip of an intense frost, the men were ordered to light a fire for the Emperor in the middle of the Guard. Each mess had to provide a log and a potato for him. Then, the victor of Austerlitz, the ruler of millions, got down on his haunches and baked 'tatees for his aide-de-camps.16 Whatever the weather, Napoleon was in his element, First amongst equals. He was king of a castle whose ramparts were the living bodies of the Guardsmen, his grousers.

To pass the time, Coignet became a barber. Sitting his punters on the rump of a frozen dead horse, he shaved them with soap and snow melted over the fire: "Perched on top of his bundles of straw, the Emperor watched this strange spectacle, and burst into peals of laughter."17

Such propinquity, such shared experiences, forged bonds of camaraderie between Napoleon and his Guard that were virtually unbreakable. He was one of them, he shared their meagre fare, their disappointments, as well as the same dangers of shot and steel. Is it a wonder that they revered him?

On February 8th the Russians fired twenty-two siege guns brought from Koenigsberg and caused havoc in the French lines.18 Bringing his Army forward, Napoleon stood near the church at Eylau. Like at Gettysburg in 1863, both sides engaged in savage fighting to control the cemetery – ironic to say the least. Although the French held on to the position, in front of Coignet, the 14th of the Line was destroyed and the 43rd crippled.19

Sénot, the drum major to the Guard,20 was told that his son had been killed: "So much the worse for him, I told him he was too young yet to follow me."21 For once, the story turned out to be false and the youth was later found alive. But things were hotting up in God's acre and amongst the snows. Even the pole carrying Coignet's regimental eagle was cut in two by a bullet.22

Napoleon had to send in the Guard to stabilize the situation. While the grenadiers charged with the bayonet, the horse grenadiers and chasseurs smashed into the Russian lines, returning with prisoners who were left later at Koenigsberg. The Emperor sent them fifty napoleons – 1,000 francs – in aid.23

Both armies had had enough and Coignet was realistic in his assessment of it: "We did not lose the battle, but neither did we win it."24 Napoleon was relieved: "Dorsenne, that was no joke for you and my grousers; I am very pleased with you."25

The survivors were in a wretched position. The following day as the dead were being buried and the wounded taken to the hospitals, some Jews came from Warsaw with casks of brandy. For six francs per man, a glass could be dipped, once only, into a barrel: "The four casks saved the army, and the Jews made their fortune."26 Even the soldiers escorting them were paid three francs a day, about ten times the normal daily rate. Brandy kept out the cold, restored circulation, settled upset stomachs and boosted morale. Well did the French call it eau-de-vie.

After a truce was agreed, the Army headed for Thorn and Marienburg. At Osterode, another deserted village, some potatoes were found. However, after diligent searching, the men also found hordes of buried treasure in the shape of food of all kinds. Coignet adds: "Our beloved Emperor did everything he could to procure provisions for us; but they did not come... So we had to go out, in all that terrible weather, in search of food."27

Coignet decided to form a hunting party to track deer amongst the snow, but the venison remained on the hoof and aloof, while hares bounded away unscathed. But as so often in a tight spot, providence seemed to smile on Jean-Roch. As he looked for the place in the forest where a hare had vanished some of the small pine trees came away in his hands. He had discovered a massive store of food buried underground, a cache that extended for a hundred square feet. Then, he noticed boxes high up in the trees – yet more stores hidden by the peasants.28

Back at the bivouac his comrades said: "Here is out ferret, it was he who found it all."29 Hence the smallest member of the Guard made the greatest contribution to their collective survival in those desolate wintry wastes. It took fifty men a whole day to unearth the stores of wheat, flour, rice, bacon and salted meat. There were twenty-five wagonloads of it. No wonder Coignet became a virtual mascot for his friends.

Coignet felt somewhat less charitable towards the Poles: "who wanted to starve us, for in our winter quarters we had passed fifty days without tasting bread... When we asked them for food, they always refused."30 It used to be said that a French radical had his heart on the left but his wallet on the right. For the Poles, Napoleon might have been in their hearts, but their food was in *their* stomachs.

Even the Russians came to the French begging for food. Coignet had an incredible sixth sense. When he noticed a peasant going to a garden every morning, as if checking it for something, he had it dug up. Beneath two stinking corpses of cows, there to dissuade anyone from further exploration, he discovered another huge cache – 1,500 pounds of rice and bacon. Without him, the Regiment would have starved.31

When the weather began to improve, a large camp was made at Finkenstein. Barracks were built and a palace of brick was constructed for Napoleon. Streets were named after battles and when provisions and wine came from Danzig morale was restored.32

Then, on June 5th Ney was attacked. At six the next morning, the Army marched towards Friedland. The Russians were waiting for them in a strong position at a ford across a river. Lannes came up from Warsaw in a bad mood with the Poles: "The blood of one Frenchman is worth all of Poland," he told Napoleon who replied: "If you are not satisfied, go away." Lannes said: "No, you need me,"33 addressing his Emperor with the familiar *'tu'*.

He was immediately sent to help Ney, opposing forces twice the size of their own. Eventually, Napoleon brought the rest of the Army up to the river: "The Russians fought like lions; they preferred to be drowned rather than to surrender."34 Coignet states that the Emperor slept on the battlefield as usual to make certain that the wounded were cared for.

On June 19th, the River Niemen was reached and there was a standoff as the bridges had been destroyed. When Napoleon arrived he sent bread to the Russians on the other side. Finally, Tsar Alexander saw reason and an envoy came to parley. The famous meeting at Tilsit was about to take place.[35]

A large raft was secured in the middle of the Niemen and a tent was erected upon it. Both rulers set off from opposite banks at the same time but, reaching the raft first, Napoleon went to offer Alexander his hand: "The two great men embraced each other as if they had been brothers returning from exile; and from every side rose shouts of '*Vive L'Empereur!*' "[36]

The following day the King of Prussia appeared alongside the Tsar. He did not impress Coignet, although Jean-Roch was struck by the beauty of Frederick William's queen. He adds that despite his victory, Napoleon was magnanimous and harboured no malice towards them.[37]

After the monarchs had reviewed Davout's Third Corps and the Guard, Coignet and his comrades were ordered to entertain their Russian counterparts. On June 30th there was a feast. The Russian soldiers did not seem to be au fait with French etiquette however. As they gorged themselves, they loosened their coats and filthy rags, used to beef up their appearance, tumbled out. Even worse, when they had eaten their fill they simply stuffed their fingers down their throats and the contents of their bellies tumbled out as well. Then they began eating all over again. Coignet was horrified.[38]

On July 10th, Napoleon left to go to Koenigsberg. Coignet and the Guard joined him by way of Eylau, remembering their fallen comrades. Only a few years later, they would pass another field of glorious dead - Borodino - as they retreated from Russia. At Koenigsberg, an English vessel came into port with supplies for the Russian army and the sailors were forced to surrender.[39]

When the Emperor received a visit from the Prussian rulers, Coignet got another look at Louise: "Lord how beautiful she looked with her turban on her head. It was said that she was the beautiful queen of an ugly king, but I think that she was both king and queen."40 Coignet was on duty only feet away from her. He adds that he would have given one of his ears to be with her as long as Napoleon was. Her charms were wasted on the Emperor. If there was one thing that Napoleon did not like, it was women engaging in politics.

When his Adjutant–Major, Belcourt, sent for Coignet to tell him he was being promoted to Corporal he reminded him that he could not read or write. Belcourt told him that when he was presented to the General he was to say he was literate and that he, Belcourt would see that he was taught by good men in the Regiment. Once again, a superior officer took his part.41

Put in charge of a mess of nineteen, he was given seven lazy but well-educated men. He was to shake them up, and they were to teach him his letters. This arrangement worked very well. His incredible memoirs attest to the fact. In celebration of his stripes and in thanks for his belated education, Coignet treated his 'teachers' and friends to a brandy in a café at a cost of twelve francs. On July 13th, he set off for Berlin.42

The atmosphere in the city was relaxed for everyone knew that peace had been made. When the occupants said that their own soldiers had not fought well, unlike the French and the Russians, Coignet corrected them: "Your soldiers are as brave as the Russians, and the Emperor had your wounded men well cared for; we carried them to the field-hospitals, as we did out own." In reply he was told: "How kind you are, corporal! You make us very happy. You have behaved in Berlin as though you were our own countrymen."43 In 1815, the Prussians would come to Wellington's rescue, having adopted Napoleon's own corps system. Imitation is the best form of flattery – unfortunately, in this case, for the French.

When he got back to Paris, Coignet continued his education, receiving instruction twice a day from his young soldiers. And deep in the Bois de Boulogne he perfected his drill. When Napoleon set up a swimming school, he had to admit that he was afraid of the water. The Emperor himself excused him from the compulsory lessons for the Guard. Belcourt decided to teach the tone of command to some of his men, Coignet amongst them. He applied himself with his usual diligence.44

In August 1808, there was a rash of parades and reviews - it was obvious that another war was brewing. The reign in Spain was falling down everywhere. Napoleon decided to spread some enlightenment, expecting the ideas of liberty and equality to be welcomed there as they had been elsewhere in the Empire. In October the order came to march to Bayonne. Coignet told his men what to expect, especially in regard to the local firewater.45

Yet, after a week in Valladolid, French soldiers were once again being spoon-fed their soup. In Burgos, the war took an even nastier turn. When some horse-grenadiers stabled their mounts by the church, a little boy beckoned one of them up some stairs by the side of the building to the belfry. When he vanished through a door, the soldier followed him. This happened twice and neither of the men reappeared. A third man was suspicious so a group of armed soldiers went up the stairs together. Firing a volley through the door, they opened it and discovered the decapitated bodies of their comrades. There were eight monks in the room and they and the boy were given a lesson in flying from the top of the belfry.46

In primitive Spain, the teachings of Christ had been perverted by ignorant priests and fanatics into a religion of assassination and torture. As the French were treated, so did they respond in kind and the outrages and atrocities duly increased. Even before the Grand Army arrived, many a village priest rutted amongst his flock rather than attempting to save their souls. Spain was still in the Dark Ages. It was an appalling situation for the French soldiers to be in, many of whom were nominally Catholics themselves.

Shortly after, Coignet joined the new King of Spain, Joseph Bonaparte, who was on his way to meet his brother. Napoleon was already on his way to Madrid. They caught up with the advance guard and on November 30th 1808, the battle of Somosierra took place. Here the Polish lancers covered themselves with glory, charging the Spanish guns high up in the mountains and clearing the way for an entry into the capital.47

Madrid did not immediately fall as even though the garrison was weak, the inhabitants, including the ubiquitous monks, had taken up arms. It took a sustained artillery bombardment to force them to surrender. Lannes then took Saragossa, but it was a bloodbath. Spanish civilians were virtually irregulars in their own right. When news came of an English army commanded by Sir John Moore that was trying to cut the French line of communications, Napoleon set out to destroy it. Yet more mountains had to be crossed, it was like the St. Bernard Pass all over again. The conditions were horrendous, the snowstorms blinding: "It was necessary to have an Emperor like ours to follow, in order to be able to resist it."[48]

The English army had bolted for the coast, closely followed by the French. In bleak January weather the Guard had to cross a freezing river that rose to their waists. On the far side Coignet marched to Benevento, which had been sacked by Moore's fleeing troops: "They killed all their horses and abandoned all their baggage-wagons and artillery."[49] For some reason, this episode is not as well known as Waterloo. Although Moore died, the bulk of his army escaped via the port of Corunna.

The Guard was ordered back to Paris. From Limoges they were conveyed in wagons to spare their legs. At Courbevoie they were reviewed by Napoleon, before being sent on their travels again, by coach and wagon to Lorraine. At Metz they could finally change their linen and put on their full uniforms. Thousands of people came out to see the famous Guard, including those of the fairer sex: "A high wind was blowing at the time, with the result that our shirts flew up in the air, and we had the field to ourselves in no time, for the ladies screamed with horror when they saw the handsomest men in France stark naked."[50]

Once dressed, the Grand Army was once again on its way – destination Vienna. Coignet volunteered to be one of twenty-five men who were to join the Emperor and mount guard at Schoenbrunn. This march turned out to be more than a marathon.

Reaching Schoenbrunn at midnight, the officers gave the men fifteen minutes' rest while they waited for Napoleon's orders an hour's march from the castle. When they finally arrived, he was furious. "What," said he, "have you marched my veterans more than forty leagues in two days."[51] Coignet had walked over 120 miles in 48 hours!

His legs and those of his companions had set like concrete. When Napoleon saw them all bent over and hobbling: "he became like a raging lion."[52] He ordered sweetened wine and had cavalrymen running around in order to see to their welfare, a nice sight for footsloggers used to the haughty attitude of their mounted troops, nicknamed 'the gods' for their aloofness. Coignet says: "The Emperor never left us; he stayed with us more than an hour."[53]

Soon Vienna fell, and the Austrian army crossed to the other side of the Danube after blowing the bridges. The river was in spate and crossing it in the face of the enemy was doubly dangerous. On May 18th, promotions were announced and Coignet became a Sergeant, the equivalent of a Lieutenant in the Line, with the right to carry a sword and cane in Paris.[54]

Lannes was ordered to lead the men across the river and take Essling, seconded by Marshal Bessières. When the French opened fire, 100,000 Austrians turned to face Lannes' single corps. Leaving Schoenbrunn with the Guard, Napoleon raced to his aid. At eleven o'clock Coignet was in the front line as were the rest of the bearskins. Rushing across Lobau island they stormed over the bridge at the far end: "As soon as the fight began a cannon-ball struck the Emperor's horse on the hip. At once all shouted, "We will lay down our arms, if the Emperor does not go to the rear instantly."[55]

To the left of Essling, fifty enemy guns were pointed at the Guard. At this somewhat inconvenient time, Coignet felt an urgent call of nature. The orders were that no one was allowed to retreat. So, with his usual sang-froid, Jean-Roch moved forward, turned his back to the enemy and dropped his trousers. A cannon ball ricocheted close by, bombarding his backside with stones. When he resumed his post Captain Renard said: "that was a near thing," to which Coignet replied: "It was sir; their paper's too hard, I couldn't use it."[56]

All the Guard had to fire back at the enemy were four cannons. Austrian cannon balls felled three men at a time and blew their bearskins twenty feet into the air. When the French gunners had been killed, Dorsenne replaced them with his grenadiers. They too were blown to pieces along with the guns. When a shell burst near the General, knocking him over and covering him with dust, Dorsenne got up and said: "Your general is not hurt. You may depend upon him, he will know how to die at his post."57

Coignet felt a pain in his arm and he thought it had been blown off. Then, he noticed a piece of flesh from one of his comrades sticking to his uniform. The cost of this battle was enormous for Lannes himself was hit by a cannon ball. Jean Lannes, the equal to Ney in audacity and bravery, had been at the spearhead of many a French victory. His own courage had often rallied his more nervous companions. Had he been at Waterloo, along with Davout, history would have been very different.58

Lannes' battered leg was amputated, he seemed to be recovering, but gangrene set in. In 1809 and for many years afterwards, that meant only one thing. Napoleon was distraught at the loss of his friend and he wept bitterly. This is another reflection upon Napoleon's character that is hardly ever mentioned in English history books. Once he had made a friend, he found it impossible to lose them. Coignet says: "We were all filled with dismay at our great loss."59

Lannes' corps panicked and retreated. By now, the Guard was stretched out in a single line and they rallied behind that inviolable wall. Bessières gave them a pep talk and even took them forward as sharpshooters. At this stage of the fighting a quarter of the Guard had fallen to the withering cannon fire without being able to fire a musket in reply. Behind them the bridges had been carried away by the fast flowing Danube. Had the Austrians realized this, it would have been an even worse day for the Grand Army.60

Coignet says that: "The battle was neither lost nor won,"61 but in the Courts of Europe and to Napoleon's enemies, it was viewed as an Austrian victory. What with the persistent troubles in Spain and a torrent of English gold ready to flow towards any enemy of France, the Empire itself was under siege. Archduke Charles asked for a three months' truce and this was quickly agreed to.62

The French withdrew to the island of Lobau and were stuck there for three days without bread. The Austrians had let loose their floating mills and these had smashed into the bridges linking Lobau to the mainland. Horses were eaten while in the background the screechings of amputees rent the air. As always, Larrey was doing his best to save men's lives.63

In the hiatus between battles, Napoleon fortified Lobau and prepared for the renewal of hostilities. Some 100,000 men prepared earthworks and redoubts. This time, nothing was to be left to chance. On July 5th the Army got ready. Eugene arrived with his Italians in time for the river crossing the next day, when the truce expired. Seven hundred French cannons waited. 64

The barrage began on both sides. The noise was tremendous, it was like the Ragnarok65 or the Day of Judgment, men were scattered like chaff, stilled in an instant by the projectiles fired by the devouring cannon. When his main Guard battery had lost so many men that they needed replacements, Napoleon was anxious lest the Austrians perceive how great was the damage they were doing to his centre. So he called for volunteers from the grenadiers. Everyone wanted to go.66

Fifty pieces were served by willing hands. They were like the hammers of Thor, such was the destruction they wrought. Napoleon paced up and down, taking snuff while, off to the right Davout was seizing the heights held by the enemy and driving them back upon the Olmütz road.67

At the critical moment, the Emperor sent forward his cuirassiers in one tumultuous body, the ground shaking as if in awe of their passing. They returned with fifty Austrian cannon. Eugene galloped up to tell Napoleon he had the victory. So ended the battle of Wagram. Such was the 'interest' returned to Emperor Francis for his investment in English gold.68

That night the Guard formed a square and Napoleon slept in the middle of it. The wounded were sent to Vienna: "The next day we found thirty cannon-balls which had fallen in one spot. It is impossible to give any idea of such a battle."[69] The hilt of Coignet's sword had been blown away, his arm was numbed, and he had seen many of his comrades die – but Jean-Roch Coignet was lucky, he had survived.

NOTES

1. Jean-Claude Damamme article: *Did Napoleon Merit The Reputation That Surrounds His Name*. See INS website: www.napoleonicsociety.com
2. Jean-Roch Coignet *Captain Coignet* 135
3. The Vistula river is the Wista in Polish and the Weichsel in German.
4. Coignet op.cit. 135
5. Ibid. 135
6. Ibid. 136 I take this incredible age with a pinch of salt. It reminds me of the Georgians that were supposed to be 160 a couple of decades ago. The oldest person ever was French - Jeanne Calment lived to be 122. (Feb 21st 1875 – Aug 4th 1997) She sold crayons to Van Gogh when she was a little girl.
7. Ibid. 136
8. Ibid. 136 It was as a result of these experiences in Poland that Napoleon organized such a massive supply chain prior to the invasion of Russia in 1812. Unfortunately, the roads in Poland, Lithuania and Russia were not up to the task. The weather and the poor quality of Supply troops did not help either. And, of course, it meant that there was no chance of a lightning, blitzkrieg-type of attack to separate Bagration's forces from Barclay's. Thus, no quick victory.
9. Ibid. 137
10. Ibid. 138
11. Jack London's stories about the Klondike Goldrush remind me of the experiences of Coignet and Bourgogne in Poland and Russia - accounts of Man versus raw Nature. See Jack London *Selected Short Stories* (New York, Airmont 1969)
12. See *Napoleon's Soldier - Little Big Man, Chapter One*
13. *Captain Coignet* op.cit.138
14. Ibid. 139
15. Ibid. 139-140
16. 'tatees is English slang for potatoes. In deepest Lincolnshire they once said 'tay'ats. The humble potato helped sustain the mighty Incan Empire – there are dozens of varieties. The Potato Famine in Ireland revealed the dependence of the Irish upon this simple tuber. Similarly, it was often the

mainstay of Napoleon's armies. Well indeed, did he say that an army marches on its stomach. Coignet would certainly have vouched for that.

17. Captain Coignet op.cit. 141 Here, Coignet reveals a side of Napoleon that is totally absent from many 'history' books. Napoleon had a sense of humour and he was happier when the people around him were happy. All this is very human, not *ogre-like* at all.

18. The writer lives in Conisbrough, England. Koenigsberg and Conisbrough mean exactly the same thing: the king's burh. Burh is Anglo-Saxon for a fortified place. This is a reminder of the ancient links between Germanic people and the Angles and Saxons who founded the English nation a thousand years ago.

19. Captain Coignet op.cit. 142

20. "Drum majors had their swords and usually a brace of pistols, but their best weapon was often their long baton with its loaded head." John R. Elting *Swords Around A Throne* 340

21. Captain Coignet op.cit. 142

22. Ibid. 142

23. Ibid. 142

24. Ibid. 143

25. Ibid. 143

26. Ibid. 143

27. Ibid. 144

28. Ibid. 144-146

29. Ibid. 145

30. Ibid. 146

31. Ibid. 147

32. Ibid. 147

33. Ibid. 148

34. Ibid. 149

35. Ibid. 149-150

36. Ibid. 150

37. Ibid. 151

38. Ibid. 152-153

39. Ibid. 153

40. Ibid. 154

41. Ibid 153 Coignet had literally *fed* many of his superior officers, hence their support for him.

42. Ibid. 156-157

43. Ibid. 157

44. Ibid. 158-159

45. Ibid. 161-162

46. Ibid. 162

47. Ibid. 163

48. Ibid. 164

49. Ibid. 165 Moore gained a tactical victory over Soult at Corunna, as the French failed to prevent the embarkation of the British troops. However,

this was a strategic defeat for the English in terms of the larger picture, as their influence was massively reduced in the Peninsular. Moore was killed in action, dying bravely. Soult ordered that a monument be erected over his grave – a tribute from one soldier to another.

50. Ibid. 167
51. Ibid. 169
52. Ibid. 169
53. Ibid. 169
54. Ibid, 171
55. Ibid. 172
56. Ibid, 173
57. Ibid, 173
58. Ibid. 174   The death of men like Lannes and Lasalle deprived Napoleon of some of his most aggressive and talented captains. Davout was kept in Paris in 1815 to quell treacherous spirits. Had he been at Waterloo in place of Ney, Wellington would not have stood a chance.
59. Ibid. 174
60. Ibid. 175
61. Ibid. 175
62. Ibid. 175
63. Ibid. 176
64. Ibid. 177-178
65. The Ragnarok is the Viking Day of Judgment when Odin, Thor and the gods from Asgard take on the renegade god Loki and his allies the Frost, Fire and Mountain Giants at the Final Battle to decide the fate of gods and men.
66. Captain Coignet op.cit. 178
67. Ibid. 179 See also David Chandler *The Campaigns Of Napoleon* (London, Weidenfeld Nicolson 1966) 714-715 for a detailed map of this battle.

COIGNET OF THE GUARD: PART FOUR
FIRE AND ICE IN RUSSIA

When Coignet left Schoenbrunn after Wagram, he was warmly received in the Confederation of the Rhine. Prior to Napoleon's rule, the smaller German states that made up the Confederation had been little more than counters in the great game played by Prussia and Austria to dominate them.1

When he returned to Paris, there was a great funeral ceremony for Marshal Lannes, including a cortège of 100,000 men. Jean-Roch was one of the sixteen men who carried his bier. Now a Sergeant on 43 sous a day, he continued with his drill practice and his education. However, Coignet felt self-conscious because his calves were not impressive in the silk stockings he now wore to go with his sword. So he bought a pair of false calves.2

When Captain Renard invited him for a meal with his family, he accepted, but he felt uncomfortable with all the well-to-do people around him – it was a bit much for someone from his peasant stock. Seated between two beauties, he was their centre of attention. Unlike the officers at the party, he was too shy to brag of his exploits either on campaign or between the sheets. Renard sang his praises instead adding: "In fact ladies, I should have been dead but for him."3

The next day, he received a letter from one of his admirers asking him to visit her. He found her: "dressed in a most captivating negligee. I could hardly contain myself."4 So began one of Coignet's most arduous campaigns, but the thrice weekly 'skirmishes' that followed exhausted him and he had a devil of a job hiding his false calves: "the task was too much for my strength; I had found my master, and should have been forced to surrender."5

She facilitated his escape by demanding he show her how well he could write a letter. When she criticised his style his pride was affronted. He refused to see her again even though she still pursued him. Instead, he put his energy into studying writing and military tactics, becoming expert in the drill. Then news came of Napoleon's quest for a new wife: "But though the Emperor was pleased with us, we were not pleased with him."[6] The Guard regarded Josephine as their personal good luck talisman, and wanted her to remain Empress.

Marie-Louise of Austria duly arrived at St. Cloud. She was overjoyed to find her pet dog, which she was loathe to leave behind in Vienna, awaiting her arrival and Napoleon did everything in his power to make her happy. At a huge party given to celebrate the marriage, Coignet was on duty, tasked with serving refreshments to the ladies. Despite his own recent exploits, Jean-Roch was rather prudish at heart. He describes their costume: "Low behind, down to the middle of their backs, and low in front so that you could see half their breasts; their shoulders and arms bare... I had never before seen the ladies of Paris, half naked, so near. I did not like it."[7]

Some time later: "The Emperor gave a magnificent ball; he opened it himself with Marie Louise. There never was seen a better formed man. He really was a perfect model; his hands and feet were unequalled for beauty."[8] Most people associate Napoleon's name with the plump figure of Waterloo. When he was younger he was very thin, even skeletal in his impoverished youth. His smile was said to be captivating when he became Emperor, while his grey eyes could be both gentle and terrifying. Sometimes he reduced his grousers to tears, even with a minor rebuke, so highly did they rate his opinion of them.

In 1811 there was great rejoicing because on March 20th a son and heir, The King of Rome was born. Coignet was on duty at St. Cloud when Marshal Duroc, a close personal friend of the Emperor's, gestured for him to approach. Then: "the dear child held out his little hands for my plume. I stooped and he began to pull at my plumes. The marshal said, "Let him do it." The child laughed..." Coignet, proud of his uniform, was somewhat depressed. But then Duroc told the nurse to let Coignet hold the baby: "Good Lord! How eagerly I stretched out my arms to receive that precious burden!" Sadly, Coignet was never to see the boy again.[9]

When Napoleon invited all the princes of the Confederation of the Rhine to Paris, and Prince Charles was chosen to be a godfather to the baby, a huge review was held in front of the Tuileries Palace. Coignet was asked to relay Napoleon's orders to the massed ranks of soldiers. He later admitted to his officers: "I heard him, but I could not look at him: he would have frightened me; I saw only his horse."[10]

In the early months of 1812, a hundred men began making 100,000 cartridges, manoeuvres took place on the plain of St. Denis, and reviews were held at the Tuileries. It was obvious to Coignet that war preparations were being made. He was made quartermaster of grenadiers and took charge of four wagons, two of which contained 28,000 francs. The Guard started for Meaux on May 1st 1812.[11]

Napoleon was in Dresden with the Empress and for ten days he entertained the other rulers of Europe – with the exception of the Tsar and the King of England. He was about to attack Russia because the Tsar, despite the Treaty of Tilsit, had failed to support him against his most implacable foe, the English. By June 23rd, the Grand Army was at the Russian border.[12]

On June 26th, the Guard crossed the River Niemen. Murat led the way with his cavalry and Davout's highly trained First Corps accompanied the guardsmen. Elting remarks that: "Undoubtedly the best-equipped infantry the Grand Armeé ever saw was Davout's I Corps at the beginning of the 1812 campaign..."[13] This campaign is often castigated from the outset by historians, but Napoleon's preparations had been extensive and meticulous.

Coignet had his own personal philosophy: "Providence and courage never abandon a good soldier."[14] This belief was exemplified in his own actions and bravery during this campaign.

At first, it was Poland all over again – until it got even worse than Poland. On June 29th the weather took a severe turn for the worse: "at three o'clock, a violent storm arose... The storm of sleet and snow was so terrible that we could scarcely keep our horses still; we had to fasten them to the wheels..."[15] Frozen to the marrow, Coignet crept beneath the cover of one of his wagons. The next day dead horse were strewn everywhere – 10,000 died in a single night. He had lost three of his own and had he not immediately harnessed the survivors they too would have perished. It was not an auspicious start to the campaign.

The Army plodded on through immense tracts of dark and gloomy forest. Many educated officers who were well versed in history must have been reminded of the annihilation of Varus' three legions in the Teutoberg forest by Arminius in AD 9. No one would ever have dreamt that their own fate was going to be even worse.

On July 13th Coignet was told by Major Belcourt that he was going to become a Lieutenant in the Line. With the ethos of the Guard fixed in his soldierly DNA, Coignet replied: "Thank you, but I do not wish to return to the line."16 Belcourt said he would get him transferred right back. When Napoleon inspected the twenty men due promotion, Coignet repeated that he wanted to remain a guardsman. As a consequence he was appointed to the Emperor's minor staff.

He soon rued his decision for he was given command of three battalions of stragglers by Count Monthyon. He suddenly found himself in charge of 700 men he was supposed to escort back to Third Corps with just a drummer and a bugle-boy to help him. Amongst them were 133 Spaniards of the Joseph Napoleon Regiment. After they left Vilna, they were lost amongst the huge forests. On the very first night there were deserters. The whole bunch were unmanageable, stopping whenever they saw fit and virtually ignoring him.17

Far from any habitation, in a place where the trees had been burnt, the Spaniards took off into the blackened forest. When he galloped after them, they fired at him and he had to let them go. Later, he reported this to a cavalry Colonel who had the fugitives arrested. They were forced to draw lots and half - 62 of them - were summarily executed. In the days to come their fate would be envied.18

At Vitebsk he went ahead expecting to give over his charges to the Third Corps, but the corps had moved on. When he got back to where he had left his men all of them had vanished save for the drummer. He caught up with Monthyon's staff with just the drummer and his servant, and they all laughed at him. The chief of staff asked him what had happened: "Ah, general, I sweated blood." When he was told he was going to be presented to the Marshal he added: "I know him, and he knows me; he will not laugh at me as your officers did. They hurt me very much."[19]

The Marshal was none other than his old friend Davout who remembered him very well. When the young scoffers heard he was so well in with the Iron Marshal they looked at him with renewed respect. Then he set off with despatches from Davout to Napoleon. From Vitebsk the Emperor headed for Smolensk were a terrible battle ensued, the Russians trying to deny entry to the town to the Grand Army. Stores of salt and sugar caught fire and lurid rainbow hues swirled amongst the flames. Against this background, Napoleon sent for Coignet. He was to take two good horses and ride for Vitebsk yet again with orders.[20]

Jean-Roch rode his first mount like an Apache, until it was almost driven into the ground, then he scrambled onto the back of the other. Delivering his despatches, he had a lie down for an hour and then set about on the return journey. In the woods that flew by on either side there was no sign of the French cavalry stations, only an ominous silence. He wisely slowed down for he almost rode into the midst of some Cossacks. A peasant warned him of the danger. Seizing him, Coignet demanded he show him a way around the obstacle, waving a pistol in one hand and holding out gold with the other.[21]

After a diversion, the peasant took him back to the main road up ahead and got three napoleons as a reward. Even when he got back to the main French Army it took him a long time to find the Emperor, who asked him for an account of his adventures. Satisfied he said: "Monthyon, pay him for all the expenses of his journey: for his two horses, and the sixty francs which the peasant well deserved. Give my old grouser time to remount himself. For his two horses, sixteen hundred francs and expenses. I am well pleased with you."[22]

Moscow was 93 leagues away through dense forest. Many of his captains urged caution and, at first, Napoleon seemed to be considering staying at Smolensk for the winter. But then he changed his mind and decided to press on. That single change of mind was to cost him his Empire.

A sharp action took place at Valutina where Ney fought the Russian rearguard. Napoleon heard that Davout had gone on ahead without searching the forest for Russian troops. Coignet was sent to warn him of the danger. Davout's men turned back but as they were blocking Coignet's way he veered off to the left and took a parallel road. Soon he found himself in the midst of retreating Russian soldiers crossing the road ahead of him. With great presence of mind he shouted "Forward!" and continued on his way.[23]

Everywhere, there were signs of the panic that had afflicted Russian troops and clear evidence of the victims of the conflict: "If they did not have time to bury them, they left them in piles for us to see. It was a heart-rending sight."[24] Berated by the Tsar for constantly retreating, Kutuzov decided to make a stand at the little village of Borodino.

Borodino, or the battle of the Moskwa as it is known in France, was like a preview of trench warfare during the Battle of the Somme. The carnage was even greater than at Waterloo. The Russians, stubborn and courageous in defence stood like a wall, in Napoleon's own words, it wasn't enough to kill them, they had to be pushed over afterwards. There was very little manoeuvre because the last thing that the Emperor wanted was for Kutuzov to retreat yet again. Hence he 'fixed' the front of their forces and the battle turned into a brutal slogging match. Davout urged him to send Poniatowski's Poles far to the right along the Utitsa road to envelop the Russian left wing and get behind their prepared earthworks, while others begged him to throw in the Guard, but he rejected both suggestions. He was proved right about the Guard for without them, he would either have been killed or captured at Krasny during the retreat. But on the day of the battle he was also unwell: "his ill-health seems to have taken heavy toll of his efficiency on this occasion,"[25] Chandler remarks.

The key to the enemy's defences were their prepared redoubts which resisted all the forces thrown at them. Finally, Napoleon sent for Coignet. He instructed him to go to Caulaincourt[26] and tell him to charge the redoubts with his cuirassiers. Caulaincourt told Coignet to follow him closely. In a joint operation, the ironclads and the grenadiers moved forward together. Coignet's life hung by a thread and he knew it: "Cuirassiers and French grenadiers struggled pell-mell with the Russians. The brave Caulaincourt fell stone dead beside me. I followed the old colonel who took the command, and never lost sight of him."[27] With death and destruction all around him he must have expected his end would come at any moment.

With bodies piled high in the redoubts, and the French in possession of them, the Colonel sent him to tell Napoleon that victory was his. As he charged back, cannon balls ploughed up the ground all around him, like marbles thrown by a furious giant. It was Wagram all over again. When he took his hat off to give the Emperor the good news he noticed that the back of it had been blown away. 'Coignet's luck' had held: "We passed the night on the battle-field, and the next day the Emperor had all the wounded taken up. This task made us shudder; the ground was covered with Russian muskets: near their field hospitals there were piles of dead bodies and heaps of limbs which had been amputated."[28]

During his pursuit, Murat came across charred skeletons. The retreating Russians had set fire to everything, including buildings housing their own helpless wounded: "That shows how much they valued their soldiers."[29] Coignet was sent on ahead to join Murat and give him despatches. The King of Naples laughed when he saw Coignet's battered hat. Napoleon had also given Coignet twenty gendarmes and told him to secure the Kremlin when Murat entered Moscow.

Many writers imply that Moscow was deserted when the French arrived, but Coignet says: "When we reached the bridge we found the city authorities there and a Russian general, who presented the keys to the prince." Furthermore, once they entered the city: "all the people came to the widows to see us pass, and the ladies presented us with bottles of wine..."[30]

While Murat continued through Moscow to the Kaluga road, Coignet took his gendarmes to the Kremlin. As if he had had a premonition, when off duty, he bought a fur robe and a bearskin for forty francs each from other soldiers. Then the great Moscow fire broke out.31

Like Bourgogne, he saw the sheet-iron used in roofing flying like chaff through the scorched air. As all the 800 fire engines had been removed on the Russian Rostopchin's orders there was little the French could do. Although the order have been given not to loot, when the common soldiers realized the Russians were burning their *own* city discipline collapsed and men took whatever they fancied, especially food and valuables.32

The toughness of the Russians was not restricted to the men. Coignet noticed that: "Two or three thousand women were there, with their children in their arms, looking upon the horrors of the fire, and I am sure I never saw one of them shed a tear."33

It is often said that the Great Fire meant that it was impossible for Napoleon's troops to winter in Moscow. Although 10,000 houses and 500 palaces and churches were burnt out, a third of the city remained untouched and colossal stocks of foodstuffs were found by the Army buried in cellars and hiding places. Once the flames had died down, Coignet was lodged in the house of a princess. Of his own grandiose billet he states: "We had thousands of bottles of Bordeaux wine, champagne, and thousands of pounds of white and brown sugar."34

He certainly got his share of unpleasant duties to perform. One of which was to take the dead bodies from the hospitals and bury them in holes twenty feet deep. After that thankless task his General spared him and Coignet was able to join him at his table. He adds: "We had provisions enough for the winter, both for ourselves and our horses."35 Had the stocks of food been gathered together and used wisely, they would have lasted through the worst of the winter months. Politically, however, Napoleon could not afford to be bottled-up in Moscow for that long.

As early as September 20th, anxious to disassociate himself from the ravages of the fire, Napoleon wrote to Alexander: "If your Majesty still conserves for me some remnant of your former feelings, you will take this letter in good part." As Chandler remarks, this message is devoid of confidence and is "Almost the tone of a suppliant asking a favor."[36] The Emperor had been stunned by the sight of a people destroying their own wonderful city, just to prevent him from occupying it. In his heart, he had hoped for a gentlemanly conflict, a quick campaign, a good battle, followed by victory and peace. As he waited in the Kremlin for an answer to his several letters to Alexander, it dawned on him that this was simply not going to happen. The silence said everything.

Once again, Coignet was where the action was. He was actually on his way to Murat with orders, when he came across French cavalrymen riding bareback in a panicky retreat. Murat's men, the advance guard of the Grand Army, had just been surprised at Winkovo.[37]

This setback precipitated the famous retreat of the whole Army. The Russians were growing ever stronger while the French forces were growing ever weaker. It stung a formerly lethargic Napoleon into action. He swung his Army south hoping to gather provisions in the warmer and more fertile areas south of Kaluga, but despite his subsequent victory at Malojaroslavets, he turned back north – into the teeth of one of the worst winters on record.

Utterly exhausted, Coignet had returned to the house of the princess. There, in the cellar, he found some horses which had been hidden throughout his stay. He took a carriage full of provisions but soon transferred these to horses as the hordes of retreating soldiers and camp-followers blocked the road.[38]

At the ghastly battlefield of Borodino: "the Emperor... sighed when he saw the dead still unburied."[39] Coignet says the worst of the winter weather began on November 6th, three days before they reached the burnt-out shell of Smolensk: "I took every possible care of myself."[40] He describes how he made tea for his General and made sure he was put in front of a good fire – helping others as he had the whole of his military career. He was fortunate to have enough tea to last all the way to Vilna. Man died around him like flies: "There were three captains, and only death separated us, which means that I alone am left alive."41

Coignet kept as close to the Emperor and the Guard as possible. Stragglers were picked off by Cossacks or perhaps worse, captured and tortured by irate peasants. When he got to the Berezina River, he saw the half-burnt bridge that had been the Army's only hope of salvation. Thanks to the Olympian heroics of General Eblé and his engineers, two trestle bridges were thrown across the freezing waters. The bulk of the Army crossed over on the nights of the 27th and 28th and Coignet found himself guarding the head of the artillery bridge to stop civilians trying to cross. On the far side of the same end of the bridge was none other than Davout – fate having brought them together yet again.42

When the pursuing Russians fired their big guns at the crowds on the bridges Coignet, like Bourgogne, was a witness to the mayhem that resulted. It would be interesting to know if the two of them knew each other, they must have met or been close to each other on many occasions. After reviewing some Russian prisoners, Napoleon sent for Jean-Roch. He was given despatches to take along the Vilna road and a guide went with him.43

At a village he does not name, Coignet met the mayor. He was instructed by the Emperor to gather a mass of provisions, an impossible task he told Coignet. But he was a Francophile and he made Jean-Roch welcome. He did much more, because he probably saved his life. As they were talking Cossacks approached and in an instant Coignet found himself bundled into a huge low oven by the mayor.44

After what seemed like ages, he was let out – but his despatches had been taken by the Cossacks. Little did he know, but that was exactly what Napoleon wanted to happen. Retracing his steps, Coignet inched his way over the glass-like road, dead and dying soldiers all around him. It was so cold that musket barrels stuck to bare hands. It had reached twenty-eight degrees below zero.45

When he finally saw the Emperor, he went to make his report. Napoleon seemed amazed: "What! They did not capture you? And your despatches, where are they?" He then ordered Coignet a week's rest and the payment of twice his expenses. Not that he had much chance of taking a rest! Coignet adds the following: "(I learned afterwards that the Emperor had sacrificed me in order to have my despatches captured and deceive the enemy)." Yet he makes no criticism of him.46

The Army was falling apart: "There was no longer any discipline or any human feeling for one another. Each man looked out for himself."47 Stronger men pushed weaker ones away from the fires, often to be pushed away in their turn. The weak oppressed the weaker – it seemed like the end.

At Smorgoni, Napoleon left for France. The Malet conspiracy had alerted him to the dangers of being away from Paris. He is often criticized for 'deserting' his Army yet, in 1814, his absence allowed the arch-traitor Talleyrand to deliver the capital over to the Allies. He can be blamed, however, for leaving Murat in charge. His brother-in-law was next in line in terms of Court precedence and it might have been perceived as an insult to have chosen someone else. But here political considerations were diametrically opposed to the good of the Army.

Coignet states: "We remained under the command of the King of Naples and were not too happy in out minds, for, though he was always the first to draw a sabre or brave danger, he may truly be said to have been the executioner of our cavalry."48 He did not take care of his horses, keeping his men mounted for hours at a time and doing little or nothing to provide the men or animals with food. Coignet says that in Davout's opinion, Murat lost them 40,000 horses through his incompetence. If so, then Murat, in effect, lost Napoleon his Empire as well, for it was the shortage of cavalry in 1813 that severely hampered Napoleon's attempt to hold the Allies at bay. When Eugene took over – Murat thinking of only himself, yet again, had fled to Naples – the survivors breathed a sigh of relief.49

When he got to Vilna, Coignet was lucky enough to find shelter with a comrade in a warm school. When he went to his

General for orders, he returned to find his companion refusing to budge. He struck him several times with the flat of his sword to make him move. Had he remained there he would have surely died. The Russians broke into the Vilna soon after: "They committed the most horrible acts in the town. All the unfortunate men still asleep in their lodgings, were murdered, and the streets were strewn with the dead bodies of Frenchmen."50

Like his compatriot Bourgogne, Coignet had only admiration for Ney: "It may be said in praise of Marshal Ney that he kept the enemy at bay at Kowno by his own bravery. I saw him take a musket and five men and face the enemy. The country ought to be grateful for such men."51 Had other senior officers had the same mettle as Ney and Eugene, the Army might have been able to rally at Vilna. As it was, the retreat continued.

The writing was on the wall. When the starving, often defenceless remnants of Napoleon's once proud Army reached Prussia they were abused by Prussian sentries. Denied access to shelter, many of them died in the frozen streets. Coignet took two men to the town hall at Koenigsberg and through sheer persistence got them all shelter. The owners of the billet were indifferent until he offered them twenty francs a day for the privilege. A Prussian doctor was kind enough to treat Coignet's frozen foot for free and added "Farewell, brave Frenchmen," as he left them.52

When he caught up with Count Montyhon, Coignet was put in charge of all the vehicles left with the Army. That was on December 28th 1812. His first task was to get rid of those that were unnecessary. Soon the French forces retreated to Berlin and then Magdeburg. Eugene got the survivors into some sort of shape at the Elbe, taking up a good defensive position according to Coignet: "he looked after everything..."53 Eugene had only 15,000 infantry, 800 cavalry and eight guns left.

Jean-Roch Coignet had demonstrated immense courage and resilience yet again. Even when nearly every one else turned their backs on their comrades, he continued to give other struggling fugitives a helping hand, be they generals or simple grenadiers. His indomitable spirit and resourceful nature kept his body and soul together, no matter what the hardships he had to endure. Coignet was fashioned in a mould all of his own. Soon he would face yet more danger and this time the very soil of France would be at stake.

NOTES

1. Jean-Roch Coignet *Captain Coignet* 180
2. Ibid. 180-181
3. Ibid. 181-182
4. Ibid. 183
5. Ibid. 185-186
6. Ibid. 186
7. Ibid. 188
8. Ibid. 191
9. Ibid. 194
10. Ibid. 197
11. Ibid. 197-198
12. Ibid. 200
13..John R. Elting *Swords Around A Throne* 217
14. Coignet op.cit. 200
15. Ibid. 201
16. Ibid. 202
17. Ibid. 203-209
18. Ibid. 208-209
19. Ibid. 209
20. Ibid. 212
21. Ibid. 213
22. Ibid. 215
23. Ibid. 216
24. Ibid. 217
25. David Chandler *The Campaigns Of Napoleon* (1966) 799. He also adds on 807: "Illness made him both fretful and excessively cautious."
26. This is not Armand Caulaincourt, the former ambassador to Moscow, but his brother, Auguste.
27. Coignet op.cit. 218
28. Ibid. 219
29. Ibid. 219
30. Ibid. 220
31. Ibid. 222
32. Ibid. 223
33. Ibid 223
34 Ibid. 223-224

35. Ibid. 225
36. Chandler op.cit. 813
37. Coignet op.cit. 225
38. Ibid. 226
39. Ibid. 226
40. Ibid. 227
41. Ibid. 227
42. Ibid. 228
43. Ibid. 228
44. Ibid. 229
45. Ibid. 231
46. Ibid. 230-231
47. Ibid. 231
48. Ibid. 233
49. Ibid. 233
50. Ibid. 234
51. Ibid. 234
52. Ibid. 235-236
53. Ibid. 237

COIGNET OF THE GUARD: PART FIVE
COIGNET'S WATERLOO[1]

"I can still see the long dark columns of the Old Guard with their proud eagles, tall bearskins, and martial faces hovering like gloomy dream pictures; first the warlike sound of drums and pipes, then the ghostly figures of the pioneers with glinting axes and long black beards, and behind them the endless columns of transport."[2]

So said Wilhelm von Kügelgen as he recalled being a young boy when the Grand Army passed through Dresden on its way to the Russian border in 1812. The vast majority of those soldiers died in the snows of a bitter winter. But the spirit of the Guard, the soul of the Immortals, did not die, it lived on in the memories of the survivors and in the cadres at the depots back in France. It imbued the men that flocked to the ranks with enthusiasm and resolve when Père Violet returned along with the flowers of a wondrous Spring. A whole new adventure was about to begin and Jean-Roch Coignet, who had served in Italy, Spain, Austria and Russia was one of the men who enthusiatically greeted the Emperor upon his return.

But then came the Battle of Waterloo and as darkness fell on the night of June 18th 1815, it also seemed to be the twilight of the idol.

The unbelievable cry of "La Garde recule!" was still ringing in their ears, as thousands of men ran for their lives down the road towards Genappe. For hours they had endured the cannons spitting death from hungry maws, the volleys of musket fire and the whine of Congreve rockets. Fear had mixed with sweat and anguish as they bravely fought for Le Tondu between the ever-tightening pincers of the forces of Wellington and Blücher. It was an impossible task that they had *almost* made possible.

As the sun set on that forlorn day, not just upon the vanquished soldiers but upon a whole Empire, the thunderous roar of the cannon abated, the stuttering crackle of musketry subsided and the chaotic whirl of dragoons and cuirassiers around the British squares became just a memory. Soon even the screams and shouts of the wounded and dying faded as the fugitives were cloaked in darkness.

That darkness still lingers in France. In the minds of many, the battle has become an embarrassment, like a cenotaph to lost glory, a tomb for Napoleon's greatness and a cross that France has had to bear ever since. A battle had been lost but *France* had not been conquered. *Defeatists* who lost their nerve allowed the country to sleepwalk into the arms of the Bourbons. Ever since, Waterloo has been a perpetual stain upon French honour. But things *could* have been different. It need not have been that way.

The events of that frenetic summer have certainly overshadowed the campaign of 1814. Napoleon's achievements with a small army against overwhelming odds were incredible. When the Emperor was allowed to be *just* a soldier there was no contemporary military leader who came anyway near him in terms of inspiration and ability - in his day he was nonpareil.

Jean-Roch Coignet was there, and in his memoirs he vividly recreates the highs and lows of this illustrious chapter in Napoleon's life.

We left Coignet on the Elbe with Eugene's meagre forces. In 1813, before Napoleon could join his stepson, the Russians and Prussians attacked. On May 2nd the 'Marie-Louises'[3] were blooded at the battle of Lutzen: "the success of which was due to the French infantry, and chiefly to the valour of our young conscripts, entirely unsupported by cavalry. It is impossible to give an idea of the desperate valour of our troops."[4] The wounded were rescued by thirty young local couples that repeatedly returned to the battlefield on their mercy mission. This again belies the oft-quoted assertion that Napoleon and the French were by now hated by all the Germans.[5]

At Dresden it was Coignet's job to requisition horses from unauthorized wagons and carriages. He passed two hundred horses on to the artillery and he impounded oxen as well.[6] Murat's profligacy with his cavalry in Russia was having extremely serious repercussions. Without a strong cavalry arm,

Napoleon could not reconnoitre properly and neither could he follow up any victories – he was fighting with one hand tied behind his back.

As Sun-Tzu states: "Intelligence is the essence of warfare – it is what the armies depend upon in their every move."7 Coignet became notorious for his strict adherence to orders. Berthier remarked to General Monython: "That old grouser is making everyone go on foot."8 Supported by his General, Berthier must also have agreed with Coignet's methods because he made him a Captain on Napoleon's General Staff.9

"You will always be near the Emperor," Monython said to Coignet when he told him the good news.10 It cost him 250 francs to buy epaulets and the tassels for his hat. No wonder scavengers rifled the bodies of the dead and dying on the battlefields of the period. There was more than just money for the taking.

At Bautzen on May 20th, the French were again victorious and two days later Latour-Maubourg's cavalry mauled the Russians. Coignet was with the Emperor, following the retreating Russians, when some cannon were fired nearby. Napoleon asked Duroc to go and investigate. Seconds later, Duroc was dying, struck by a cannonball. The Guard was ordered to halt and Napoleon sat for hours in front of his tent with his head bowed and his hands clasped.11

Napoleon went to embrace his old friend for the last time: "When he returned to camp he walked up and down in front of his tent. No one dared go near him; we all stood around with bowed heads."12 First it was Lannes and now Duroc. Napoleon's greatest and best friends were being taken from him and lesser men were starting to question his authority and to look to their own futures. As if that wasn't enough, traitors like Talleyrand and Fouché were causing trouble in Paris, turncoats like Bernadotte and Moreau were actively helping the enemy, and his own Marshals upon whom he had lavished wealth and high position would soon desert him.

Peace was declared on June 4th and Napoleon headed for Dresden. He no longer had the Army seen by young Kügelgen only a year before. When the armistice ended on August 10th he was badly outnumbered – the Allies had 800,000 men while he had little more than 300,000. Even Papa Francis, his vacillating father-in-law, had gone over to the other side. Despite achieving another victory at Dresden where he returned to help Marshal St. Cyr, the French forces were badly overstretched.13

Even the news that Moreau had fallen failed to raise the spirits of some of the French officers. Coignet was stunned by their reaction: 'This was a memorable victory; but our generals had had enough of it. I had my place among the staff, and I heard all sorts of things said in conversation. They cursed the Emperor: 'He is a ---,' they said, 'who will have us all killed.' I was dumb with astonishment. I said to myself, 'We are lost.' "14

The next day Coignet himself ventured the opinion that they would be better off at the Rhine. His General agreed and said: "but the Emperor is obstinate: no one can make him listen to reason."15

One wonders what these men expected from the Allies. When Napoleon went they got the White Terror in his place. If they avoided D'Artois' and Lord Liverpool's purges they were sent out to pasture on half-pay, their places taken by the dilettantes returning in Louis XVIII's baggage-train. Large parts of France were ransacked by the invading armies. It was a strange sort of 'liberation'.

Napoleon did his best, pushing himself to the limit. At Pirna he became sick and ill, overtaken by exhaustion. Defeats followed in quick succession as his Marshals failed to emulate his brilliance - Vandamme, Macdonald and Oudinot were beaten in the field. On September 14th Bavaria defected to the Allies. At Leipzig Napoleon hoped to turn back the tide.16

On the second day of this epic three-day battle, Coignet was sent for. The Emperor instructed him to get the seventeen wagons of the Imperial household clear of the city. They contained the treasure and all his maps. The following morning, as Coignet was preparing to leave, the Allies attacked again. The Saxon contingent of Napoleon's forces took the opportunity to change sides, making the Army's position untenable.17

As cannonballs fell amongst the wagons, Coignet got them moving towards the long bridge that led to safety. That evening he learnt that the French had repulsed the combined forces of four armies but their ammunition was running out. A retreat was imminent. Tragedy occurred when the sappers, instructed to blow the bridge when the Army had crossed, blew it up too soon, stranding thousands on the far bank. Marshal Poniatowski drowned trying to swim his horse across.[18]

The shattered remains of the Army crossed the Saale on October 20th. Murat left soon after for Naples. It did not take him long to start secret negotiations with the Austrians. From Erfurt Napoleon headed for Hanau where the Bavarians had the temerity to bar his path.[19]

In a forest just in front of the town he spoke to the Guard. Some 40,000 Bavarians, greatly outnumbering the two battalions Napoleon was sending against them, were waiting in a strong position. Coignet rode up to his Emperor: "Would your Majesty permit me to follow the horse-grenadiers?" Napoleon answered: "Go, there will be one good man the more."[20]

With mud up to their knees the grousers pressed on and managed to turn the position of the enemy. The Bavarians wavered: "unable to resist them for a moment, and were cut to pieces… the most fearful carnage ensued that I ever saw in my life."[21] Coignet, on a small horse, struggled to keep up. On the extreme left by the city wall, he found himself faced by an enemy platoon. Their mounted officer charged him with a long sword. Coignet parried the stroke and then cut his head off with his sabre, returning to his own side with a captured Arab horse.[22]

The Bavarians thought they would be Napoleon's last straw, but it was they that turned out to be but a broken Wrede.[23]

From Frankfort the remnants of the Army retired to Mayence where yellow fever struck. Coignet again had the unenviable task of managing the burial parties. Then the minor headquarters stayed in Metz for two months, awaiting events.[24]

The campaign of 1814 was about to begin. Napoleon's attitude can de summed up in the words of Charles Ist of

England when a prisoner: *"Dum spiro spero"* – 'While I breathe, I hope'.25 His Army might have been weak in numbers, but he used them in a tour de force.

On January 27th at St. Dizier there was a sharp battle and after losing badly the Allies were forced to fall back on Brienne. St. Dizier was a shattered ruin and the inhabitants had to flee the town. Here was a stark warning of what an invasion and occupation would really mean.26

From the heights of Brienne the enemy rained down shot and shell upon the French forces, struggling through the muddy landscape. The Emperor was determined to take the town where he had studied as a boy. Riding out in front of his men he said: "Soldiers, I am your colonel; I shall lead you. Brienne must be taken."27 Coignet writes of the electric response that surged through the listeners: "each soldier became equal to four. Our troops were so transported that the Emperor could not control them; they rushed past the staff."28 When historians try to pretend that the 'individual' is unimportant in the scheme of things, they forget human nature and the immense effect that impassioned words can have upon the human psyche. Brienne duly fell.

On the pursuit to Mézières, in virtual darkness, Napoleon was attacked by a Cossack. Colonel Gourgaud shot him at point-blank range with his pistol. After twenty-four hours in the saddle it was clearly time to rest. The small Army then went to Troyes and on February 1st pushed back the Allies at Chaumpaubert. At La Rothière, although he retained the battlefield, Napoleon could only manage a draw. The battles now came thick and fast: Château-Thierry on the 12th; Gennevilliers on the 15th; Montereau on the 18th. A French corps had failed to arrive in time to support the Emperor so he sent Marshal Lefebvre to seize the bridge at Montereau, Coignet along with him. He was on his Arab mount captured at Hanau. Lefebvre's blood was up and Coignet saw him foaming at the mouth as he hacked at the enemy.29

On the road to St. Dizier, Allied cavalry counterattacked. The French were rescued by a battalion of chasseurs who had cast of their knapsacks in order to help all the more quickly. In the meantime Napoleon and the Old Guard were setting up the artillery on a hill before Montereau. The Emperor himself sighted the pieces despite the soldiers pleading for him to go to the rear: "No," he said, "the bullet which is to kill me is not yet moulded."30 Coignet laments that he ought to have met a glorious death there rather than be betrayed later by those he had raised to prominence.

The furious pace continued, there was a battle at Méry-sur-Seine on the 21th; Sézanne on the 28th; Berryau-Bac on 5th of March and a terrible clash at Craonne on the 7th. On March 13th Coignet was at the gates of Reims. The Russians held the city. A surprise sortie by them literally caught Napoleon napping - he had been exhausted by the struggle at Craonne. With alacrity and choice expletives, he urged his staff to bring up the siege artillery. After a bombardment the cuirassiers stormed into the place and wreaked havoc: "The Emperor, at the head of his staff, was in Reims by midnight, and the Russians utterly routed."31 Coignet's only regret was that these amazing achievements were not echoed elsewhere in France. At Fontainebleau: "We wanted to make a last effort, and march upon Paris; but it was too late... Paris had surrendered without resistance."32

Coignet hoped to follow Napoleon to Elba but as he was no longer a member of the Guard he could not be taken. After he had chosen the 600 men he was allowed to have as his bodyguard, Napoleon ordered General Drouot to take the rest to Louis XVIII in Paris. Those men stepped from the sublime to the ridiculous. Coignet wept as the Emperor took his last farewell.33

He says: "If Paris had held out twenty-four hours, France would have been saved."34 Instead, the forces of reaction plunged the nation into heartbreak and sorrow, returning émigrés landing like vultures on what they thought was Napoleon's political corpse.

Coignet was sent home on half-pay of 73 francs a month and made to plant cabbages. At Auxerre in the spring of 1815, he heard some incredible news from a drinking companion, the return of the grey coat: "I withdrew, overwhelmed with joy... I felt as if my Emperor was already back again."35 Ney arrived with the 14th Regiment, determined to arrest Napoleon. The thought that he intended to lay his hand upon the Emperor made Coignet tremble.

Depressed when he heard shouts of 'Down with Bonaparte' and 'Long live the King', his hopes revived when the soldiers of the 14th put their shakos on their bayonets and cried "Long live the Emperor!' The same commissioner of police came out for the King in the morning and the Emperor in the evening. Coignet laughed his head off.36

The next day he waited with other officers at the Place St. Etienne for Napoleon's coach. When he saw Coignet, Napoleon gestured to him: "So you are here, old grouser?"37 He then made him quartermaster of the palace and baggage-master general. Coignet set off to join Monthyon in Paris.

In the capital, Coignet went to collect the 300 francs due him, but an old émigré who had taken a position with the Emperor said the pay had been stopped. There must have been many such men who did their best to sabotage Napoleon's forces. Coignet appealed to his General and got his funds, before seeing to his duties of billeting the Army and getting rations of forage. He paid 2,700 francs for two fine horses for himself – his brother Alexander loaning him most of the money. On his 1,800 franc charger he was better mounted than Monthyon.38

On June 1st there was a gathering at the Champ de Mars. Napoleon distributed eagles to the Army. He cried: "Swear to defend your eagles! Do you swear it?"39 Coignet noticed that the vows were made without warmth and Napoleon himself was well aware of it. The morale of the men was fragile – it was one of the reasons for defeat two weeks later. The soldiers had not forgotten the betrayal of Marmont, Ney and other Marshals the year before. When Bourmont went over to the Allies on the eve of the Waterloo campaign, taking Napoleon's plan of attack, it confirmed their worst fears about traitors in their midst.40

During Napoleon's march on Paris, Bourmont: "had been appointed by the Comte d'Artois to supervise Ney's operations in attempting to stop his former master. Bourmont was a dyed-in-the-wool royalist..."41 who Napoleon had taken in only after

Ney had sworn to his loyalty. Davout, the most perceptive of men, had warned the Emperor in a letter about him: "Who would trust such a man".42 Even though the regimental commanders of the 14th detested Bourmont, Gérard spoke in his favour as well, so Napoleon acquiesced. Bourmont deliberately 'held back' the right wing of the Army at the outset of the campaign – treason apparent from the very beginning. He followed that up by taking the plan of attack to Blücher's headquarters.43

So why did Napoleon employ such men? The main reason was undoubtedly political, his wish to show that all men could serve under him, if they were prepared to loyally serve France. He had allowed hundreds of émigrés to return in the past and he wanted to show he would tolerate *former* enemies, if they had mended their ways. Even the likes of Cadoudal had been given a chance to reform. He could not be just a General, Napoleon had to play the role of Emperor as well. And part of his role he saw as healing the nation, not just defending it.

He was obviously upset by this treachery because Coignet heard him say to Ney: "your favorite has gone over to the enemy with all his officers."44 It was far worse than that – it meant that the common soldiers was *expecting* betrayal from then on and were constantly looking over their shoulders.

On the plain of Fleurus, the Emperor spied some dismounted cavalry in the distance. Coignet was sent to investigate: "Do not get caught,"45 Napoleon added. At the foot of a steep hill Coignet saw three English officers mount their horses and move towards him. Saluting the enemy, he turned to leave as others were trying to get behind him. Urging Coco, his charger on, he noticed one of the officers following him. When he shouted 'surrender' Coignet demanded the same of him. Then he wheeled left and in a lightning stroke pierced him with his sabre. This was one Englishman who was not 'sharp' enough.46

The captured horse revealed the regimental number. When an officer begged Coignet for the animal, he sold it - fifteen napoleons went to his servant and twenty francs to the grenadiers. The Emperor said: "Make a note of this old grouser. After the campaign, we will see him."47

On June 16th, having taken command of the Army in person, Napoleon sent Gerard's corps and the Old Guard against the Prussians. Coignet was later sent to Gerard to see how the battle was progressing. He found the General covered in mud amid hand-to-hand fighting. With reinforcements victory was assured he told Coignet, who states that Ligny was: "Not a battle, it was butchery."48 When he returned to Napoleon, despite the Emperor having earlier upbraided Gerard about Bourmont, he said generously: "Ah! If I had four men like Gerard to rely on the Prussians would be lost."49

After Coignet's report, Napoleon rubbed his hands. Things were going well. But, for a twist of fate, it could have been all over. Blücher had been unhorsed during the conflict and French cavalry had ridden by him several times as he lay trapped under his mount. Had they picked him up, or finished him off, there would have been *no Waterloo*. It was Blücher's pathalogical hatred of Napoleon that ensured the Prussians rallied in time to march to Wellington's aid at Mont St. Jean. Gneisenau, his deputy, despised his English ally and felt that Wellington had done nothing to assist the Prussians at Ligny. He was all for heading back to Prussia tout de suite. Then Alte Vorwarts returned to the Prussian headquarters, bruised but not bowed.50

That night, according to Coignet, Napoleon: "sent out officers in every direction... We were all on duty that night; no one had any rest."51 This contradicts the view that Napoleon felt lethargic after Ligny as many have said. At 3am on June 17th came the order to advance. By 7am the French columns had come up and only the English were left ahead of them. When Ney arrived he was rebuked for not pursuing Wellington's men then told: "Go, marshal, and take possession of those heights; the enemy are drawn up in front of the woods. When I hear from Grouchy, I will give you the order for a general attack."52

Coignet was ordered to find the position of the English left wing: "I must mention that we were drenched with rain and very muddy; our artillery could not manoeuvre."53 This was to delay the start of battle for a critical few hours. Ney was finally given the order to attack. Coignet describes how he repeatedly asked Napoleon for reinforcements. News also came from the right wing that French soldiers were withdrawing. The Prussians had started to arrive in force.[54]

Napoleon had to weaken his centre to reinforce that sector and this allowed Wellington to breathe: "The Prussian army moved into line, and the junction was complete; there were two or even three of the enemy to one of us; there was no means of holding out."[55] Taking the Guard, the Emperor marched it forward and spurred his horse towards Cambronne's square, but the staff officers forced him to retire. Then suddenly, it was every man for himself.

At Jemappes, Napoleon tried to re-establish order but Coignet: "found myself taking part in another rout as complete as that of Moscow. 'We are betrayed,' they cried."[56] He adds that it was when the right wing was broken that the panic started. In other words, because of the Prussians. The impression is often given that the Prussians arrived at Waterloo late in the evening, when Wellington had virtually won the battle. The truth is different: "in view of Napoleon's heavy attack on the Anglo-Allied centre and fearing that Wellington might break before his men could cut off the line of retreat of the French army, Blücher had decided to attack with his IV Corps cavalry and two brigades. At some time between 4 and 4.30pm Nostitz brought Bülow the order to attack."[57] And it was the Prussian cavalry that harassed the retreating French, the English were exhausted.

Wellington's men had fought magnificently and the Dutch-Belgians deserve much more credit than they are usually given but as Chandler states: "Wellington's army had hardly any chance of ultimate victory on its own, and the opportune arrival of a growing flood of Prussian troops on the French right flank undoubtedly swung the fortunes of the day."[58]

John Keegan, however, in 'The Face of Battle' says that "the most perceptive of all the comments about Waterloo is the best known and apparently the most banal; that it was 'won on the playing fields of Eton'... He (Wellington) was proposing a much more subtle idea: that the French had been beaten... by the coolness and endurance, the pursuit of excellence... which are learnt in game-playing - that game-playing which was already becoming the most important activity of the English gentleman's life."59 What utter tosh.

Perhaps all those thousands of Prussians were 'foreign boarders' at Eton? In his own badly written book, its introduction as glutinous as the field of Waterloo itself after the rain, he describes the dense smoke from musket and cannon that reduced visibility to a matter of yards. Wellington literally *did not see* what was happening far off to his left and, after the battle he took most of the credit for the victory.

So, a battle had been lost but *France* had not fallen – "The path is not a 'given', but it is made in the treading of it. Thus one's own actions are always a significant factor in the shaping of one's world."60 Everything now depended on Napoleon.

The Emperor rode to Charleroi and then to Laon. Grouchy was ordered to report there. At a meeting with his Generals, Napoleon found that some wanted him to go to Paris and others to stay with the Army. He replied: "How can you advise such a thing. My place is here."61 Soon after the Old Guard arrived: "returning in good order from the battlefield."62 There was no 'last stand' at Waterloo as many assume.

Coignet says Napoleon was compelled to go to Paris by his Generals: "We were never to see him again."63 By then, the National Guard were flocking to Laon. They were expecting to fight, not to arrive just in time to surrender like thousands of Australians at Singapore in WWII. Coignet travelled on with Monthyon and other demoralised men. The Prussians caught up with them at Villers-Cotterets. They escaped with minutes to spare: "Desolation reigned everywhere... Everyone was on the way to Paris with his valuables."64 But in Paris there remained a man of iron – Davout.

Both sides had lost heavily during the Waterloo campaign, the French 60,000 and the Allies 55,000. Yet: "the Emperor's military position was not necessarily hopeless, providing he continued to enjoy the support of the army, the French populace and government."65 By the end of June there were 117,000 troops to defend Paris. Blücher had only 66,000 men and Wellington a mere 52,000 troops to take the capital.

Davout urged Napoleon to seize control of the Government – but the Emperor hesitated. Physically and mentally exhausted, Napoleon failed to act. Meanwhile, Fouché persuaded the Chambers to declare themselves indissoluble and called for Napoleon's abdication. Ney had not helped by giving a long and rambling speech and insisting that there was no Army left.66

When Blücher got to the gates of Paris on June 30th he was *repulsed*. The Allies were strung-out like Varus in the Teutoburg forest. Napoleon offered his services as a mere General, but the politicians turned him down.67 Had he ignored them and joined forces with Davout, Blücher and Wellington could have been chased ignominiously out of the country.

When he had failed to move earlier, Davout, his most able and loyal officer, looked to his own future and even he deserted Napoleon.68 The Emperor had no wish to bring civil war to his adopted country and so he naively turned for succour to 'the greatest of his enemies' – England. Louis XVIII had claimed asylum there, Napoleon convinced himself he could retire to the same place. He had a chance to sail for the United States, but he waited too long and Fouché alerted the British navy to his presence on the coast. Had he arrested Fouché before the campaign: "the Chambers would have remained passive and Waterloo, although still a disaster, would not then have been a decisive battle in providing ammunition for Fouché to use against him."69

Even now, France could have been spared the blight of the Bourbons and the White Terror. On July 1st Coignet received orders to move to the south of Paris: "where the army was reunited and entrenched... When I reached the Barrière d'Enfer, where the army had collected, I found Marshal Davout on foot, his arms folded. Gazing at that *splendid army*, who were shouting, "*Forward.*"... The troops wanted to move against the enemy force which had crossed the Seine... Marshal Davout was doubtful what to do..."70 Davout was a very able lieutenant, but he was no Napoleon.

We shall leave Jean-Roch Coignet on the plain of Les Vertus before Paris a short while before, the Old Guard to his right and the National Guard to his left – the former with orders *not* to attack. Coignet had been galled at the sight of a Prussian officer who repeatedly cavorted ahead of his own troops in an arrogant manner. With him, Coignet had two rifled pistols that had cost him 100 francs. And he had plan that he explained to some gentlemen onlookers: "I know my trade. I shall have him out in front of the line, and make him angry, if possible. If he gets angry, he is mine."71

Approaching the Prussian lines, Coignet was taken for a deserter by the enemy – until he fired his pistols. The Prussian then charged him in a rage. When he tried to sabre Coignet: "I struck his sabre up above his head, and, with the same stroke, brought my sabre down upon his face with such force that his nose went down to find his chin. He fell stone-dead."72

Little Big Man, Jean-Roch Coignet, knew how to defend his country. When everyone else was running away, ingratiating themselves with the invaders or the Bourbons, or vacillating with indecision, he alone knew how to uphold the honour of France.

NOTES

1. There is a famous painting by Vernet called The Last Grenadier at Waterloo, which suggests it was all over for Napoleon after that battle. There is much more to Waterloo and its aftermath than is often realized. The Emperor could have fought on as will be shown later in this chapter. Napoleon said that a great man is consumed in illuminating his century. As the greatest man of the C19th, this can clearly be said to apply to himself. He was devoured by the hatred and animosity of the so-called 'legitimate' divine right monarchies of the day. Napoleon had been elected by plebiscite several times, unlike them – their aristocratic blue blood came before the common man and they caused the blood of thousands to be shed in their inveterate opposition to him. Chief amongst the nations responsible for that carnage was England, which bribed others to fight him.

When Napoleon returned to Paris in 1815 from Elba, Thiébault said: "One moment and one man had sufficed to give France back to the French, the French to France." Quoted in Paul Britten Austin 1815 The Return of Napoleon (London: Greenhill Books, 2002) 284.

2. Antony Brett-James 1812 (London: Macmillan Ltd, 1966) 18 Wilhelm von Kügelgen was 9 at the time. He had been born in St. Petersburg.

3. The Marie-Louises was the name given to the new conscripts because they were so young – like Marie-Louise, Napoleon's second wife and the new Empress of France.

4. Jean-Roch Coignet *Captain Coignet* 239

5. Ibid. 239

6. Ibid. 240

7. Sun-Tzu *The Art Of War* (London: Folio, 2007) 66 Translated by Roger.T. Ames

8. Coignet op.cit. 240

9. Ibid. 240

10. Ibid. 241

11. Ibid. 241-242

12. Ibid. 242

13. Ibid. 243-244

14. Ibid. 245

15. Ibid. 245

16. Ibid. 245

17. Ibid. 246

18. Ibid. 250

19. Ibid. 251 In 1809, without a declaration of war, Austria attacked Bavaria, Napoleon's ally. He had quickly gone to the aid of that country. This is a reminder of how quickly alliances shifted in those turbulent years.

20. Ibid. 252

21. Ibid. 252

22. Ibid. 253

23. General Wrede commanded the Bavarian forces. Only a year before they had been on the same side in the Grand Army of 1812.

24. Ibid. 254

25. John Adair *By The Sword Divided* (London: Century Publishing, 1983) 230. Charles Ist had believed in divine right. He famously said just before his execution: "A subject and a sovereign are clean different things..." 236

26. Coignet op.cit. 254

27. Ibid. 255

28. Ibid. 255

29. Ibid. 256-257

30. Ibid. 257

31. Ibid. 259

32. Ibid. 259

33. Ibid. 260

34. Ibid. 260

35. Ibid. 261

36. Ibid. 262

37. Ibid. 262

38. Ibid. 264

39. Ibid. 266

40. Ibid. 269

41. David Hamilton-Williams *Waterloo New Perspectives* 154-155
42. Ibid. 155
43. Ibid. 155 "Blücher was contemptuous of de Bourmont as a traitor and said so, shouting in de Bourmont's face, "Cockade be damned! A dirty dog is always a dirty dog!' " For once, he and Napoleon would have agreed on something.
44. Coignet op.cit. 266
45. Ibid. 267
46. Ibid. 267
47. Ibid. 268
48. Ibid. 269
49. Ibid. 269
50. Hamilton-Williams op.cit. 230
51. Coignet op.cit. 270
52. Ibid. 271
53. Ibid. 271
54. Ibid. 272
55. Ibid. 272
56. Ibid. 273
57. Hamilton-Williams op.cit. 327
58. David Chandler *The Campaigns of Napoleon* (1966) 1,093
59. John Keegan *The Face Of Battle* (London: The Folio Society, 2008) 175. His map of the Battle of Waterloo is also very inaccurate. The arrow showing the Prussians on 109 says 'THE PRUSSIANS ADVANCE (*Evening*)'. As we have seen, hundreds of Prussians had been engaged long before this. Around 7,000 Prussians were killed at the battle – hardly a tally for johnnie-come-latelys. This is yet another book that wallows in English prejudice.
60. Sun-Tzu op.cit. 42
61. Coignet op.cit. 273
62. Ibid. 274
63. Ibid. 274
64. Ibid. 275
65. Chandler op.cit. 1,094
66. Ibid. 1,094-1,095. See also Hamilton-Williams op.cit. 358: "Ney, exasperated by Napoleon's seeming ingratitude for all he had done for the Emperor since his return, now extracted a terrible revenge...Ney said that he had no reason not to tell the truth, and that he was convinced that the country would be overrun by the Allies within two weeks."
67. Chandler op.cit. 1,095
68. Davout allowed himself to be manipulated by Fouché. Hamilton-Williams op.cit. 359-360: "Napoleon pleaded with Marshal Davout to let him use the 117,000 men Davout controlled to reverse his defeat at Mont St-Jean and then combine these with the 150,000 depot troops to use against the other Allies... But Davout was now Minister of War and Commander-in-Chief of Fouché's provisional government, and had an eye to holding office under Louis. He refused Napoleon's plea. In fact, he went

further and threatened that if Napoleon did not leave Paris he would have him arrested."

69. Ibid. 361

70. Coignet op.cit. 279 (My italics) He adds: "With our left wing on Versailles, not a Prussian nor an Englishman could have stood against the fury of our men." On 280 he says of Davout: "He was no longer the warrior whom I had formerly seen in his brilliance on the field of battle..."

71. Ibid. 277

72. Ibid. 277

NAPOLEON AND RUSSIA

"they were Russians... entirely set upon the single goal of expanding their empire by whatever means might be necessary..."*

When Napoleon came to power in France, the diplomatic and military cards had already been dealt. He came late to the table, for the four houses of England, Austria, Prussia and Russia were used to dividing the spoils of the continent amongst themselves. To these empire builders, Napoleon was an upstart, the joker in the pack, intruding into their private game. The monarchs were the dealers and they bitterly resented the arrival of someone who could not only play their game but also beat them at it.

To help understand Napoleon's position we can go back to his future. For what the German chancellor Bethmann-Hollweg said in 1914 was just as apposite in 1814: "The future belongs to Russia, which grows and grows, looming above us as an increasingly terrifying nightmare."[1] Centuries before that remark, the Russian bear had been pawing at the territory of others. Ever since the failure of the Ottomans to take Vienna in 1683, the door to the west lay open for Russian expansionism.

In the Great Northern War of 1700-1721, Tsar Peter defeated Sweden and Poland-Lithuania. He grabbed Livonia and Ingria from the Swedes and founded Saint Petersburg in 1703.[2] Later that century, Russia was more than happy to keep her share of Poland during the infamous partitions by bribing the Austrians and the Prussians with other portions of that unfortunate country. In Napoleon's own time, Tsar Alexander had the ambition to seize the whole of Poland for himself. Although he was a dumb blond in appearance, the Russian leader was as greedy for territory as his illustrious forebear and not averse to treachery, scheming and the abandonment of diplomatic niceties to get his way. After all, he allowed his own father Tsar Paul to be murdered and he had been an ally of Napoleon.

When the Ottoman Turks were forced to leave Vienna in 1683, it was the Russians who gained most: "For the moment it was Russia's territorial expansion which stunned the rest of Europe: it absorbed the whole of the Ottomans' provinces on the north coast of the Black Sea and the Crimea before moving into the Caucasus and central Asia."[3] Ukraine was annexed and soon Russian explorers were sweeping through Siberia on their way to the Pacific Ocean. In the 1740s, long before Sarah Palin cast a wary eye across the Bering Straits, the Russians were in Alaska.

When it comes to territorial acquisitions, the Russians have form. Catherine the Great, whom Elting calls an 'imperial bitch,'[4] could not understand how England gave up its former colonies in America. She said: "Rather than have granted America her Independence, as my brother-monarch, King George has done, I would have fired a pistol at my own head."[5]

Napoleon's attack on Russia in 1812 is often portrayed as if it were some sort of violation of a retiring Snow White. The invasion was actually a consequence of the Emperor being driven to distraction by Alexander's machinations and treacherous duplicity. Alexander had professed eternal friendship at the treaty of Tilsit in 1807. Despite having crushed the Russian army at Friedland, which left Russian provinces his for the taking, Napoleon was generous to the young Tsar. The main thing he wanted was for Russia to make common cause against the most treacherous power of the day - England. Alexander promised to blockade his ports against British shipping and Napoleon was satisfied. He also happened to like the jejeune Alexander personally. To him, personal friendship and one-to-one relationships mattered; to the Romanovs, they didn't mean a damn. Tsar Paul's brutal strangulation certainly proves this point.

Napoleon has often been portrayed as a monster and called a Corsican Ogre, unjustifiably so. However, Alexander was a lot like Frankenstein's original creature. Although beautiful on the outside, behind those blue eyes there lurked a feverish dichotomy of enlightenment and repression. The young Tsar's views on kingship and the right way to rule were given impulse not just by the spark of 'divine right', but by an abruptly terminated liberal education and the clandestine murder of his father.

Alexander was a haunted, troubled soul, a guilty man fearful that he would share the same fate as Tsar Paul. Indolent, deceitful and devious, he was yet sensitive and impressionable. He yearned for political guidance and a suitable mentor, for he was only twenty-three years old when he came to the throne. Later he was to harbour a secret bitterness because his one-time hero had shown himself to have feet of clay when he declared himself Consul for life. No wonder then that his love-hate relationship with Napoleon was to poison the agreements between them.

It is interesting that Alexander, born on December 23rd, was eventually to see himself as a divinely inspired saviour whose task was to free Europe from the scourge of Napoleon. But he began his life under the influence of his grandmother, Catherine the Great. In the Age of Enlightenment, Catherine had toyed with the idea of emancipating the serfs. She had chosen a Swiss tutor for Alexander, Frederic-Cesar La Harpe, who taught him about the virtues of the ancient republics.

Things changed in 1793 when Louis XVI and Marie-Antoinette received the kiss of death at the guillotine. Liberal and enlightened ideas were no longer the order of the day. La Harpe was sent packing, leaving a sixteen-year-old Alexander unsure of the ways of the world. He had no wish to emulate his father, Tsar Paul, who, after his accession to the throne in 1796 began "by declaring war on all forms of "modernism".'[6]

Paul ruled like a petty tyrant and his murder by strangulation rocked Alexander to the core. Inspired by angry nobles, the deed traumatised his tender, young heir and as Curtis Cate remarks: "This was greatly to affect his dealings with Napoleon."[7] It was not the first palace revolt with which he was familiar. Catherine had had Emperor Peter III murdered. Alexander quickly realized that, if he wanted to stay alive, he would have to pander to the whims of mighty nobles, most of which were great Anglophiles and no friends of France.

When Napoleon first appeared on the European stage, Alexander felt that it was the dawn of a new age of enlightenment. He saw him as a virtual demi-god: "had Alexander himself not once said to the French ambassador in Petersburg that that extraordinary man Napoleon could accomplish in one year what it would take another individual twenty years of even a lifetime to complete?"[8]

It was a time when Napoleon was receiving praise from unexpected quarters. Madame de Stael wrote in 1797 of "that intrepid warrior, the most profound thinker, the most extraordinary genius in history."[9] Later, when Napoleon had repeatedly shown her that he was not interested in her physical charms, she adopted the role of the 'woman scorned'. In a strange parallel, Alexander also fell out of love with his hero.

Despite Napoleon's sweeping victory in the plebiscite of 1802, endorsing his decision to become Consul for life, Alexander took it as an act of betrayal. He wrote in a letter to la Harpe: "... the veil is now fallen. Since then, things have gone from bad to worse... Now he is one of the most egregious tyrants History has produced."[10]

As for Napoleon, "he regarded Russia as a natural ally rather than as an enemy of France."[11] After all, Paris and Saint Petersburg were 1,400 miles apart and with Russian's traditional focus being to the east, he saw no need for territorial disputes between the two countries. Had Alexander been confident enough to decide his own foreign policy then, despite his earlier disillusionment, he and Napoleon might have maintained their friendship after Tilsit in 1807. However, there was already a history of conflict between the Russian colossus and the nascent French Republic.

It was Alexander's grandmother, Catherine the Great, who promoted the First Coalition by "encouraging Austria and Prussia to strangle the revolutionary "bastard" in its cradle by attacking the young French Republic..."[12] She was wily enough not to commit any Russian troops to the conflict. Similarly, Tsar Paul, Alexander's father, promoted the Second Coalition allying himself with Austria, Portugal, Britain and the Turks.

By April 1799 Suvorov's Austrians and Russians were in Milan and "Not only was there a threat of an invasion of southern France but an Anglo-Russian force had landed in Holland."13 Massena defeated the Russians at Zurich on September 26th of that year and therefore prevented them from invading France by the 'back door'. It is worth asking at this stage, what threat were the French to Russia at a time when France was assailed from all sides?

So, when the Grand Army crossed the Niemen in 1812, just who had fired the first shot?

Despite that, Napoleon was prepared to make a friendly gesture. He returned Russian prisoners of war unconditionally, even decking them out in brand new uniforms. Knowing that Tsar Paul felt badly let down by his erstwhile allies, especially the English, Napoleon further suggested that the newly elected Grand Master of the Order of Saint John, Paul himself, should have Malta. When the English took Malta, the Tsar became incensed: "The Tsar turned right round and revived the Armed Neutrality of the Northern Powers against England."14

Like Alexander after him, Paul could turn his allegiance around on a sixpence, as his former allies the English might say. Both father and son had a Jekyll and Hyde personality, certainly dualistic, probably even bordering upon the schizophrenic. Surprisingly, considering his earlier attitude to Napoleon, Paul sent an envoy to Paris and broached the topic of a joint Russo-French expedition to India to teach perfidious Albion a lesson. The same idea was, of course, later suggested to Alexander by Napoleon himself.

Napoleon wrote to his brother Joseph in 1801: "The Russian attitude is very hostile towards England... peace with the Emperor (of Austria) is nothing compared with an alliance that would master England and keep Egypt for us."15 He was well aware of the value of a Franco-Russian alliance.

Unfortunately for Napoleon, all this came to nothing when a silk scarf tightened around Tsar Paul's neck. However, despite his disappointment, he was to repeat his lenient policy. After the battle of Friedland in 1807, when he destroyed the Russian army, "as he had done in 1800 with Tsar Paul, Napoleon offered a gesture of friendship to Tsar Alexander by sending back several thousand Russian prisoners newly uniformed and armed."16

There was a backlash from Napoleon's own army this time, when his cold and hungry troops saw ragged, sick Frenchmen returning from Russian imprisonment. Some French prisoners were reviewed by the Tsar and given a ducat apiece, but others were withheld after various lame excuses. Napoleon was forced to get rougher with other Russian prisoners in order to achieve their release.

Even worse was to follow in 1812 when Russian soldiers, especially Cossacks, marched naked French prisoners through the snow in temperatures way below zero, or sold them to vengeful peasants so that their brains could be dashed out against logs. Partly because of this, Napoleon made strenuous efforts to evacuate the French sick from Moscow before the disastrous retreat began. Comparing the two rulers over a period of years, it can clearly be seen that Napoleon's treatment of prisoners was the more humane.

Other problems developed between the two countries. As Felix Markham states: "Napoleon never succeeded in gaining moral acceptance by the European powers as a legitimate ruler."17 Even worse, cowardly terrorist attacks upon his life, promoted by the Comte d'Artois and secretly paid for by the English Cabinet, killed many innocent civilians and were obviously a great shock to the First Consul. Markham adds: "In the minds of his opponents a code of conduct prevailed which they would never have presumed to apply to a legitimate monarch."18

When Napoleon had the duc d'Enghien arrested for his alleged part in another plot on his life and to show that he was not powerless in the face of these criminal attacks, the Courts of Europe were in uproar, especially when d'Enghien was summarily shot by an overzealous subordinate. Alexander was especially shocked by this turn of events.

Furthermore, although d'Enghien had served with Suvorov in Italy, and was undoubtedly a traitor, he had been a friend of Princess Amelie, the mother of Princess Elizabeth of Russia.

Baden, where d'Enghien was arrested, was also linked to Alexander by marriage. Shortly after this, the Tsar's Foreign Minister, Czartoryski played a major role in the formation of the Third Coalition.

Then, there was Austerlitz, Napoleon's crowning triumph against the old reactionary monarchs of Europe. In tears, Alexander fled the battlefield crying: "We are infants, in the hands of a giant!"[19]

Before the battle, Napoleon had sent his ADC Savary to the Russian camp to suggest a personal meeting between the two Emperors. Scorned by the dandies surrounding Alexander, who could have come straight from the pages of Pushkin or Turgenev, this idea was rejected. It is often said that Napoleon, with his proffered olive branch, was only trying to lull the Allies into a false sense of security prior to his coup de main.

Yet, after his greatest ever victory, he sent a Russian prisoner, Colonel Repnin with a personal message to the Tsar: "Tell him that if he had heeded my proposals and accepted an interview between our outposts, I would have submitted myself to his lovely soul. He would have declared to me his intentions to give Europe a respite, and I would have agreed to them."[20]

Unfortunately, after the battle, the Russian elite had been like a 'duck hit on the head' as Abraham Lincoln might have put it – they did not know what else to do but vanish in a cloud of dust. Only Czartoryski remained long enough to receive the message, and he saw to it that Alexander never heard about the offer. Years later, after his return from Elba, and before Waterloo, Napoleon sent a letter to George, the Prince Regent, requesting peace. This too, never got to its intended recipient. Yet it is always Napoleon who is blamed for 'causing' these wars.

The Tsar took no part in the subsequent peace negotiations and later, he allowed himself to be dragged into the conflict caused by Prussia's unilateral declaration of war against France in 1806. Lovely, his soul might have been, but sensible it was not.

Alexander also lost the considerable backing of the British taxpayer. For every 100,000 troops Russia had put into the field, he had been getting £1,250,000 – a huge sum in those days.21 In 1805, as well as his catastrophic intervention into Austrian territory, he had sent armies into Naples and Hanover. His support for the Prussian claim to Hanover was not popular with his paymaster and this had serious repercussions: "Prussia, Austria, and Russia were more or less impoverished nations; only English subsidies enabled them to raise and pay vast armies for year after year of hard campaigning."22 And now the gold stopped flowing.

It is worth stressing that, without all this money from the British Treasury, there could have been no 1805 campaign and Alexander would have been forced to agree to some accommodation with France, perhaps the very alliance Napoleon had always hoped for. There would also have been no need for the French invasion of 1812. Alexander's love of money to buy himself the influence in Europe that his ego craved, the pecuniary appetites of the other monarchs, and the propensity of the English to dispense their largesse, was what really plunged Europe into a series of debilitating wars. Napoleon's greatest enemy had no troops - it was the Bank of England.

Like all weak rulers, Alexander was flattered by the attention and the affected adoration of others. Even though Napoleon took a genuine liking to him at Tilsit in 1807, once Alexander left the 'love-in' on the raft in the middle of the river Niemen, he was soon flirting with the other powers: "Within a year he was dickering with England and had reached a tacit understanding with Austria. He had interfered with the Polish military operations in 1809 and was now attempting to persuade Poland to make him its king, while massing troops along his western frontier."23

At Erfurt in 1808 all the Tsar was prepared to offer Napoleon in the case of renewed hostility with Austria was Russian neutrality. Alexander had offered Austria exactly the same thing. Yet, despite not a single Russian soldier coming to the aid of the French at Wagram in 1809, after his victory, Napoleon gave parts of Galicia to both Russia and the Grand Duchy of Warsaw.

Alexander cynically explained his attitude to his mother, the Dowager Empress. He wanted: "to gain a breathing-space, and, during that precious interval, build up our resources... must we spoil all our work and raise suspicion of our true intentions, just because Napoleon is temporarily embarrassed?"[24] And, if Alexander's attitude was not bad enough, Talleyrand and Caulaincourt were going to him behind Napoleon's back.[25]

Once again, Napoleon had been the victim of an Austrian attack. He had not wanted war and was right to assume that his alliance with Russia ought to have prevented it – but for Alexander's double-dealing. Wagram had been a tough and costly battle and Marshal Lannes, Napoleon's friend, had been one of the casualties. This time it was Napoleon's turn to weep after an epic confrontation. Meanwhile, the war in Spain was going badly and was a constant drain on French manpower and resources. Far from being the warmonger of legend, he was deeply realistic: "Battle should only be offered when there is no other turn of fortune to be hoped for, as from its nature the fate of a battle is always dubious."[26]

At Erfurt, aware of his own precarious position as ruler and his need for an heir, Napoleon raised the idea of his marrying the Grand Duchess Catherine, the Tsar's sister. But the Dowager Empress, who had already berated Alexander for having anything at all to do with the French Emperor, was not impressed. She regarded Napoleon as the Antichrist and the treaty of Tilsit as nothing less than a 'pact with the devil'.[27] Curtis Cate suggests that Napoleon's "highly personal feud with his imperial "brother," Alexander of Russia was influenced by his jilted hope of being able to marry into the Romanov dynasty."[28] Perhaps that is going too far, but Alexander's prevarications and lack of enthusiasm for the idea did not bode well. As late as February 1810, Napoleon was being denied a final answer in regard to a younger Russian princess, as Catherine had already been married off to someone else. Hence, he married Marie–Louise of Austria.

The full extent of Napoleon's problem with Russia was revealed by Savary who replaced Caulaincourt as French Ambassador to Saint Petersburg in December 1807. He said:

"The Emperor and Count Roumiantsov are the only friends of France in Russia."29 And he was only half-right there. It is no surprise to learn that Savary would never get as close to Alexander as Caulaincourt had done. In fact, Napoleon faced the implacable hostility of most of the Russian Court.

Also, by now, Alexander was no doubt looking over his own shoulder and recalling what had happened to his father, Tsar Paul, because Napoleon's Continental System, curtailing trade with the English, was having a devastating effect upon the incomes of Russian nobles. There was not enough gold flowing into their troughs and the pigs were squealing. Alexander simply did not have enough courage to stand up to them.

When it came to the Grand Duchy of Warsaw, Napoleon and Alexander were poles apart. To the latter, it was not so much an encroachment upon Russia's back yard as a take over of its front garden. It was the territory Alexander coveted most. He was jealous of Napoleon's acquisitions and he wanted some of his own: he saw it as little less than his birthright. Alexander had no one to blame but himself. He had entered into a Coalition against France willingly – after all, someone else was paying for it, but Russia had gambled and lost.

Yet, it was as a direct consequence of his clumsy interference in European affairs that Napoleon decided to set up the Grand Duchy as a buffer state. What really stuck in Alexander's craw was the fact that "Nowhere in Europe were the inhabitants more rabidly pro-French and – as Tsar Alexander was chagrined to realize – so disturbingly anti-Russia."30 The former Polish provinces that had 'belonged' to Austria and Prussia, a land of four million people, stretching from the Oder river to the border of Russia at the Niemen, had been restored to the Polish people by Napoleon, thus correcting part of the misdeeds performed by Austria, Prussia and Russia all those years before.

Despite the further clamourings of Polish patriots, Napoleon resisted the pressure to reconstitute Poland itself as a nation state, primarily in deference to Alexander. He did not want to strain relations between them further, even when his 1812 campaign was underway. Had he given in to the tremendous wave of Polish nationalism, it might well have tipped the balance in the early stages of the invasion, particularly if he had accompanied it with the emancipation of the serfs.

In 1811, Alexander had planned an attack of his own and had massed a considerable force on his western border. The Polish Prince Poniatowski warned Napoleon that: "Alexander was planning a surprise attack on the relatively weak French forces left beyond the Elbe."[31] However, his possible allies, Austria and Prussia, the usual suspects, had no stomach for it, so he backed down.

The idea that the 1812 campaign was simply a result of Napoleonic megalomania must be put to rest, despite Alexander's all-innocent line to John Quincy Adams, the American minister at Saint Petersburg, in March of that year: "And so it is, after all, that war is coming which I have done so much to avoid."[32]

Considering all the above, one must agree with colonel Elting when he states that: "All of this Russian military adventuring occurred before one armed French soldier stepped onto Russian soil."[33]

That Napoleon's final decision to invade Russia was a mistake there can be no doubt, but we have the benefit of hindsight. After years of frustration as a consequence of the slippery policies of his former protégé, and the never-ending enmity of England, Napoleon prepared for the campaign of 1812. He hoped that one decisive battle would sweep Alexander back into the fold, close Russian ports to British vessels, and so precipitate a lasting peace. Sadly for him, what followed was not the equivalent of a second Cannae but another Zama. Like Hannibal, he was doomed to die in exile.

On the eve of the invasion, with the French Grand Army preparing to cross the river, Napoleon made a last reconnaissance along the banks of the Niemen. His horse stumbled and threw him. It was nothing but a slight fall, he reassured his superstitious staff. He had long since fallen from the pedestal in Alexander's eyes and consequently, Napoleon's hopes for a gentlemanly war with his 'brother' Alexander were misplaced.

To Alexander, friendship and enmity were two sides of the same coin. He had come out from behind the shadow of Tsar Paul a long time ago and now he was bent on a little political assassination of his own. What Alexander wanted was Napoleon's complete and utter downfall, and he was prepared to go to the gates of Paris if need be in order to achieve it.

NOTES

*   Elting 526
1. Hywel Williams *Fifty Days That Changed The World* (London: Folio, 2008) 211
2. Ibid. 113
3. Ibid. 114
4. Elting 521
5. John Clarke *The Life And Times Of George III* (London: Book Club Associates, 1972) 110
6. Curtis Cate *The War Of The Two Emperors* (New York: Random House, 1985) 14-15
7. Ibid. 15
8. Ibid. 8-9
9. Felix Markham 133
10. Cate 16
11. Ibid. Preface x
12. Ibid. 6
13. Markham 70
14. Ibid. 89
15. Ibid. 89-90
16. Elting 618
17. Markham 113
18. Ibid. 113
19. Cate 19
20. Ibid. 19
21. Ibid. 7 He adds that there were "four thousand English bankers and merchants who had once inhabited the port of Kronstadt, at the mouth of the Petersburg isthmus..."
23. Ibid. 63
24. Markham 187
25. Ibid. 187
26. Ibid. 183
27. Ibid. 186
28. Cate Preface x

29. Markham 186
30. Cate 8
31. Markham 188
32. Cate 5
33. Elting 521
34. See Dexter Hoyos *Hannibal's Dynasty* (London: Routledge, 2003)
Hannibal's greatest victory occurred at the Battle of Cannae when he
destroyed a Roman army of nearly 80,000 men. More men were killed that
day than on the first day of the Battle of the Somme in the First World War.
Hannibal was defeated by Scipio Africanus at Zama. He was later hounded
by the Romans and after a period as a naval commander, he committed
suicide to avoid capture by taking poison. Napoleon as a youth applied to
join the British navy! He was later poisoned by the Comte de Montholon on
Saint Helena.

MARCH OR DIE:
THE RETREAT FROM RUSSIA IN 1812

"We left behind us an enormous number of dead and dying. Further on it was worse still, as we had to stride over the dead bodies left on the road by the regiments going before us."*

Few events in the whole of human history can compare with the retreat of the Grand Army from Moscow in 1812. To the brutal horrors of war were added the cruelties of what Marshal Ney called 'General Winter'.1 Bourgogne recalls these events with a stark, bare prose, for what actually happened to him and his comrades needed no embellishment. Tolstoy's *War and Peace* is like a fairy tale in comparison, and his Napoleon little more than a caricature of the real French Emperor.

There were military disasters before and after this campaign, for example: Pickett's charge at Gettysburg in 1863; the defeat of the Swedish King Charles XII at Poltava in 1709 - an earlier ill-fated invasion of Russia; and the loss of the French paratroopers at Dien Bien Phu in 1954. But none of these had such elements of Greek tragedy about them. Clausewitz said that: "in war the simplest thing is difficult,"2 and Napoleon himself made the remark that from the sublime to the ridiculous is only one step.

That the Emperor overreached himself there can be no question. Those hastily constructed trestle bridges at the Berezina really did prove to be 'bridges too far', but before the campaign began, young French soldiers and others anxious to gain a commission, had been enthusiastic to join what they feared might be Napoleon's last military venture. He had put all his amazing resourcefulness into preparing for this conflict and every contingency had been provided for. All that is, except the weather.

It very nearly was Napoleon's last campaign for, after the battle of Malojaroslavetz – which led him to make the fateful decision to return over the same burnt out desert his man had traversed on their way to Moscow – he decided to go on a reconnaissance in the very early hours of a dank and foggy morning. He was almost immediately surrounded by 6,000 of Platov's Cossacks and, but for the immense bravery of his personal staff and the timely arrival of Bourgogne and a contingent of the Imperial Guard, he would either have been killed or captured.[3]

At Dresden in May 1812, he had been at the apogee of imperial power. As his Army died of cold and starvation amidst the Russian wastes, did Napoleon realize that his days were numbered? He literally left his cavalry behind – for 60,000 horses died in Russia. Some 10,000 died in one night in a freezing downpour in June. Many more of the unfortunate animals were eaten by their former riders, or by the snow-blind infantry stumbling along behind the cavalry and artillery. And that was before the cannibalism began.

Of all the memoirs of this period, Bourgogne's is the best.

Sergeant Bourgogne had a soul of iron, not just a constitution made from it. He had his own conception of la gloire: "I felt that the greater the danger and suffering, the greater the glory and honour..."[4] Here is what it meant to be a member of Napoleon's Imperial Guard. These were men forged by hardship, tempered with courage and tested by fire. Napoleon could not have achieved the things he did without them. And the campaign of 1812 tested their mettle to breaking point. In agonizing and harrowing detail, Bourgogne tells how the whole Grand Army was tested to destruction.

Bourgogne's story touches the common humanity amongst us all. It shows a modern world, where people wallow in physical laziness and vapid conspicuous consumption, just what it takes to make a real hero. When a man's in a tight spot his greatest need is to be able to draw on his own inner well of strength and fortitude. Bourgogne's well was very deep. When he had absolutely nothing and was freezing and starving to death – he had himself. The pride and honour of France were encapsulated in his indomitable spirit and physical toughness.

Admiration for such qualities extends across continents and through time. Sir Arthur Conan Doyle states: "There is no better writing and no easier reading, than the records of these men of action."[5] And as an Englishman, he speculated on 'what might have been', had Napoleon's army managed to cross La Manche and tuck Britain up its sleeve: "A Briton cannot help asking himself, as he realizes what men these were, what would have happened if 150,000 Coignets and Bourgognes, with Marbots to lead them, and the great captain of all time in the prime of his vigour at their head, had made their landing in Kent."[6]

The answer is elementary my dear Doyle.

Murat, who was not as bright as the buttons on his uniform, was in charge of the advance guard of the Grand Army that was based at Winkovo to the south of Moscow. Lulled into a false sense of security by the Russians, his forces were suddenly attacked, sustaining a large number of casualties. When Napoleon heard of this he realized that the game was up. Tsar Alexander was never going to make peace. And the retreat began.

Bourgogne says that: "I cannot possibly describe all the sufferings, anguish, and scenes of desolation I had seen and passed through, nor those which I was fated still to see and endure; they left deep and terrible memories, which I have never forgotten."[7] His descent into the valley of the shadow of death was a passage into abject terror, a living nightmare that lasted weeks. On many occasions he thought his time had come.

Adrien-Jean-Baptiste-François Bourgogne never expected to see his home at Condé again. Born in 1785, he was already a veteran of Eylau and Essling, having fought Austrians, Prussians, Spaniards and Russians before in the service of his Emperor. His attitude is summed up in the third verse of Roland's song:

> 'Eh! demande où sont les perils
> C'est là qu'est aussi la victoire!'
> 'Eh! Ask where the dangers are,
> That is where victory is too!"[8]

When he arrived in Moscow he was proud of the fact that "we of the Imperial Guard had marched more than twelve hundred leagues without resting."9 Having survived the firestorms that had greeted the French Army, he rather enjoyed his stay: "On the days off duty we drank, smoked, and laughed, talking of France and the distance separating it from us, and the possibility of being sent still further off."10

Those rumours of a possible march to India were premature. In clement weather, from Paris to Moscow by fast horseback courier took around fourteen days. Long before the Army left Moscow, those couriers had been failing to appear. The journey had become fraught with dangers and presaged the Pony Express of America in the 1860s. Instead of Indians, there were Cossacks and furious peasants. The fact that the mail no longer got through was, in effect, the writing on the wall. The summer was long since over and all the Emperor's horses would soon be falling like autumn leaves.

One of the first gruesome sights that met the retreating warriors was the battlefield at Borodino, with its hundreds of rotting corpses.11 This did not do wonders for morale. Many arms and legs had been eaten away by wild animals. An incredible story came to Bourgogne's attention. A French Grenadier, whose legs had been blown off during the battle, had kept himself alive by sheltering inside a dead horse. The flesh of the poor beast had sustained him along with bloodstained water from a nearby stream.12

The very next night of October 29th-30th, the first snow fell. Bourgogne's star must have been shining, because he acquired a bearskin coat that was to save his life on many future occasions when other unfortunates froze to death all around him. There were many far worse off than he.13

That same day a Portuguese officer sidled up to the fire at which Bourgogne was warming himself. He was escorting several hundred Russian prisoners: "They had no food, and were reduced to eating each other. Literally, when one of them died, he was cut up and divided between them, and afterwards eaten."14

For several days Bourgogne himself had had only horseflesh to eat. The food carted from Moscow by the fleeing troops had all been used up. He adds: "with the cold weather, our real miseries began."15 It distressed even the veterans when they had to start leaving their sick and wounded behind to the tender mercies of their Russian pursuers. As the snow deepened, the going got ever harder.

By November 5th soldiers were constantly falling by the wayside. Bourgogne tells of the superhuman efforts they had made thus far in the hope of reaching Smolensk. That day a baby was born to the cantinière Madame Dubois: "in the midst of the falling snow, with twenty degrees of frost, i.e., about ten below zero, she was delivered of a fine boy..."16 The poor child lasted only a few days. "That same night our men killed a white bear, which was eaten at once. After spending a miserable night, on account of the fearful cold, we set out again."17

November 6th brought dense fog and a punishing frost: "Our lips were frozen, our brains too; the whole atmosphere was icy. There was a fearful wind, and the snow fell in enormous flakes."18 A passing horseman turned out to be a General searching for Napoleon to tell him of the Malet conspiracy in distant Paris.19

With the Cossacks picking off the stragglers, the shattered Grand Army had to be constantly on the march. There was not even time to light a fire and cook a proper meal. The menu was simple – horsemeat. Many men made do with bleeding the horses. It was so cold that the animals barely noticed. Soon Bourgogne and his comrades resembled vampires: "The blood was caught in a saucepan, cooked, and eaten... The saucepan was carried with us, and each man, as he marched, dipped his hands in and took what he wanted; his face in consequence became smeared with blood."20

Haggard soldiers with hollow eyes and sunken cheeks, their uniforms in tatters, dressed in anything they could lay their hands on in a futile effort to stay warm, dragged themselves along, their beards bristling with icicles of blood. The conditions became so dreadful that even the bond of friendship between old comrades broke down. Men began killing each other for morsels of food. Frosts became so hard that even with an axe it was impossible to chop up the carcass of a horse for meat. Not having slept properly for days, the refugees grew ever weaker.

If things weren't bad enough, they got even worse at the posting station in Gara. Over seven hundred men had crammed themselves inside the long barn-like building when fire broke out in two places within. Fortunately for Bourgogne there had been no room for him inside. Instead, he bore witness to the tragedy that followed: "Then cries and shrieks of rage were heard, the fire became a vast tossing mass, through the convulsive efforts of the poor wretches to escape. It was the picture of hell."[21]

Bourgogne managed to save a handful of men, but other outsiders, half-crazed with cold and starvation, rushed towards the building crying "What a beautiful fire!"[22] He later heard that roasted bodies were dragged out and eaten by Croats. Bourgogne added ruefully: "failing a man to eat, we would have demolished the devil himself, if he were only cooked."[23] Nevertheless, he personally eschewed such horrific human sustenance.

Despite all the misery, Bourgogne also relates a tale of extreme devotion. Just before he got to Smolensk there was a terrible snowstorm with twenty-seven degrees of frost. Anyone caught in the open stood no chance of survival. Yet that was the situation faced by the twenty-year-old prince Émile of Hesse-Cassel. With him were several hundred of his men. All night, blasted by a screaming wind, they surrounded him, protecting him from the arctic cold. As the hours went by, they died off like the rings of an onion: "The next morning three-quarters of them were dead and buried beneath the snow, along with ten thousand others from different corps."[24]

When Bourgogne staggered into Smolensk he was met by utter chaos. At one stage Napoleon had considered staying there for the winter but the few food stores left in the burnt out city were soon devoured by desperate men. An old Chasseur said to Bourgogne: "I have been in Egypt, and, by God! it was nothing compared with this."[25] He was lucky enough to find his friend Grangier who gave him a piece of cooked beef – his first proper meal in twenty-three days.

Beyond Smolensk, 90,000 Russians were barring the path at Krasnoi. It looked like the Grand Army was doomed: "But the Emperor wished to show them it was not quite so easy as they imagined: for although we were most wretched, and dying of cold and hunger, we still preserved two things – courage and honour."[26]

Battle commenced at two o'clock in the morning. The French moved forward through deep snow in three columns and charged with their bayonets at the ready. Passing through the Russian camp, making great slaughter, they reached the village of Krasnoi itself. A murderous hand-to-hand conflict ensued with spectral shadows flickering in the lurid flames cast by burning huts. [27]

A second fight occurred on November 17th. As the French got into order of battle, Bourgogne was detailed to be the *guide général* at the right of the line. He stood for over an hour holding the butt-end of his musket in the air as the bullets whistled all around him.[28] A few thousand men of the Grand Army faced 50,000 Russians and they had to withdraw. Passing Krasnoi by another route, the survivors were mortified when they had to leave the wounded behind: "to a savage and brutal enemy, who stripped and robbed these unfortunates without pity for their wounds or their condition."[29]

On the way to Orsha, Bourgogne saw Napoleon himself on foot, walking with the aid of a stick. Once there, he noticed the boats of a pontoon train being burnt so that the extra horses could be used to pull the remaining guns. This calamitous decision almost sealed the fate of the Army. By now, of some thirty-five thousand former men of the Guard, barely seven thousand were left with the colours.[30]

Spirits lifted however, when news came that Marshal Ney had arrived with the remnants of the rearguard. He had long since been given up for dead: "The Emperor's joy was unbounded when he heard that the Marshal was safe."[31] Napoleon had said that he would have given all the gold in the Tuileries vaults just to see him again. Strange it is to relate then, that less than two years later, Ney would betray his Emperor when the Allies closed in on Paris.

The power of Napoleon's own magnetism was undimmed. He had heard that the Russians were waiting at the Berezina. Gathering the Grenadiers and Chasseurs around him, he drew his sword and raised his voice: "Let us all swear to die fighting than not see our country again!" Cries of 'Vive l'Empereur' rose majestically into the frozen air: "It was a splendid moment, and for a time made us forget our miseries."32

At that time of the year, it was dark by four o'clock in the afternoon and the exhausted men were reduced to calling out for their corps to bivouac alongside at the day's end, not for their once proud regiments. The thought of his dead friends plagued Bourgogne and his depression deepened. Then he got left behind.33

The North wind was howling and all his comrades had disappeared: "Soon I was alone, with only the dead bodies along the road to guide me."34 A sixth sense made him pause and turn his bearskin coat inside out so that the fur was closest to his skin. This helped him survive but, even so, he stumbled as sleep threatened to overwhelm him. To sleep was certain death.

He had been through so much and his physical weakness meant that he was close to collapse. Now came his *noche triste*, what the Spanish call a night of tears: "In this immense country and the awful silence I was alone, a prey to the most gloomy thoughts – of my comrades from whom I was separated, my country, my relations – and I began to cry like a child. The tears relieved me, and gradually my courage came back."35

Then, as if by a miracle, he fell down a steep embankment and he found, sheltering in a wagon at the bottom, his old friend Picart.36 He had not seen him since Napoleon reviewed the Imperial Guard on the eve of the departure from Moscow. Picart had been sent on ahead on escort duty and was in reasonable physical shape. He was also one of the best marksmen in the whole Army. For Bourgogne, came the hour, came the man.

Bourgogne told Picart the appalling news. Of 40,000 cavalry, only 1,000 were left, formed into a Doomed Squadron led by a General in which the 'private' soldiers were all officers, itself part of a similar Doomed Battalion. Picart was stunned and berated Napoleon: "He is a regular fool of a conscript to have waited so long in Moscow... to stay there thirty-four days just waiting for winter to come on! I call that folly."[37]

Picart had a treasure beyond compare – a saucepan, and he gave Bourgogne a cooked meal: "I do not think I ever enjoyed, or ever shall enjoy, anything so much."[38] Together, the comrades headed for the Berezina, Russian cavalry all around them. In an encounter with Cossacks they came off best and captured a horse into the bargain. Picart became the 'advance guard' sitting at the front of the horse and Bourgogne, facing backwards, was the 'rearguard'. They dismounted and hid in the trees when 200 half-naked French prisoners and their escort approached.[39]

The 'Russian' officer turned out to be a Frenchman who, after twenty years in Russia, longed to return to France. They overheard him talk to a prisoner: "I know quite well you have not been conquered by force of arms, but by this unendurable Russian climate."[40] The 'Russian' also said that Napoleon had been captured along with all his Guard. This devastating news upset Picart but, in the end, he refused to believe it and said to Bourgogne: "Cheer up, *mon pays*... if we are lucky enough to find the Emperor, it will be all right."[41] Bourgogne adds: "Picart, along with all the veterans, who idolised the Emperor, thought that once with him everything was bound to succeed, and that, in fact, nothing was impossible."[42]

Saint Peter might have denied his Lord, but now he was ready to die for him again.

They were hopelessly lost in dense forest when Picart noticed two women in the distance, so they decided to follow them. One must have been lady luck, for they were led to the door of a very welcoming Polish family. When they told an old peasant man they were members of Napoleon's Guard: "At that name the Pole bowed, and would have kissed our feet." Great care and attention was lavished on the pair, food was brought to them and their wounds were bathed.43

Wanting to reward their host, Bourgogne recalled a portmanteau that was attached to the captured Cossack horse. Amongst the contents was a commander's cross with Napoleon's portrait upon it. The old peasant eyed it greedily and duly received it as a gift: "I cannot describe his pleasure. He pressed it several times to his lips and heart," and obviously, only death would subsequently part him from it.44

So it was, that in the depths of the Lithuanian forest, miles from anywhere and hundreds of miles from France, they came across a simple peasant whose adoration for the Emperor equalled their own. This demonstrates vividly, the colossal impact Napoleon had upon the whole of Europe, including the most distant, far-flung, and isolated parts.

A Jewish guide, known to the family, then took them towards the Berezina, where the sound of cannon fire could already be heard. Ironically, they were now ahead of the remnants of the main Army and, waiting by the high road, they saw Napoleon himself approaching. The state of the survivors shocked Picart, who had not seen the Grand Army for a month, and he shed tears openly: "It breaks my heart to see our Emperor on foot, a stick in his hand. He, so great, who made us all so proud of him!" Picart added: "Did you see the way he looked at us?"45

Bourgogne wrote: "The Emperor had turned his head towards us as he passed. He looked at us as he always looked at the men of his Guard when he met them alone. He seemed, in this hour of misfortune, to inspire us by his glance with confidence."46

Many of the refugees stumbling along the road had lost fingers and toes to the frosts. Their eyes were red, their faces blackened, from having been too close to the windblown campfires. Dressed in rags and tatters, they had burnt cloaks and coats and only sheepskin wrapped around their frozen feet.

Having rejoined his regiment, Bourgogne saw the *pontonniers* up to their necks in the icy waters of the Berezina, valiantly building two trestle bridges.47 He had developed a fever and, but for the help of his comrades, he would probably have been left behind and taken prisoner. As Oudinot's men crossed to the far side to secure the bridgehead, Victor's corps kept the Russians at bay to the rear. At seven o'clock on the morning of November 28th, although still ill, Bourgogne slipped across the river alone. Thousands of others, exhausted and reluctant to abandon their fires, stayed behind only to fall into the clutches of the enemy.48

It might be assumed that by now everyone would be cursing Napoleon for being responsible for all this misery. Yet, when some Grenadiers went around the bivouacs asking for wood for him: "Everyone willingly gave the best they had. Even dying men raised their heads to say, 'Take what you can for the Emperor.' " Was there ever such devotion as this?49

When the Russians shelled the bridges, pandemonium broke loose amongst the hundreds of stragglers. As a body, they rushed towards the bridges and chaos ensued. Men, woman and children, fought each other as they clawed their way to the opposite bank. When Marshal Victor retreated: "He and his men had to cross the bridge over a perfect mountain of corpses."50

Still in a fever, Bourgogne continued on his way, the Russians following the fleeing Army on either side of the road. Meeting some officers in charge of a hundred men of all nationalities up ahead, he soon realized that no one knew the right route to take. When this became known amongst the ranks, many men wept like children. Soon after, his shelter blown away by a ferocious gale, Bourgogne had to walk around all night to stop himself from freezing.51

He then reached Molodechno on the way to Vilna: "I heard later that it was from this place that the Emperor despatched his twenty-ninth bulletin, which caused such a sensation in France, announcing the destruction of our army."52

Anyone who was unable to walk faced certain death, but even those well enough to travel had no idea where they were going. Bourgogne followed 10,000 men who were plodding along, many so close to death that they no longer cared about anything.

When Bourgogne arrived at Smorgoni on December 6th, he heard that Napoleon had left for Paris the evening before. He states that many foreigners then began criticizing the Emperor, but: "owing to Malet's conspiracy, his presence was necessary in France, not only for the administration, but to organize a new army."53 He put the trouble down to surprisingly well-dressed and hearty men who suddenly appeared amongst the stragglers. Bourgogne even wondered if they were English agents sent to cause trouble.54

General Wilson, the English officer, was attached to Kutusov's army at that time, and English gold had certainly been behind many of the earlier wars between Russia and France. Even today, many so-called 'historians' from Britain continue to castigate Napoleon for 'abandoning' his Army in 1812, seeking to blacken his reputation in any way they can. In fact, all the senior French officers supported his decision to return to Paris and, on Bourgogne's testimony, even the rank and file understood the reasons behind it.

Although it seems hard to believe, for poor Bourgogne, the weather got even worse. On the road to Vilna he says: "I should call the efforts we made superhuman. This terrible cold was more than I had ever felt before. I was almost fainting, and we seemed to walk through an atmosphere of ice."55 The anarchy in Vilna was virtually indescribable as some 50,000 famished wraiths descended upon the place, banging on every door in the hope of finding food.56

To Bourgogne's immense joy, he bumped into Picart again, better still, his old comrade had some freshly baked bread: "For fifty days I had not tasted any, and it seemed that if only I could eat a little I should forget all my miseries."57 An alarm sounded and, after driving off some Cossacks from the outskirts of town, they became separated again.

King Murat was supposed to have held Vilna and reorganised the troops there, but he lacked what Napoleon called two o'clock in the morning courage. When he left for Kowno with his bodyguard, Picart amongst them, everyone else tried to follow his example. By now Bourgogne was in a desperate state. Not only was his right foot frozen, he had an open wound, the middle fingertip of his right hand was at the point of dropping off, and he had colic, having been poisoned by a Jew who coveted his possessions.58

A crowd of 10,000 fought to get out of Vilna, Bourgogne amongst them. Soon, he found himself being left behind. Only Marshal Ney's rearguard of 300 men prevented everyone from being captured by Cossacks. Bourgogne pays him tribute: "I shall never forget the Marshal's commanding air at this moment, his splendid attitude towards the enemy, and the confidence with which he inspired the unhappy sick and wounded around him. In this moment he was like one of the heroes of old times. In these last days of this disastrous retreat he was the saviour of the remnants of the army."59

Almost killed by a Cossack, Bourgogne climbed Ponari hill where abandoned wagons full of Army gold, were being ransacked by Cossack and Frenchman alike.60 Had he not rejoined Grangier and his comrades, he would have been just another body in the snow. Every road now resembled a battlefield.

"At last we reached Kowno," he says, and "we heard at intervals the sound of artillery, which seemed to us like the expiring sigh of our army."61 In one night, 1,500 men froze to death after getting drunk. They were so weak that just a small amount of brandy caused intoxication. When he got to the Niemen and the Russian border, Bourgogne found himself to be one of only 60 survivors in his regiment – some 2,000 men had marched into Russia five months before.62

Further hardship awaited him in Prussia, yet he had already been marching for sixty days. In temperatures way below zero, with little food, never more than two or three hours' sleep a night, and under constant pressure and attack from Cossacks and the Russian army, he had doggedly kept going. His achievement was incredible, his will to survive inviolable and his fortitude indomitable.

"One day, perhaps – who knows? - my memoirs, although badly written, will interest those who read them. The great genius is no more, but his name will live for ever."63

So will yours Bourgogne, so will yours. En avant, marche!

NOTES

*Sergeant Bourgogne: *The Retreat from Moscow* (London: The Folio Society, 1985) 57

1. Felix Markham 197 Marshal Ney in a letter to his wife Aglae.
2. Kevin J. Dougherty et al, *Battles of The American Civil War 1861-1865* (Stroud, England: Spellmount) 143
3. Markham 195 "On October 24 he found the way barred by the Russians at Malojaroslavets, and in a desperate day's fighting, in which Eugene's Italian corps distinguished themselves, he lost five thousand casualties." And Bourgogne, 49: "I remember that, just after this incident, the Emperor was talking to Murat, laughing at his narrow escape from being captured."
4. Bourgogne Ibid. 98
5. Sir Arthur Conan Doyle *Through The Magic Door* See: books.google.com/books?isbn=1426415796 (2007) 80
6. Ibid. as above.
7. Bourgogne 41
8. Ibid. 13. Third verse of *Roland à Roncevaux.* Words and music by Rouget de L'Isle.
9. Ibid. 18. One league equals three miles.
10. Ibid. 45
11. Markham 193 "The main French attack started at dawn on September 7, and by the end of the day the Russian positions had been captured, but the Russian Army had not been broken; only seven hundred prisoners were taken. On the same page he quotes Clausewitz, who, in his 1812 account wrote, 'Kutuzov, it is certain, would not have fought at Borodino when he obviously did not expect to win. But the voice of the Court, of the Army, of all Russia forced his hand.'
12. Bourgogne, 50. He heard this story on October 28th 1812.
13. Markham, 196 states that: "The first snow did not fall until November 5..." In this he is mistaken. He obviously did not read Bourgogne, 50 carefully enough!
14. Bourgogne 51
15. Ibid. 51
16. Ibid. 54
17. Ibid. 54. This could not have been a polar bear, of course, but 'brown' bears can be any colour from yellow to tan through to black. This does show however, just how wild the forest was through which they were passing. Wolves and bears were very common in Lithuania and Russia. When they were with the Polish family, a pack of wolves repeatedly came up to the door and began howling, even after Picart chased them off with a firebrand.
18. Ibid. 54
19. Malet was an unbalanced former General who briefly seized power in Paris after declaring that Napoleon had died in Russia. The fact that no one

thought to proclaim The King of Rome Napoleon II, greatly concerned the Emperor.

20. Ibid. 55
21. Ibid. 61
22. Ibid. 61
23. Ibid. 62
24. Ibid. 65
25. Ibid. 70
26. Ibid. 84
27. Ibid. 83-86
28. Ibid. 89-90
29. Ibid. 91
30. Ibid. 96
31. Ibid. 96. When Napoleon heard the news, he said Ney was not a man, he was a lion. Bourgogne and his comrades had the pride of lions, an inflexible sense of honour and duty that saw them through this disaster.
32. Ibid. 98
33. Ibid. 98-99
34. Ibid. 101
35. Ibid. 103
36. Ibid.,108-110. Picart must have been a real character: 108-143 deal with Bourgogne and Picarts' adventures together. A great film could be made of just this small section of Bourgogne's epic journey.
37. Ibid. 113
38. Ibid. 117
39. Ibid. 125-126
40. Ibid. 126
41. Ibid. 128
42. Ibid. 128
43. Ibid. 130
44. Ibid. 132
45. Ibid. 142
46. Ibid. 142
47. Ibid. 145. The first bridge was finished at two o'clock in the afternoon of November 26th. The second, for the artillery and cavalry, at four o'clock. "These brave men sacrificed their lives to save the army. One of my friends told me as a fact that he had seen the Emperor himself handing wine to them." General Eblé was in charge of this operation.
48. Ibid. 148-151. The scene at the crossing was so awful that even Bourgogne, despite all the horrors he had so far witnessed, had to turn away.
49. Ibid. 150
50. Ibid. 151
51. Ibid. 158
52. Ibid. 158
53. Ibid. 159

54. Ibid. 159
55. Ibid. 161
56. Ibid. 162
57. Ibid. 162
58. Ibid. 163. Earlier, a Jew saved Bourgogne and Picarts' lives. Here, and later, other Jews tried to poison and steal from the weakened remnants of the Army. As Picart could pass himself off as a Jew and knew their ceremonies, they usually treated him very well.
60. Ibid. 174-176
61. Ibid. 189
62. Ibid. 195
63. Ibid. 200

ASHES TO ASHES:
VOLCANOES AND NAPOLEON 1812

"Weather… is the greatest ally or the greatest enemy in the entire history of war."[1]

On June 29th, shortly after the French Grand Army entered Russia, there was a tremendous thunderstorm. Jean-Roch Coignet later recalled: "The hailstorm was so bad that we had great trouble in controlling our horses… I was half dead with cold, and unable to stand it any longer, I opened one of my wagons and took refuge inside."[2] Meanwhile, on July 4th that same year, in the land of Napoleon's inveterate enemies the English, John Constable painted *A Hayfield behind West Lodge*. He followed that with *Fields behind West Lodge* on July 7th.[3] Both pictures displayed remarkable sunsets. So what was the connection between the shivering soldier and the talented artist? The answer may come as a surprise – volcanic eruptions - or more particularly the effects produced by the ash, dust and gases that they pour into the atmosphere.

In the years prior to 1812, a plethora of volcanic eruptions across the Northern hemisphere had completed disrupted the normal weather patterns. The consequences for Napoleon's invading Army were to be absolutely dire.

Towards the end of the Eighteenth Century and throughout the years of Empire there were many such eruptions affecting the climate as far away as Siberia and Alaska, and as the French soldiers criss-crossed Europe in response to the many Coalitions arrayed against them, the sky was filled with dust, gas and ashes that resulted in fantastic sunsets and beautiful rosy dawns. The power of Nature should never be underestimated. The eruption of the Deccan Traps in India 65 million years ago, which continued for a period of over a million years, helped wipe out the dinosaurs. The French Revolution of 1789, which destroyed the dinosaurs of the ancien regime, was itself partly a product of conditions created by a spate of volcanic activity in Europe. Thus volcanoes indirectly helped Napoleon gain power and the fateful eruption of Tambora in April 1815 played a significant part in his downfall.[4]

In the preceding generation similar events had had momentous effects. A series of major eruptions in 1783-1785 almost seemed to announce the coming of the French Revolution. The cataclysm that occurred at Asama, Japan[5] in 1783 was well matched by that of Laki in Iceland. That island nestling in the far north well deserves to be called the Land of Fire and Ice. Over an eight-month period, clouds of poisonous sulphur dioxide billowed into the atmosphere killing half the livestock and over a quarter of the population.[6]

A local Icelandic priest wrote: "This past week, and the two prior to it, more poison fell from the sky than words can describe: ash... rain full of sulphur and saltpetre, all of it mixed with sand."[7] This 'Laki haze' spread all over Europe. The hottest summer on record created a high-pressure system that funnelled the air south-east towards the Continent. Meanwhile, in the merciless sky there hovered a blood coloured sun, a vivid portent of disaster.

The sky above Norfolk in the East of England was described as copper coloured in 1783.[8] Up to 23,000 British people died that August and September from aerial pollution and its after-effects. A bitter winter followed with hailstones that knocked cattle senseless in the fields. This cold snap in 1783-1784 is estimated to have taken 8,000 more lives.

In America the Mississippi froze at New Orleans and ice was seen in the Gulf of Mexico. Benjamin Franklin said "there existed a constant fog all over Europe and a great part of North America."[9] Tree ring data backs this up for "it was very cold in 1783 in the extreme northwest" of America.[10] It would appear that volcanic eruptions have their greatest influence in high latitudes - as the Grand Army would find out nearly thirty years later. Tree ring data from Alaska, the Yukon and the Mackenzie valley show that "1810 was the coldest summer over the whole region..."[11] Of added importance, in respect of the invasion of 1812, an 'unknown' eruption had taken place in

1809 according to tree ring data: "The severity and spatial extent of severe conditions across western North America in the summer of 1810 supports earlier hypotheses of a major volcanic eruption in 1809 for which there is no historical evidence."[12] We shall see the full ramifications of this 'extra' eruption on top of everything else later.

In 1783 and subsequent years, the abnormally cold temperatures led to crop failure and widespread food shortages across Europe. Thus: "The great French Revolution, one of the greatest events in modern history, was brought to a head by famine. This was the 'Three Year Freeze' of 1784-1786."[13] Those who have only heard of the social and political conditions that brought about the Revolution need to consider how a hungry belly affects 'politics'. Interestingly, in the Great Retreat of 1812 it wasn't the cold that finished the men off but lack of food according to Dominique Jean Larrey, Napoleon's respected Chief Surgeon. He also noted how coffee helped keep the hunger pangs at bay.

Napoleon was particularly susceptible to the cold and he complained constantly of it when he and Caulaincourt returned to Paris by sledge after news of the Malet Conspiracy reached them near Vilna in 1812. The remnants of the Grand Army then still struggling out of Russia were left in Murat's incapable hands and order was only restored when Eugene Beauharnais took over command.

Napoleon lived during the last decades of the so-called Little Ice Age that lasted from about 1500 to 1850.[14] So it has to be borne in mind that the atmospheric cooling that followed volcanic eruptions, which filled the sky with particulates and gases that blocked out the sun, occurred against a background of already low temperatures by historical standards. Ironically, the last Frost Fair on the River Thames was held in 1814, the year of Napoleon's first abdication.[15]

The Laki eruption of 1783 was only the start, the opening chord in a symphony of destruction. There followed a barrage of volcanic eruptions, each adding yet more dust to the atmosphere. Mount Etna was active in 1780, 1792-93, 1802, and 1809 and there was a major eruption from October 27th

1811 to May 1812 – a *month* before the Grand Army entered Russia. The Urzelina volcano in the Azores erupted in 1808. That year in England, Luke Howard noted an abnormally brilliant twilight.[16] The following year Constable painted another marvellous dust-inspired painting with *The River Stour at Sunset* as Etna spewed forth.[17] And the effects of the 'unknown' volcano have also to be factored in. In 1811 as well as the major eruption underway on Etna, there was more volcanic activity on the Azores and Vesuvius also erupted that year. In the West Indies on the isle of Saint Vincent, La Soufriere erupted in 1811 and April 1812 – again just before the invasion of Russia.

So it should come as no surprise that in Russia itself, spring came late in 1812 and thus the crops were unripe when the French arrived; the summer was incredibly hot and dusty, broken by torrential arctic downpours as described by Coignet; the autumn was unusually mild and the winter was one of the very worst on record. It was almost as if Nature had conspired to test an Army of 500,000 to destruction – to see just what human beings were capable of enduring.

In *The Boy with the U.S. Weather Men* of 1917, it states: "There had been some marvellous sunsets during the years 1810 and 1811 and the spring of 1812, but none of the scientists of that time thought of observing them or finding any significance in them, nor did any of them imagine that such could have any effect on the weather.'"[18]

Before the invasion and with his usually thorough attention to detail, Napoleon had made enquiries as to the nature of the Russian climate and he had been told that as long as he retreated before the middle of November, the worst of the winter weather would not affect his plans. However, with the eruptions of Saint George in the West Indies in 1810, Etna in Sicily in 1811 and La Soufriere in 1812, there was a "continual replenishment of the stores of volcanic dust,"[19] in the atmosphere - and it was Napoleon's glorious Empire that was about to vanish in these combined dust-fuelled sunsets.

Now we can return to a trembling Coignet as he surveys the devastation wrought by that epic hailstorm on June 29th 1812:

"Next morning a heart-rending sight met our eyes... the ground was covered with horses which had died of cold. More than ten thousand had died during this night of horror."[20] That figure is worth repeating – *ten thousand!* No wonder that in the months ahead there would not be enough remounts for the exhausted French cavalry to hold the marauding Cossacks at bay. So less than a week after the Grand Army entered Russia, many of the French cavalry were forced to walk on foot and in over-sized riding boots this wasn't easy. The lucky dismounted soldiers found a ride on the small horses indigenous to Lithuania and Russia and looked comical with their feet trailing only inches from the ground. But this disaster was no laughing matter.

There was precious little to feed to the horses that had survived the storm. Green rye found in the abandoned fields killed the animals that foraged upon it and the supply trains could neither keep up with nor find the units they were supposed to be resupplying. Without nourishing oats, the horses pulling the artillery in particular would soon succumb to disease and exhaustion. And this was without Murat's stupidity, for he kept his men on the qui vivre and did not allow them to rest either themselves or their animals. The saddled horses developed sores on their backs and were exhausted by futile expeditions chasing Cossacks who constantly spooked the Army. Everything seemed to be going wrong and all the while the heavens were preparing a winter of biblical proportions.

An instinctive dread seemed to overcome the Army. Karl von Suckow later wrote: "Not a soul in sight, not an inhabitant in the villages we passed through... These exceptional marches, added to the great shortages we had to put up with, thinned our ranks to an unexpected degree, and thousands of men disappeared within a very short time. Hundreds killed themselves..."[21]

Captain Fritz ---, serving with the Russians adds: "The air along the wide sandy tracks running through endless pine woods was really like an oven, so oppressively hot was it and so unrelieved by the slightest puff of wind."[22] Already he had served with Wellington in Portugal and Spain but he had never experienced such intolerable weather before. The retreating Russians travelled by night to escape the furnace-like conditions.

Count Wedel who was serving in the Polish Lancers described life on outpost duty: "the horses were seldom unsaddled, and never at night, because we always had to be specially prepared for night attacks, since a hundred Cossacks, knowing the district and every track in it, could without danger to themselves put the wind up an entire army corps."[23] All this before a single major engagement had been fought. Lithuania, a whole province had fallen without a shot and now hundreds if not thousands of soldiers of the Grand Army fell in turn, of starvation, the cold, the heat or simply unmitigated despair.

Those that plodded on were often far from healthy. Heinrich von Roos a senior doctor with Mountbrun's cavalry corps heading for Smolensk describes how: "On 23 July we came in pouring rain to the River Dvina, which we had orders to cross. There was no bridge. For several days we had not been dry, and now such a cold bath was pleasant for nobody, all the more so because we were in a sickly condition."[24] Many of them had diarrhoea and Roos tried to ease their discomfort with camomile and peppermint tea until it was discovered that thick broth helped the sufferers. It was easy to tell if a campsite belonged to the French or the retreating Russians – the excreta of the enemy was normal, that of the Grand Army can be guessed at. Dealing with the symptoms of diarrhoea whilst on horseback was messy and difficult to say the least.

Both the torrential rainfall and the otherwise oppressive dry and dusty conditions were the direct result of all those volcanic eruptions. The real enemy of the Grand Army was the weather.

By the time Napoleon reached the city of Smolensk in the middle of August his position both politically and militarily was extremely awkward. He had failed to bring the Russians to battle and the state of his Army, particularly the cavalry, left a lot to be desired. If he paused for the winter to reorganize, the whole of Europe might consider him beaten. Here, Antony Brett-James points out more human failings: "Whereas Davout, rigid, unpopular martinet that he was, tried to conserve his men and horses the dashing King of Naples (Murat) fatigued and thinned his regiments, not only by losing no chance to attack Cossacks encountered along the way, but also, in the expectation of a decisive battle, by keeping most of his cavalry massed centrally, thus increasing the already unmanageable problem of feeding and watering the horses."25

It was as if Fate had been preparing the demoralised men and exhausted, sick horses for total oblivion. Hungry, if not starving, weak and disoriented, they would be drawn on to the gates of Moscow and after the Battle of Borodino, which would cut a bloody swathe through those who had endured it thus far, the decimated survivors would find themselves facing a retreat of hundreds of miles into the teeth of the worst winter weather in a hundred years. The stage had been set – now they faced the final curtain.

But before the temperature plummeted there was a very unusual autumnal interlude. Napoleon declared that Moscow, which he had now occupied, was as mild as Paris at the same time of the year. Fatally, he dawdled in the city, awaiting peace proposals from Tsar Alexander that never came. And every day the steely jaws of winter began to close upon his unsuspecting Army.

Brett-James remarks: "warnings about the impending winter were ignored or treated with contempt. It is true that October was exceptionally mild for Russia… When General Rapp told him: 'The natives say we shall have a severe winter.' Napoleon retorted scornfully: "Bah! You and your natives! See how fine it is.' "26 But no one could possibly have known just how bad it was going to get and after all the horror stories he had heard about the weather, Napoleon had been lulled into a false sense of security by a mild autumn.

After Murat was surprised at Winkovo on October 18th, the Great Retreat began. By now only 107,000 men remained under arms. They left Moscow encumbered with baggage and plunder, almost sleepwalking into disaster.

When things can't get any worse – they often do. So it was in 1812 for the fleeing French and Allied contingents that made up the remnants of the once proud Grand Army. For as well as lower temperatures caused by the many volcanic eruptions prior to 1812, there was also much less solar activity - the so-called Dalton Minimum: "The sun's activity undergoes long-term changes in intensity... The Dalton Minimum, which occurred around 1790-1820... The year 1810 was the last full calendar year without any sunspots being observed... This solar behaviour is consistent with a reduced solar luminosity and should be accompanied by a cooler climate on Earth."27 Although the effects of such solar behaviour has still to be fully understood and explained, the lack of sun spots indicating *lower temperatures on Earth* might have exacerbated an already terrible concaternation of events pertaining to the weather over Russia in 1812.

And there is still more. The El Niño effect might also have played a part in the destruction of the biggest army the world had so far seen. In his book *El Nino in History: Storming Through The Ages*, Cesar Caviedes describes how a transition from an El Niño to a La Niña can effect the weather: "Another quick El Niño-La Niña transition in 1812 – *when autumn turned to a brutal winter in a few weeks* – plunged temperatures to -30 degrees Fahrenheit, making Napoleon's retreat from Moscow a disaster. He lost 90 per cent of the remains of his army during the seven-week ordeal."28 (My italics)

And if all this wasn't bad enough, Napoleon's men still had to fight the Russian Army and swarms of Cossacks as it made its way out of the benighted country.

Now the high latitudes had another debilitating effect: "The rapidly shortening days meant long cold nights... Ever the days grew shorter and the red sunrises and the red sunsets – which would have meant so much had any one understood – continued."29 To add to the growing nightmare, the troops were clad in summer uniforms and many, from warmer southern climes, were totally unused to such arctic weather.

By now it was every man for himself. Stumbling, freezing spectres - no longer could they be called soldiers - froze solid around their pathetic campfires. They died off in layers like an onion, those at the back succumbing first until the very innermost victims' spirits were given to the night. Around the bodies howled the wolves that feasted as never before. Merciless Cossacks pursued those that staggered on, stripping them naked after making them prisoner and forcing them to walk bare foot in the arctic hell. Or else furious peasants bought the prisoners for a few kopecks so that they could bash their brains out on logs arranged for the purpose. It was no longer war, it was sheer butchery, outright murder. After earlier battles like Austerlitz and Friedland, Napoleon had been generous to his captives, even returning some Russian prisoners in brand new uniforms. The Russian Army cared little for the way their irregulars were operating and they themselves were in the grip of the terrible freeze. It was a war of annihilation and the biggest killer was the weather.

Sergeant Bourgogne gives all the harrowing details in his memoir *Retreat From Moscow*. Starving men were reduced to eating horseflesh and the thin ragged crows that fell out of the frozen sky. Men walked like zombies across the snowy wastes their faces and beards covered in matted horses' blood. To the survivors the dead appeared to be the lucky ones. The paths through the tractless forests and barren wilderness were covered in ice and if a man fell it was the end - everyone else was far too weak to offer assistance even if they had not been as totally selfish as they all now were. They were hardly men as the retreat progressed, they were frozen automatons, their hearts as cold and hard as the terrain over which they passed.

When the desperate fugitives reached the Berezina River there was another terrible discovery: "The French Army had now reached the marshes, but the Weather was fighting for Russia. Just at this time, a sudden and unexpected thaw set in, making the marsh a morass... Winter was before, winter behind, the Russians on the barrier."[30]

And all this was the result of those turbulent volcanoes, less heat from an almost spotless sun and that El Niño – La Niña changeover event. What chance had Napoleon and the Grand Army ever had? The campaign was doomed from the start. Hundreds of thousands of skeletons were left scattered across the plains to record this victory of Nature over Man.

In a painting by Caton Woodville's there is a superb evocation of the crossing of the Berezina where a wistful Napoleon is looking at the Army's remaining flags burning on a pyre to lost glory. The composition as a whole reflects the dire extremes to which the Grand Army had now been reduced.

In the howling winds and the deathly cold, the remnants of a once proud fighting machine were covered by the snow falling from a leaden sky. For every grain of volcanic dust that had been launched into the atmosphere there was now a tumbling, twirling flake of ice. It seemed as if every indication of the Army's passing was to be obliterated, every corpse put to rest beneath a blanket of unforgiving snow.

NOTES

1. Francis William Rolt-Wheeler *The Boy with the U.S. Weather Men* (Boston, Lothrop, Lee & Shepard Co. 1917) 62 of 154 when printed from The Project Gutenberg website.
2. Jean-Roch Coignet quoted in Antony Brett-James *1812* (London, Book Club Associates, 1973) 48
3. John E. Thomas *John Constable's Skies: A Fusion of Art and Science* (University of Birmingham Press, Edgbaston, England, 1999) 103. See the whole of *Chapter Three: Evolution of the skies in Constable's art* from 93 onwards for images and further explanation. The author adds: "Thus there were likely to have been heightened sky colours throughout the period 1808-12... It is clear that the sunrises and sunsets of this period were notable for their increased redness." 103
4. See Chapter Fifteen *Napoleon, The Tambora Eruption and Waterloo.*
5. In *The Boy with the U.S. Weather Men* 61 it says of the French Revolution: "It followed the greatest eruption in the history of the world, that of Asama, in Japan in the year 1783." However, recent ice core data from Greenland discussed on the CAT.INIST website and reported in the document *Climatic impact of the A.D. 1783 Asama (Japan) eruption was minimal: evidence from the GISP2 ice core.* Hence: "These results suggest minimal climatic effects in the Northern Hemisphere from the 1783 Asama eruption, thus any volcanically-induced cooling in the mid-1780s is probably due to the Laki eruption."
6. See *Laki* on Wikipedia for a detailed description of the effects of this 1783 eruption. The British casualty figures that follow and the consequences for America are taken from this account.
7. See *Laki* on Wikipedia. The parish priest was called Jón Steingrímsson.

8. John E. Thomas op.cit. "In Norfolk in 1783 it was reported that the sun remained coppery coloured until it was 20 degrees above the horizon." 103

9. See *Laki* on Wikipedia under *Contemporary reports*.

10. See Energy Citations Database at www.osti.gov/energycitations and the document *Summer temperatures across northern North America: Regional reconstructions from 1760 using tree-ring densities*. The quote is from the *Description/Abstract* section.

11. Ibid.

12. Ibid.

13. See *The Boy with the U.S. Weather Men* 61.

14. See Wikipedia *Little Ice Age*. The dates for this vary, especially its beginning.

15. Ibid. See *Effect on the Northern hemisphere* where is states: "The first Thames frost fair was in 1607; the last in 1814, although changes to the bridges and the addition of an embankment affected the river flow and depth, hence diminishing the possibility of freezes."

16. John E. Thomas op. cit. 103

17. Ibid. 103

18. See *The Boy with the U.S. Weather Men* 62

19. Ibid. 62

20. Antony Brett-James op. cit. 48

21. Ibid, 51

22. Ibid. 52. Captain Fritz's surname is not known.

23. Ibid. 56

24. Ibid. See 59 and 66-67

25. Ibid, 84

26. Ibid. 147

27. See *A Sun-Climate Connection?* by Douglas Hoyt in *Mercury* May-June 2003.

28. See flipkart.com for a review of Cesar Caviedes: *El Nino In History: Storming Through The Ages* (2001).

29. See The Boy with the U.S. Weather Men 63

30. Ibid. 65

NAPOLEON AND THE ENGLISH PRESS GANG

BONAPARTE BOMBARDED BY BLATANT BRITISH BIAS

"The English in general know nothing of the affairs of
the Continent, particularly those of France."
(Napoleon)*

In his lifetime Napoleon faced the most vitriolic and scabrous
attacks imaginable from the British press and Establishment.
No lie was too big, no exaggeration too outrageous, no
defamation was beyond the pale. English gold for the sweaty
palms of his would-be assassins was not enough, the Cabinet
and the warmongers in Parliament wanted to ensure his
political assassination as well. Even today, this pathetic one-
sidedness continues – and from people who consider
themselves historians. Correspondents and academics, some
with titles and others without, seem to be writing as if they still
lived in the C19th. To them it is as if the British Empire still
exists. To many, truth is a mere casualty of a continuing
propaganda war.

The worst thing for any leader or politician to face is ridicule,
as grasping members of Parliament found in the summer of
2009 in London. Ridicule was heaped upon Napoleon by the
British press in copious measure. McLynn states that: "the
British press carried on a scurrilous campaign of defamation
against the First Consul."1 Papers claimed, for example, that
Napoleon was sleeping with his stepdaughter Hortense. Then
there were the highly personal and demeaning cartoons from
the likes of Gillray, Napoleon appearing invariably as a dwarf.

It was different, of course, if it was the *English* Establishment
that was being mocked. When the cartoon showing the *British
National Assembly* came out ridiculing the monarchy, the
Prince Regent wanted it suppressed and paid for the plate to
be destroyed.2

Incidentally, it is very *unBritish* to laugh at somebody else but not be prepared to take a joke yourself. But the last thing the corrupt British Cabinet was prepared to do was extol the virtues of 'fair play'. Napoleon rightly complained to the British ambassador Whitworth about this. McLynn says his pompous reply was that: "press liberty was part of the traditional English freedoms and the government could not interfere; this from a creature of Pitt whose repressive 'Two Acts' of 1795 had silence all *pro-French* opinion."3

Because of these and other cartoons, Napoleon is still thought of as small by the vast majority of people today. He was, in fact, about 5'6" tall, the average height for a Frenchman of his time. Similarly, the ridicule continues today, if often at a more subtle level. On Dec. 5th 1977, *The Daily Mail* published a two-page spread on Bokassa, under the headline *Clown Imperial.* The article began: "Ex-paratrooper Jean-Bedel Bokassa followed his hero, Napoleon, on the path to imperial glory yesterday." The paper rightly criticized the waste of money for such a poor country as the Central African Republic was in 1977, and still is today. But the subtext implies that Napoleon himself was ridiculous and a clown.

An alternate view could be, how amazing it is that a white man who died on a small island in 1821 in the middle of the Atlantic Ocean, could become so respected and imitated by a black man in the centre of a completely landlocked country in a different continent 150 years later. In 'darkest Africa' as it was once called, the memory of Napoleon still shone.

In *Waking The Ghosts of Waterloo* from *The Daily Telegraph* of June 13th 1987, John Keegan takes a very Anglocentric route around the battlefield. Keegan pontificates in his usual way stating that: "Waterloo is the simplest of all battles to understand. As Wellington himself put it: 'They (the French) just came on in the old way and we drove them off in the old way'." The 'we' in this instance being the British. Amazing stuff indeed, seeing that there were less than 24,000 *British* soldiers at the battle against 72,000 French. Keegan does not even mention the Prussians until the very end of his article. Some 7,000 Prussians died as well. Were they knocked down crossing the road? Perhaps they fell into Victor Hugo's 'sunken lane' and were never seen again?

Keegan says: "Blücher, whose troops' arrival on the left as the day closed had robbed Napoleon of all chance of victory." Let us look at this 'as the day closed' remark. The battle was fought on June 18th at the height of summer, albeit a very wet and stormy one, when daylight would have ended around 10pm. The end of a summer's day is therefore around 9-30 when the sun goes down. Let us be generous and allow it to be 8pm 'as the day closed.' Napoleon wrote of the same events: "It was 4 o'clock. Victory ought from then on to have been assured; but General Bülow's corps carried out its powerful diversion at this moment. From 2 o'clock in the afternoon onwards General Daumont had reported that General Bülow was debouching in three columns, and that the French chasseurs were keeping up their fire all the while they were retiring before the enemy, which seemed to him very numerous. He estimated them at more than 40,000."4

Napoleon goes on: "The French army, 69,000 strong, which at 7.00pm had gained a victory over an army of 120,000 men, held half the Anglo-Dutch battlefield, and had repulsed General Bülow's corps, saw victory snatched from it by the arrival of General Blücher with 30,000 fresh troops, a reinforcement which brought the Allied army in the line up to nearly 150,000 men, that is two and a half to one."5 Not a *mention* of all this in Keegan's account.

With the necessity of fending off the newly arriving Prussians and with many of his men already committed at Hougoumont and La Haye Sainte, Napoleon only had cavalry to attack Wellington. David Hamilton Williams says: "The time was approximately 3-30p.m... Napoleon himself ordered the grand Battery to intensify its fire on the English centre...."6 He later quotes from Ensign Gronow of the 1st Foot Guards who was at the receiving end of the great French cavalry charges: "At four o' clock our square was a perfect hospital, being full of dead, dying, and mutilated soldiers."7 Had Bülow not taken some of the pressure from Wellington, let alone the succour afforded by the arrival of Blücher's men, history would have been very different.

Keegan implies it was all over by 7pm but David Chandler adds a rider to all this: "the Young Guard contrived to retain some hold over Placenoit until 9pm. The fighting withdrawal of the Old Guard was a model of valour and cool determination."[8] The film *Waterloo* with Rod Steiger is a Keeganesque tour de force – with the actions of the Prussians almost airbrushed out of the script. Chandler also tells how earlier: "the 'oldest of the old', the 1st/2nd Grenadiers and the 1st/2nd *Chasseurs* of the Old Guard swept into Placenoit with the bayonet amidst a storm of rain and expelled all of *fourteen* Prussian battalions in very short order."[9] That did not appear in the film Waterloo. It is a slur on the memory of The Immortals to imply that they 'all ran' at Waterloo.

In the book *Great Military Leaders And Campaigns* edited by Jeremy Black, below the title to a chapter on the Duke of Wellington it adds: "British Victor over Napoleon."[10] It never credits Blücher at the same time. No partisanship there then. It also states that after the battle: "Within days, Napoleon had abdicated again, ending the war he had so recklessly revived."[11] This is an absolute travesty.

One of the first things Napoleon did upon returning to power in 1815 was to write to the Allies asking for peace. His letter to the Prince Regent was never even opened let alone passed on to that rotund imbecile. As an Englishman one despairs at compatriots who have to fabricate details about the past in order to promote their own one-sided agendas. Black and his team should be thoroughly ashamed of themselves. Their version of events has more than a suspicion of the dark art of 'spin'.

The truth was somewhat different: In a personal letter, Napoleon attempted to convince the sovereigns of Europe that the Ancien Régime no longer suited the French nation: "The Bourbons no longer wished to associate themselves with French beliefs or manners. France had to separate itself from them. Its voice called for a liberator... Enough glory has already decorated the flags of various nations. Great successes have usually been followed by great reverses. A better arena is open today to sovereigns, and I am the first to enter it."

The only response to this peace offering was the formation of the Seventh Coalition..."12

The arrogant Allies, determined to snuff out equality and restore privilege, ganged up as they had with six previous coalitions to destroy the one person who had given equality of opportunity to every man throughout his former empire.

The Daily Telegraph contained a book review by Nigel Nicolson on Sept. 3rd 1988. Dorothy Carrington had just had published her book *Napoleon and his parents*. The title appeared as follows:

Nigel Nicholson on a monster's boyhood

Nappy days

Nicholson is a bigot of the first order who writes splenetically whenever he mentions Napoleon. One fears he is about to have a heart attack at the mere hint of his name. To call Napoleon a 'monster' is pathetic. Nelson murdered Caracciolo at Naples, yet he is a British 'hero' with a huge monument to his name in the centre of London. Canning ordered the British navy to attack neutral Copenhagen in 1807 and murdered hundreds of innocent, peaceful civilians in a terror campaign, yet he is written of as a 'British statesman' in the British press.

In English a nappy means the same as a diaper – yet another crude and asinine attempt to belittle Napoleon. In his diatribe *Napoleon 1812* 13 – a supposed *history* book, his version of Napoleon can barely walk upright without dragging his knuckles on the ground. On page 9 he tosses a hand grenade into Napoleon's reputation with lines like: "Both Napoleon and Hitler controlled continental Europe." And on page 8 he states: "He did not await the first attack; he was always the aggressor." This is palpable and inexcusable nonsense. France was *attacked* in 1805, 1806, 1807, 1809, 1813, 1814 and 1815. And even during the Peace of Amiens, the terms of which Britain ignored, the Cabinet allowed d'Artois and the Bourbons to plan further terrorist attempts upon Napoleon's life – paid for with *British gold.* Writers like Nicholson further tarnish the good name of their own country by spouting such ridiculous slurs.

Only a most bigoted person would compare Napoleon with Hitler. Napoleon gave the Jews rights throughout his empire and was the first person to suggest that they be given territory of their own in the Holy Land. Napoleon allowed all religions freedom of worship and put an end to the internecine religious wars in France. Nicolson adds on page 178: "he no longer seemed the liberator of nations but their oppressor. He was the enemy of the entire world. Even the United States, fighting against England, considered him a tyrant."

The 'enemy of the entire world'. How can anyone take Nicholson seriously when he speaks such drivel as this? Furthermore, thanks to the British navy attacking any ship it liked at sea, neutral or not, Napoleon sold indefensible Louisiana to the States in 1803. It was the largest *ever* peaceful transfer of territory in the history of the world. Yet Nicholson says the Americans hated Napoleon. So why did they go to war with the *British* in 1812? They did so because the same arrogance that caused England to lose its American Colonies still prevailed - only Britain was allowed to bully every other mercantile nation in the world and board their shipping.

Nicholson almost drools when he quotes Thiers on page 130 concerning the retreat from Moscow: "He saw nothing of the retreat, and didn't want to see it because he would have been brought face to face with the consequences of his mistakes. He preferred to deny them... He should have been on horseback all day supervising the passage of rivers and sustaining morale..." Anyone who bothers to read Bourgogne's *Retreat from Moscow* and Coignet's memoirs will see that that is *exactly* what Napoleon was doing – except that he was on *foot* amongst his men, as even the Emperor did not have a horse due to the freezing cold. And after flogging Napoleon with the words of others Nicholson admits: "These judgments are harsh." In the index to his book there is only one mention of Bourgogne, the account par excellence of this campaign, and none of Coignet yet he quotes the unreliable Segur many times. Bourgogne is full of praise for the inspiration and morale boosting of his Emperor – perhaps that's why Nicholson virtually ignores him.

On January 22nd 1989, *The Sunday Telegraph* published *Revolution Most Foul* about the French Revolution two hundred years before. Peter Vansittart comments: "... Napoleon remarking to Metternich that a man like himself does not worry about a million deaths. Surveying a pile of battle corpses, he was as reassuring as Danton after the Massacres: "Small change, small change! A night in Paris will repair all this!" No advance here on the Fredericks, Catherines, and Pitts, let alone on Wellington, who wept over the Waterloo casualties."

Metternich was an aristocrat who despised Napoleon and wanted to preserve the privileges of his class, he is hardly a favourable witness. Napoleon did sometimes make glib remarks, in poor taste, with Metternich it was most likely a form of braggadocio in an effort to hide the weakness of his forces.14 However, as Coignet describes time and again, in the *doing* rather than the mere saying, Napoleon always did his best to see to the wounded, remaining on the battlefield personally to see to their welfare. Indeed, when Coignet was poisoned by a Bourbon agent (whom the British ultimately paid for) Napoleon himself sent two medical orderlies to help Coignet and kept himself up-to-date with his medical condition. Wellington called his soldiers 'scum' and kept his men at a distance in accordance with his view of aristocratic superiority. British soldiers had the worst reputation in Europe for going berserk once inside towns that they had been besieging. When Moore bolted for the coast and Corunna, leaving hundreds of British women and children behind, it was *Napoleon* who took care of them!

On the retreat from Moscow Napoleon put his own coaches at the service of the wounded. Would Wellington ever have done such a thing? He also made many comments about the horrors of war which are seldom reported, *never* by British historians who churn out the same couple of sayings ad nauseum.15 Napoleon wept at the death of Lannes and he was devastated by the death of Duroc. Yet Vansittart adds: "From Napoleon is not far to Hitler..." It was the *British* who invented concentration camps in the Boer War – to corral innocent women and children in one place because they could not defeat the Boer Commando in the field. That was something Napoleon *never* did – as we have seen, he offered succour to the women and children his enemy *abandoned*. Some 26,000 Boer women and children died of disease or starved in those camps. It is a shameful aspect of British history that is never taught in our schools. Even the German ministers of the Kaiser complained about this callous treatment. Napoleon was far kinder to his prisoners than the British of the time ever were. French soldiers were stuffed in rotting hulks in England. Napoleon often allowed his former enemies to enlist in his army. There were Spaniards and Portuguese serving with his forces in Russia, for example. Even Georges Cadoudal the Royalist rebel was given the opportunity to join Napoleon's forces.15

The Daily Mail of June 17th 1989 had a piece entitled *Return to Waterloo* by Paul Johnson, another bombast of the Old School. Johnson spouts: "The British, who hated Napoleon, never believed he would rest content in his tiny kingdom of Elba..." The fact that Louis XVIII never paid the two million francs a year, as prescribed in the treaty of 1814 whereby Napoleon agreed to abdicate, meant that he could not have paid his staff and soldiers had he remained. But it is the statement that 'the British hated Napoleon' which needs addressing most. That is either a deliberate fabrication, or another example of Johnson's consummate ignorance.

The Grimsby *Evening Telegraph* of July 14th 1997 has a fascinating account of a time *When Lincs mustered to meet Napoleon's men*. At first glance it might seem as if the Lincolnshire lads were preparing to repel Napoleon if he invaded. The truth is far more interesting: "At the very end of the C18th, and the beginning of the 19th, North East Lincolnshire was under a certain amount of threat. For on the Continent, Napoleon was lending weight to the hopes of *local revolutionaries and republicans.* These were railing against both the monarchy and the church. Levellers, whose origins were in the Civil War, called for the end of monarchy. To counter those who would *positively welcome* Napoleon's troops and the opportunity for revolution they would bring, the establishment – the Constitutionalists – raised bodies of armed men... militia..."[16]

These were the same sort of armed brigands who murdered peaceful protesters at the infamous Peterloo Massacre of 1819. Yet according to Johnson *everyone* hated Napoleon! Franceschi and Weider also belie this nonsense, quoting opposition members of Parliament in 1815: "Bonaparte was received in France as a liberator. It would be a monstrous act to make war on a nation to impose on it the government it did not want."[17] They also repeat the words of the *Morning Chronicle* which "lectured Lord Castlereagh, the foreign secretary, 'English patriots think that the powers of the continent are unified not so much against Bonaparte as against the spirit of liberty.' "[18]

Byron hated Wellington and Castlereagh, not Napoleon, and he was certainly not alone. When Napoleon was prevented from landing on British territory in 1815, after Waterloo, he had many defenders in Parliament and hundreds of people flocked to see him from all over the country. The likes of Johnson seem to believe that if you repeat nonsense long enough a gullible people will believe it to be true. If they only hear the same old rubbish, perhaps so.

Johnson also repeats the Waterloo canard: "By the time he used his guards, at 7pm, he was already under pressure from the Prussians." As we have seen, the influence of the Prussians was operating hours before that. He recounts Wellington shyly admitting: "By God, I don't think it would have done if I had not been there." It would not have been done without tens of thousands of Prussians either m'lud.

The Sunday Times of Oct 20th 1996 declares: *Napoleon's bodice ripper found in Moscow archive.* As well as part of a romance turning up in the Moscow archive so did: "Napoleon's own account of the disastrous campaign against Russia in 1812, in which he rejects the conventional view that his army was destroyed by winter blizzards." They report a comment of his which was incredibly relevant to the problems of the Labour Government in London in 2009: "A government that does not know how to admit guilt is a government that cannot command." However, the paper then flies its own ignorance like a kite. It actually says: "Notes from the archives also suggest the ageing soldier was unwilling to accept that invading Russia *too close to winter* was the biggest blunder of his life."

Napoleon's Grand Army began crossing the River Niemen on June 24th 1812, when he was 42 years old. British winters might be bad - but they don't start on June 24th – neither do winters in Russia.

The Sunday Times then claims he admitted that he had been defeated by Kutuzov at Borodino. They quote Professor John Mcmanners, lecturer in French history at Oxford, who opines: "It is fascinating to realise Napoleon was willing to admit to being out-generalled rather than confess he made such a fundamental mistake as picking the wrong time to take on the Russians." Again this seems to infer he chose the wrong 'season'. As Coignet, who went through the campaign attests, along with the many eyewitness accounts collected by Anthony Brett James and Paul Britten Austin, the summer weather was appalling as well as that in winter.[19] The roads were virtually impassable and supplies failed to reach the troops. A good case can be made that Napoleon should have paused at Vilna or Smolensk, or that he ought not to have embarked upon the project at all, but that is not what the Professor seems to be saying. Good manners might make a man, but Mcmanners is a poor historian.

The Sunday Times of Nov 3rd 1996 had a review by Alan Judd of Alastair Horne's book *How Far From Austerlitz*, entitled *His Ticket To Waterloo*. Judd says Napoleon: "saw a way of evicting the British from Toulon and seized the chance with both hands. Later, sick leave in Paris confirmed his early good impression: the famous 'whiff of grapeshot' with which he introduced himself to the Paris mob (killing 400) concisely established not only his initiative but one of the fundamentals of his relationship with the people of France – and with any others he could reach."

In effect, Judd says Napoleon was born to kill and loved killing people for the mere hell of it. This begs the question just what were the British doing in Toulon? If French ships had seized Bristol, Hull or Portsmouth and had been kicked out and their men slaughtered in droves by Nelson – this would have been 'a good thing' to Judd and his ilk and Nelson would be all the more a 'hero'. Similarly, the Royalist mob that attacked the Convention was determined to remove by violence a legitimate government. Barras commanded the forces that defeated the rebels. Napoleon was in charge of the troops under his command. Napoleon quelled an armed insurrection whilst he was under legitimate authority. When the British militia murdered and mutilated at Peterloo, they were attacking innocent civilians who were merely *discussing* the way their country should be run.

In a letter to the *Sunday Telegraph* of May 21st 1995, Cleo Shaw makes this very point: "All too often the violence was on the side of oppressive authority. For example at the Peterloo Massacre, on August 16, 1819, about 60,000 unarmed people, including many women and children, gathered in St Peter's Fields in Manchester… They had many grievances, including the starvation price of food. But the violence came not from them but from the untrained yeomanry that the magistrates called out. With their sabres they killed eleven people and injured hundreds."

One has to be very careful about being Judd and jury.

The reviewer then quotes Horne himself: "If Austerlitz raised Napoleon to the pinnacle of his success, it also turned his head and filled it with the delusion that no force could now stop him conquering the world." This is trite nonsense and likens Napoleon to some evil genius in a James Bond film who gets up in the morning planning world domination even before he has had his breakfast. The *very next year* after Austerlitz - 1806 - Napoleon bent over backwards to avoid war with Prussia as Jean-Claude Damamme proves in his excellent article '*Jena – 1806, The Battle that Napoleon did not want.*'[20] Similarly, it was the Austrians who invaded Bavaria in 1809, an ally of France, starting a new war, despite Napoleon asking Marshal Davout to keep his patrols away from the Austrian border so as not to provoke them. And it was the Allies who refused to let Napoleon rule France in peace in 1815 as we have already seen.

Judd then writes in fine Orwellian style: "France warred with Europe for 25 years." Of course, the £66,000,000 paid in bribes by the British Government to entice Austria and Russia and other poorer countries into their coalitions was done merely to promote 'peace and prosperity' as Big Brother might have put it. The truth is very simple – *England was the cause of most of the wars of that time.* It was England that provoked the Americans to rebel; it was England that bankrolled the other continental powers to *attack* France; it was the *British navy* that considered the sea and oceans their own domain – where other countries could only ply their trade under British sufferance. And all this for a rapacious clique of corrupt politicians in Whitehall and a later crew of nasty Bourbon exiles.

Judd adds: "each conquest needs another to protect it. Talleyrand, the subtextual hero of this book, tried and failed to persuade his master of this before deserting him..." Talleyrand as 'hero' – that would certainly have amused his contemporaries – especially Fouché - his equal in duplicity and treachery.

Judd too, has to get in the Hitler slur: "Horne makes telling comparisons with Hitler throughout... Napoleon buried at least a million Frenchmen..." What Judd doesn't say, is that most of them were killed because of the repeated wars of aggression started by *England* even though he admits: "it was Britain that stood against him throughout, bankrolling the allies to the tune of an astonishing £66 m."

In *The Grand Old Duke* which appeared in *The Sunday Times* of March 30th 1997, Robert Blake oozes over the "great man" and speaks of "the two heroes of the war against Napoleon. Wellington and Nelson..." He quotes Wellington saying: "take my word for it, if you have seen but one day of war, you would pray to Almighty God that you might never see a thing again."

Quite so, so what was Wellington doing in another country *looking* for war? Why didn't he agree to the peace proposals Napoleon urgently requested as soon as he returned from Elba? Was Mont Saint-Jean some strange extension of the Home Counties that does not appear on British maps? Just what was he doing there?

He was trying to destroy a man who had just staged a bloodless takeover of a country that was glad to see the back of the Bourbons. As the English Opposition member had said, why go to war to prevent the French people from having the ruler *they wanted*? The answer is in a simple phrase – *it was a war to maintain privilege.*

That same year, Blake wrote in *The Sunday Times* – Nov 16th 1997 – a review of Frank McLynn's book on Napoleon, catchily entitled with complete impartiality: *He detested freedom and liberty.* The old Tory warhorse trots out the same tosh. He asserts that: "McLynn has a bit of a chip on his shoulder about England." Yet so did his hero Wellington, who never forgave providence for causing him to be born in Ireland. When confronted by his non-English birth, Wellington said with eminent modesty: 'Because a man is born in a stable, that does not make him a horse'. He certainly considered himself a god set above the ordinary man, and he was dead set against extending the franchise to the common people.

Blake says of Lord Liverpool: "He may not have been very exciting figure but he was honourable, conscientious and efficient." This appraisal concerns the man who bullied Louis XVIII into persecuting former Napoleonic soldiers and officials after Waterloo, and who launched harsh and repressive measures against the native British population. As David Hamilton-Williams states: "D'Artois used both the police force and his agents to terrorize and murder Bonapartist officers and supporters as requested by the British Prime Minister Lord Liverpool."[21]

This is the same sort of 'honour' no doubt that led to the construction of those concentration camps in South Africa – victory at all costs, vengeance at every turn. Lord Blake might be all in favour of such men, but the British public, if they knew of such events, would be suitably ashamed of what was done in their name by corrupt aristocratic 'leaders'.

Maurice Chittenden comments on Peter Hofschröer's work in *The Sunday Times* of Jan 25th 1998: "Hofschröer, who spent eight years researching evidence in the Prussian archives and in accounts by British, German and Dutch officers present in the allied headquarters, said: 'The Duke of Wellington very carefully nurtured his reputation. The whole truth was, at times, a casualty in the process'." Hofschröer made a case for Wellington deliberately hanging back when Blücher faced Napoleon at Ligny. Chittenden adds: "John Elting, a retired American army colonel whose own history of the Napoleonic wars became a textbook at Westpoint military academy, supports Hofschröer: 'I knew this was going to produce howls of anguish. American historians have always been suspicious why Wellington was so slow,' he said."

There will undoubtedly be more revelations as more old documents, letters and accounts come to light. Suffice it to say, Wellington certainly did not win the battle of Waterloo *alone* as Keegan and Blake and the like seem to insist. A letter to the *Sunday Telegraph* of Oct 23rd 1994 brings out another important contrast between Napoleon and Wellington. Dr John Adamson writes: "Wellington's battles were relatively small-scale operations. None approached the scale of Napoleon's engagements at Jena or Wagram. At Leipzig... the combined forces involved on both sides totalled more than 400,000 men. Generalship in those circumstances was a test Wellington never faced." Napoleon was also an Emperor, with a whole country to run, and he was aware of the treachery that could always occur behind his back as it had in 1814. Such colossal responsibilities were never faced by Wellington, who made a reactionary Prime Minister when he did climb to the top of the 'greasy pole' in England.

Perhaps one day, a film will be made that does Napoleon justice. It has been a long time since Abel Gance. *The Daily Express* reported on August 1st 1986 that Jack Nicolson paid $250,000 for the rights to *The Murder of Napoleon*. The actor said: "I look at him as thinkers like Bernard Shaw and Nietzsche did who considered Napoleon THE man."

In Britain, the same jaded biased stories have kept recurring over the past few decades. Right-wing publications give space for the same elderly generation of High Tory apologists to chant the same old mantras. The English Press Gang continue to mug Napoleon's memory and seek to attain the historical apotheosis of Wellington and Nelson. They might be journalists, but what they write is definitely not *history*.

NOTES

* Quoted in Somerset De Chair *Napoleon on Napoleon* (London: Brockhampton Press, 1992) Frontispiece.
1. McLynn 264
2. See Wikipedia under Gillray
3. McLynn 265 (My italics)
4. Somerset De Chair 266
5. Ibid. 271
6. Hamilton-Williams *Waterloo New Perspectives* 320
7. Ibid. 324
8. Chandler *Waterloo The Hundred Days* 165
9. Ibid. 151 (My italics)
10. Jeremy Black Ed. *Great Military Leaders and their Campaigns* 198
11. Ibid. 202
12. Franceschi and Weider 195
13. Nigel Nicolson *Napoleon 1812* (London: Weidenfeld And Nicolson, 1985)
14. Felix Markham points out just why Metternich is not to be trusted when he remarks: "The saying often attributed to Napoleon that 'one night in Paris would replace the losses of a battle' is much older and, in fact, goes back to Condé in the Seventeenth Century." *Napoleon* 142-143. See also Coignet for the many occasions when Napoleon saw to the care of the wounded.
15. See my Article *Napoleon and the Art of War* on the INS website.
16. My Italics
17. Franceschi and Weider 195
18. Ibid. 195
19. Antony Brett-James *1812 Eyewitness Accounts* (London: Macmillan, 1966)

Paul Britten Austin   *1812   The March on Moscow* (London: Greenhill, 1993)

Paul Britten Austin   *1812   Napoleon in Moscow* (London: Greenhill, 1995)

Paul Britten Austin   *1812   The Great Retreat* (London: Greenhill, 1996)

20. See INS Website under Articles

21. Hamilton-Williams   *The Fall of Napoleon* 308

THIS SEPTIC ISLE:
PRIVILEGE AND PERSECUTION IN EARLY C19TH BRITAIN

Last came Anarchy: he rode
On a white horse, splashed with blood;
He was pale even to the lips,
Like Death in the Apocalypse.

And he wore a kingly crown;
And in his grasp a sceptre shone;
On his brow this mark I saw –
'I AM GOD, AND KING, AND LAW!'
(Shelley – *The Mask of Anarchy*)[1]

That was what Shelley wrote in Italy when he heard the disturbing news of the Peterloo Massacre. In Manchester, at least eleven innocent people were killed and hundreds injured after a crowd of people desperate for political representation and reform, were cut down by brutal mounted militia at the behest of British magistrates acting with the full authority of the state.[2]

Far away, on the tiny island of Saint Helena, Napoleon was dying a slow, lingering death from arsenic poisoning and had little time left to live. According to most English history books, Napoleon was the scourge of the age, the greatest danger to this country, and responsible for all the wars and bloodshed that had ravaged Europe for two decades. Nothing could be further from the truth.

British subjects were sabred and cut down in cold blood that dreadful year not because of Napoleon, but because the wealthy oligarchy that controlled the country and had paid for other powers to attack France were determined to maintain and even extend their control over the benighted population. The so-called 'sceptred isle' was in fact being crushed under the mace of divine right and privilege.

Here is the version 'spun' by Robert Stewart, Lord Castlereagh to Parliament on May 16th 1821, less than two weeks after Napoleon had died on the 5th: "The magistrates had not employed a greater force than was necessary... The servants of the magistrates, the constables, had suffered; they had been struck, injured, and trodden down. The bloodshed was not occasioned by the magistrates, but by those who under the mask of reform, had no other object than rebellion."3

One detects real sympathy for the common man and the downtrodden masses here. But this 'empathy' on behalf of the so-called monied 'elite' for their underlings was apparent time after time in what was a real Dark Age in terms of political freedom in the British Isles. While he was alive, Napoleon was used as a smokescreen by the privileged nobility to obscure the real cause of burning resentment, namely the absolute refusal of the likes of Pitt, Castlereagh, Liverpool and Wellington to share political power with the vast majority of their fellow countrymen. And even when Napoleon was thousands of miles away, they insisted that nothing must change back in Blighty. Not only must Britannia rule the waves, Parliament was sure to waive the rules where the common man was concerned.

British subjects were peasants in all but name. They could be press-ganged and forced to serve in the British Navy; they could not vote; their newspapers were censored and made prohibitively expensive; the Six Acts enforced repression upon them; and Habeas Corpus had been suspended. Oh what bliss was it to be alive in the England of George III.

And English 'historians' still maintain it was all Napoleon's fault.

It is worthwhile comparing the British monarch, his mad-jesty, to George Cruikshank's cartoon - A Free Born Englishman (1819) – where the dismal figure has his lips fastened shut and is immobilized by chains.

It should never be forgotten that it was precisely because of the King's stubbornness that the American colonies rebelled.

Not surprisingly, they did not want taxation without representation. After their epic struggle for freedom the oppressive weight of taxation fell even more heavily upon British subjects of the foolish King. While the nobility spent huge sums beyond the dreams of avarice for common people, they were seldom taxed. Pitt owed £40,000 at his death after drinking himself into oblivion, despatching a bottle of port a day – perhaps that is where the phrase 'any port in a storm' comes from? His policies certainly created a storm of protest in his native country. Parliament, crushing the general population in so many ways, 'found' £40,000 to pay off Pitt's debts – never had the nation's priorities sunk so low.4

To Pitt, Castlereagh, Liverpool and Wellington, even when the peasants weren't rebelling they were revolting. The cream of British society had little of the milk of human kindness for their fellow countrymen. The Corn Laws were passed in 1815, making extra profits for rich landowners but higher priced bread for the masses, and that same year in April there was the cataclysmic eruption of Tambora, a huge volcano on the island of Sumbawa in Indonesia. There is an old English saying: 'It never rains but it pours' and never was this more apt. Tambora led directly to a period of global cooling, temperatures falling by an average of one degree Centigrade around the world. What followed was the notorious 'year without a summer', terrible rains and widespread starvation in Europe.5

As if that was not bad enough, as bread prices soared, wages fell. Manchester spinners saw their incomes fall from 24 shillings a week in 1815 to only 18 shillings three years later. The pay of weavers had plummeted from 11 shillings to only 6 shillings a week.6 Trouble was bound to follow. The Government was able to find tens of millions of pounds to prosecute its wars against Napoleon, *billions* in the pounds of today, but they were basically prepared to let their own people starve.7

When strikes occurred, *blacklegs* – people who continued to work - were intimidated, and stones were thrown at some factories. People who are hungry often feel desperate. The Government, rather than help by fixing the price of bread or instituting a minimum wage, became alarmed. The £40,000 they voted to pay off Pitt's debts would have fed the population of whole towns.

Always looking for sinister and rebellious motives amongst the general population, senior politicians saw this as tantamount to revolution. Sir John Byng, whose table could probably boast a crust or two, wrote to John Hobhouse of the Manchester spinners' strike in July 1818: "The peaceable demeanour of so many thousand unemployed men is not natural; their regular meeting and again dispersing shows a system of organization of their actions which has some appearance of previous tuition." By Jove, most of these bounders were *well-behaved* – this was a very dangerous turn of affairs for the 'elite'.8

Many of these spinners had been working from the age of six and had recently been doing 15 or 16 hour shifts with less than an hour a day in breaks.9 It is amazing that they had the energy to do anything after such a punishing schedule. Yet, despite all this, they were forced to live in squalor and often went hungry. Manchester, like most industrial towns had no MP – no representation in the House of Commons.

No wonder Cruickshank was so scathing about a 'free born Englishman'.

To the aristocracy, the working population was best treated like a coach-and-four. They were to be bridled, kept in the traces and whipped occasionally to make them go a little faster. What they didn't want was for any mavericks to come along and 'organize' the underclass in protest against the status quo.

Hence the hymn - 'All Things Bright and Beautiful' which goes:

The rich man in his castle
The poor man at his gate
God made them high or lowly,
And ordered their estate.10

The poor were by definition disorder incarnate, almost halfway towards anarchy when they were born. Hence the gentry, the clergy and the aristocracy were determined to crush the first signs of any questioning of the Almighty's scheme of things. They felt it their divine right to do so. After all they were working for his divine majesty the King.

This state of affairs has a long history in Britain and is seldom covered in our schools and in our history books. The infamous Enclosure Acts passed by Parliament between 1750 and 1850 stole from many of the poor what little they had. As Richard Muir states, common land was: "shared among the leading farmers in the course of parliamentary enclosure. Each parish had its own Act of Enclosure, issued by parliament when petitioned *by the leading landowners of a locality...* it changed the face of many lowland counties and sent the old peasant society to its destruction."11 He adds: "that the English countryside operates according to the Biblical maxim 'to him that hath shall be given'."12 And so it proved time after time.

Taking one example, Luddington-in-the-brook in Northamptonshire was enclosed in 1807. Amazingly, the village stream *was the main road* into this village. It wasn't much of a place but the locals were probably well content with it as it was. After the Enclosure Commissioners had done their survey, the place began to change. Although new dwellings were built by a modern road the old village area became deserted, such that by 1886: "the attractive little medieval church was left with only a farmstead for company as its wonderfully grotesque gargoyles glowered over the empty pasture."13

As the 'elite' slowly destroyed the fabric of old England, that same year 1807, some 2,000 Danes were massacred in a brutal bombardment of Copenhagen by the British Navy. In equality of destruction and mayhem, the aristocratic gargoyles in Parliament saw to it that there was plenty to go around. Canning was almost sure that the neutral Danes were going to 'give' their powerful navy to Napoleon, so he destroyed it – just in case.

Muir details how the "Gods of Profit" were the new deities worshipped in the City of London.14 As if the above litany of woe was not bad enough more was to follow in Scotland with the so-called 'Highland Clearances'. But it is worth pausing here to remark that between the years 1816 to 1825, 78,400 men and women were transported to Australia because: "Unrest in the wake of the Corn Laws prompted the suspension of Habeas Corpus, and the notorious 'Six Acts' gave the agricultural squirearchy, most of whom were magistrates, swingeing powers."[15] In other words, anyone who dared question what was happening in the countryside as well as the new industrial towns could find themselves on a long voyage to the antipodes. So much for England being a green and pleasant land.

In Dorchester in Dorset, there is a cattle bridge still bearing the warning: 'Anyone found damaging this bridge, in any manner, will be liable for Transportation for Life. 1820.' And that 'damage' would include slogans against the Government![16]

So much for a Home fit for Heroes for those soldiers who fought against Napoleon. Having done their bit the Authorities would crack down hard if even they ever dared to step out of line.

Now, if the English suffered, the Scots suffered even more. Nothing in England can compare with the terrible Highland Clearances and especially the notorious and callous actions in Strathnaver by the agents of the Duke and Duchess of Sutherland.

Elizabeth Gordon, the 19th Countess of Sutherland had agents like Patrick Sellar who turned cruelty into an art. In order to 'improve' the land, it was decided to get rid of the folk who were trying to scrape a living there. [17] It was like a mini Harrying of the North of 1069-1070 AD – that terrible time when William the Conqueror had his men kill everyone and destroy all the settlements between York and Durham after the Saxon peasants had dared to revolt.[18] Although Sellar and his employees didn't directly murder the Highlanders they made it impossible for them to go on living there. Their favourite tactic was to set the crofts ablaze to drive people away.

Donald McLeod, a crofter himself, was an eyewitness to the clearances: "The consternation and confusion were extreme. Little time was given for the removal of persons or property; the people striving to remove the sick and helpless before the fire should reach them... I myself ascended a height about eleven o'clock in the evening, and counted two hundred and fifty blazing houses, many of the owners of which I personally knew..."[19]

At Strathnaver, an old man, one Donald Macbeth was almost burned alive while his son was at a christening, despite Hugh Macbeth having begged the authorities to wait until he could remove his sick father. Donald was still clinging to life when Hugh returned to find him "lying in the open where Sellars' men had dumped him".[20]

As Richard Muir says: "The bulk of these clearances took place between 1811 and 1820 and so far as virtually everyone in the remainder of Britain was concerned, the events might have been taking place on Mars."[21] Certainly the landed gentry elsewhere were more likely to take this as an example to be copied rather than behaviour to be condemned.

In 1814, Patrick Sellar decided he'd like some of the land for himself. Notice was therefore given to existing tenants to vacate their land. Not surprisingly, they stayed put and then their own religious leader, *their Minister,* told them they would be damned if they did not accept this abominable and hellish treatment. Sellar's own demons set fire to their homes and an old woman, confined to her bed, died of wounds, and a pregnant woman died when she fell through the roof of the burning home she was trying to save. When Sellar was tried for murder in 1816, he was acquitted.[22] Meanwhile British subjects were being transported for far less than this. But, of course, they were not from the 'upper and superior classes'.

It is hardly surprising, as Mark Urban has said: "Back at the time of Napoleon there were actually plenty of people in this country and Parliament who didn't believe in fighting the French. Many didn't want to pay for war, some radicals even longed for a little more liberty, equality and fraternity in this country." [23]

No English history book would fail to mention the one-eyed British 'hero', Nelson. Very few people know that in a deplorable, not to say murderous episode in Naples, Nelson behaved like a one-armed bandit.

In 1799 after Russian and Austrian troops had driven French troops from Naples, the surviving French forces held out in three forts within the city. Realizing they were trapped, they signed an armistice with their adversary Cardinal Ruffo acting on behalf of King Ferdinand. The French were given permission to leave the city with all the honours of war, their lives guaranteed. The treaty was signed by both sides, by Russian and Turkish representatives and by Captain Troubridge of the British Navy. Then along came Nelson.24

Nelson had written to Troubridge: "Send me word some proper heads are taken off, this alone will comfort me".25 Nelson also wanted to try King Ferdinand's failed generals for cowardice and "if found guilty... they shall be shot or hanged... I ever preach that rewards and punishments are the foundation of good government". 26

When Nelson arrived at Naples the treaty appalled him. The French were already in vessels ready to leave port and all the signatories refused to renege on the previous arrangements. Then, at the last minute, the King and Queen of Naples cancelled the treaty. The Queen wrote to Emma Hamilton, Nelson's mistress, to tell him: "to treat Naples as if it were a rebellious city in Ireland" – a statement revealing in more ways than one.27

The French and their allies were now cooped up on their 'rescue' ships without food and amidst squalor and disease. Ruffo resigned in disgust but Nelson wrote to his wife claiming victory: "Nelson came, the invincible Nelson, and they were all preserved and again made happy." 28

The 'victor' now decided to punish over 8,000 refugees who were tried for treason. At least 100 were executed, probably more, but as Ferdinand later had the records destroyed, the true number will never be known. Caracciolo, the most important prisoner was executed at Nelson's behest. Hanged like a common criminal, his body was tossed into the sea. Nelson refused his family permission to take the corpse for proper burial. 29

King Ferdinand gave the Dukedom of Bronte to Nelson as a reward, some 30,000 acres and an income of £3,000 a year.30

Not bad pay for mass murder. This was the work of one callous and incredibly vain British aristocrat on his 'Grand Tour' of Europe. The more he lost bits of himself, the more Nelson grew in his own estimation. What an odious man he was.

Back in England, William Hazlitt was strongly opposed to British foreign policy. He wrote widely on political corruption and the need for reform. As Tom Paine had written in *The Rights of Man* (1791): "What is government more than the management of the affairs of a Nation? It is not, and from its nature cannot be, the property of any particular man or family, but of the whole community, at whose expense it is supported..." 31 That was not the way George III saw it. Repression not only continued, it increased.

As early as 1780 Charles Fox had supported reform, especially the scrapping of rotten boroughs and pocket boroughs, and of giving the freed seats to the new industrial towns. Fox had described the French Revolution as the "greatest event that has happened in the history of the world", but he was horrified by the execution of Louis XVI. Yet when war broke out between Britain and France he desired a negotiated end to the conflict. Although he would not go as far as Paine, Fox wanted existing 'freedoms' to remain. He was all for male suffrage but not universal suffrage. 32

William Pitt had once looked up to Fox and they had both advocated peace with the Americans and political reform. But, when the French Revolution occurred, Pitt changed his tune. He soon began slapping taxes on just about everything he could think of – including horses, tobacco, tea, spirits, and sugar. Finally, in 1798 he introduced a temporary income tax – which British residents have been cursed with ever since. 33

Pitt didn't much like criticism. At the opening of Parliament in 1795 cries of 'bread', 'peace' and 'no Pitt' were heard. So he decided to change the law on treason. Things got so bad that Pitt had to have an armed bodyguard. When the King went insane, rather than allow the nation to discuss what should happen to the body politic, he decided to regulate or suppress the nation's newspapers. His default position seemed to be to make any bad situation worse. 34

He ought never to have been short of a bob or two himself, as we say in England, as his income as Prime Minister was £10,500 a year – over a million pounds in today's money.35 Yet he still died owing that £40,000. As he could not even balance his own 'budget' perhaps it is no wonder that the country was going to the dogs.

Lord Liverpool was the British Prime Minister at the time of Waterloo and he and Castlereagh, the Foreign Secretary, got a little political fillip from the conclusion of the war. However, it turned out to be little more than a dead cat bounce. Liverpool was all for increasing repression and he started by raising the tax on newspapers. When the Peterloo Massacre occurred he supported the magistrates and the Manchester and Salford Yeomanry that had orchestrated the slaughter: "thereby highlighting the fact that Liverpool's government was now willing to use the same tactics against the British people that it had used against Napoleon and the French army".36

The draconian Six Acts were passed in November 1819. Not only did they drastically curtail free speech, but also the right of assembly. Meetings of more than 50 people were banned and magistrates were empowered to search people and property for arms. (It is sometimes men without arms that cause the most trouble as we have seen with Nelson). 37

As if all the above and having a mad King was not enough for the country to stomach, his heir 'Prinny' was a self-obsessed spendthrift. Even as early as 1795 he had debts of £650,000 – which would probably be *billions* in today's money. 38 Prinny was a great supporter of the hard-line taken by Liverpool's government. When the Luddites broke new shearing frames that would put them out of work, the Prince Regent offered £50 to anyone who would give information on the perpetrators.39 In 1812, Parliament made frame-breaking a capital offence and 12,000 troops were sent to areas of 'trouble'. That same year thirteen men in Lancashire were transported and twelve executed for attacking cotton mills while in York fifteen more suffered the ultimate punishment. 40

The Prince of Wales is famous for his rebuilding of the royal Pavilion at Brighton. But a bright 'un he was not, insisting he had led the charge at Waterloo to his dinner guests. The cost of that pavilion, by the way, and his other profligate expenditures could have been of immense help to the starving unemployed poor. But, being so regal and in the celestial heights, there is little indication that he knew of their plight and still less that he would have cared had he known. He mocked his own father's affliction in London clubs. By the time he became King he was addicted to alcohol and laudanum, having been addicted to flattery and praise all his life. 41

When someone threw a missile through the glass of Prinny's coach, this was enough for Parliament to introduce the Gagging Acts. Not only did they forbid meetings of over 50 people, magistrates were now empowered to arrest anyone suspected of encouraging sedition – the exact meaning of sedition always being at the whim of the individual magistrate. 42

In reaction to all this, Byron lambasted the Government in his own inimitable and cutting style, saying in *Wellington: The Best of Cut-Throats* (1819):

> Though Britain owes (and pays you too) so much,
> Yet Europe doubtless owes you greatly more:
> You have repaired Legitimacy's crutch
> A prop not quite so certain as before
> ... You are 'the best of cut-throats': do not start
> The phrase is Shakespeare's, and not misapplied;
> ... And I shall be delighted to learn who,
> SAVE YOU AND YOURS, HAVE GAINED BY WATERLOO
> (My capitals)43

The dichotomy between the living standards of the rich and the poor in early C19th Britain was immense. Sometimes, as we have seen, it was literally a matter of life and death. The fat cats in those days had claws and the full panoply of the powers of the State. And they were neither unwilling, nor afraid to use them. The shades of the Conqueror's avenging army still stalked the land.

As to the problems in the Manchester area, the radical newspaper *The Black Dwarf* put this bluntly in an issue on September 30th, 1818: "These evils to the men have arisen from the dreadful monopoly which exists in those districts where wealth and power are got into the hands of the few, who, in the pride of heir hearts, think themselves the lords of the universe." [44]

Recently Naomi Klein has spoken of *"The Shock Doctrine"* and *'Disaster Capitalism'*. Anyone who studies Britain's economy in the early C19th will see the incipient roots of this phenomenon. The aristocrats and the powerful landowning classes back then did not need a Milton Friedman to tell them how to squeeze wealth from the common people. Those spinners in Manchester and the unfortunates transported for trivial acts would never have dreamt that Huey Long would one day speak of a minimum wage for families and of the need to "Share Our Wealth", nor could they have foreseen the Welfare State that now exists in Britain. Yet, with the current banking crisis, the rich are again getting away with financial murder – and being rewarded for it. Just like Sellar during the Highland Clearances.

Similarly, like Donald Rumsfeld and Dick Cheney, Liverpool and Castlereagh knew how to privatise 'justice'.

Napoleon had different ideas. In terms of personal wealth, to quote Rhett Butler, he 'didn't give a damn'. Jean-Roch Coignet describes how Napoleon marched into Berlin after the battle of Jena wearing the drabbest uniform amongst all his glittering entourage and wearing a one sou cockade – a few pennies in *today's* money. He saved most of his pay as Emperor and used it for the defence of France in1814. When Napoleon abdicated that year, the first thing Louis XVIII wanted to do when back in France was to get his hands on the ex-Emperor's personal fortune.

Napoleon benefited the whole Continent, not just his adopted country. As Hywel Williams states: "Napoleon's rationalist reforms of French administration, together with his legal code, shaped most western European states."[45] Clive Emsley, Professor of History at the Open University goes even further: "Go to Continental Europe and people don't have the same negative image of Napoleon. Many see his Empire as modernizing, as rational, enlightened, trying to be just. All right it was despotic but there were careers open to talent."[46] Whereas Rumsfeld would have slotted in nicely between

Liverpool and Castlereagh, in Napoleon's France he would have got nowhere because under Napoleon, careers were open to talent.

Napoleon knew the value of education for all classes of people. He founded free schools throughout his Empire.[47] He wasn't afraid of capable and remarkable men, he actively encouraged them to take up positions in his government and administration and in the Army. And he was more tolerant of different religions. Whereas the Jews were persecuted elsewhere in Europe, Napoleon gave them equal rights. Catholics in Protestant Britain were actually barred *by law* from going beyond major in the British Army, neither could they be magistrates. In France people could worship God in their own way without fear it might harm their career. [48]

The rigid class system in Britain held back reform and industrial improvement. Yes, it was the 'home' of the Industrial Revolution, but that was mainly due to brilliant engineers and industrialists, not the men in Parliament. In fact, one such man, William Cockerill from Lancashire went so far as to leave the country and seek his fortune abroad. No one wanted his machines in England, so he settled in what is now Belgium in 1799, the year of Napoleon's coup. There he set up a firm that by 1997 employed 28,000 people and had become an industrial giant. Similarly, it was Napoleon who in 1803 personally decided to have a port constructed at Antwerp – and it has gone from strength to strength ever since. The myth that Napoleon 'destroyed Europe' with constant warfare is just that – a myth. [49]

Emsley puts it this way: "Love him or loathe him, there's no dispute that Napoleon launched modern Europe. He completely redrew the map, he swept away ramshackle governments, modernized administrations, and he didn't just do this in France, but in Germany, Italy, the Netherlands and… in what is now Belgium." [50]

The poisonous class system in Britain, the very foundation of which was privilege and heredity, made this country a 'septic isle'. George Ist, the first of the Hanoverian Kings, was born in Saxony and could not speak a word of English. His grandson

George III often talked nonsense. George II wasn't even born in this country. His son was the notorious 'butcher' Cumberland who conducted the ethnic cleansing in the Highlands after the rout of the Scots at Culloden in 1745. The later clearances like Strathnaver had this infamous pedigree. 51

The British Monarchy later became known as the House of Saxe-Coburg Gotha. It only became known as the House of Windsor in 1917 as, with German U-boats sinking British vessels, that name was not really patriotic. Princess Diana used to call her in-laws 'The Germans'.

American readers will be aware of the part played by the mercenary Hessians during their War of Independence and how Washington crossed the Delaware to give them a treat at Trenton. Of the 63 million people living in Britain today, probably barely a handful know that German mercenaries were used in Ireland and that: "They were... notorious for their atrocities and brutality toward the population of Wexford in 1798",52 or that the military were used as 'police' by magistrates at this time. As has been seen recently in Iraq – when soldiers are used as a police force, problems invariably follow.

Lord Byron said in Parliament: "As the sword is the worst argument that can be used, so should it be the last."53 But no one seemed to be listening. On August 16th 1819, in Saint Peter's Field in Manchester over 50,000 people gathered peacefully to listen to Henry 'Orator' Hunt and others. Only ten minutes after he had begun his speech, the local magistrates decided that "the town was in great danger" and called for his arrest. When the crowd tried to prevent this, drawn sabres flashed in all directions as they were unleashed upon the crowd. Then mayhem followed - as the crowd fled they were slaughtered as if they had been French soldiers being pursued by the Prussian cavalry after the Battle of Waterloo. 54

Paul Fitzgerald has called this: "An extraordinary event. If you like, it was Manchester's equivalent to Tiananmen Square."55 No politician ever apologized for this outrageous act, on the contrary Parliament passed the *Six Acts* and prohibited all such future gatherings. Well might Cicero say: "The evil implanted in man by nature spreads so imperceptibly, when the habit of wrong-doing is unchecked, he himself can set no limit to his shamelessness".56

NOTES

1) Shelley – *The Mask of Anarchy* See 3-4 of section on Lord Castlereagh at
    www.spartacus.schoolnet.co.uk/PRcastlereagh.htm
2) See 1-9 of Peterloo Massacre at
    www.spartacus.schoolnet.co.uk/PRpeterloo.htm
    and 1-5 of Peterloo Massacre at The Education Forum
    www.educationforum.ipbhost.com/index.php?showtopic=10747
3) See 3 section on Lord Castlereagh as above at spartacus.schoolnet
4) See 5 section on Pitt at
    www.spartacus.schoolnet.co.uk/PRpitt.htm
5) See section on Mount Tambora on Wikipedia and Tambora The year without a summer on the Physical Geology 2005 website.
6) See section 1-2 of Industrial Unrest at
    www.spartacus.schoolnet.co.uk/PRstrikes.htm
Pounds, shillings and pence make up 'old money' to those of us in England over fifty. Britain changed over to a decimal currency on February 15th 1971. A pound used to contain 240 pence and there were 12 pence to the pound – hence 20 shillings to the pound. When I was a boy in the 1960s a shilling was still quite a lot of money. A loaf of bread then cost about one and fourpence ha'penny or 1/4½. That is one shilling, four pence and a halfpenny. You can see why we went to decimal! That is the equivalent to approximately 7pence today. (So why does a typical loaf now cost £1-60?) As late as 1973 a teacher's starting salary in England was only £1,300 a year.
7) Britain's wars against Napoleon came with a hefty price tag: "Getting rid of 'Boney' was still expensive with a total bill to Britain of £1,500 million and a consequent National Debt of £733 million." Hywel Williams *Fifty Days That Changed The World 143.* A million pounds back then is approximately equal to a *billion* pounds today. So it cost over a *trillion* in all!
8) See 2 of section on Industrial Unrest as above at Spartacus.schoolnet.
9) Ibid. 3
10) As late as the 1950s, this hymn was being taught in British schools to convey the same 'eternal verities' – i.e. that people ought to know their place. Quoted by Alun Howkins in "John Bull was a Farmer", an episode of *FRUITFUL EARTH* BBC WALES (1997).
11) Richard Muir *The Lost Villages of Britain* (London: Michael Joseph, 1982) 154 My italics.

12) Ibid. 154

13) Ibid. 155

14) Ibid. 157

15) Hamilton-Williams *The Fall of Napoleon* 330

16) Ibid. 330

17) Muir 173-174

18) Ibid. 80-82   William certainly lived up to his nickname of The Bastard.

19) See 4 of Highland Clearances on Wikipedia at
>   http://en.wikipedia.org/wiki/Highland_Clearances

See also The Cultural Impact of the Highland Clearances by Ross Noble at the BBC history website. And Muir op.cit. 173-174

20) Muir op.cit. 174

21) Ibid. 174

22) Ibid.,173

23) Mark Urban speaking as presenter in BBC programme *LEVIATHAN* (1997) as he introduced Clive Emsley's take on Napoleon and Europe.

24) See Tom Holmberg's Article Nelson's Honour (1998) at:
>   www.napoleonbonaparte.nl/html/body_nelson_s_honour.html

25) Ibid. 1

26) Ibid. 1

27) Ibid. 2

28) Ibid. 2

29) Ibid. 2 See also Caracciolo section at Wikipedia. Nelson was totally in thrall to Lady Hamilton, who encouraged him in this detestable and shocking act.

30) Ibid. 3

31) See 3 section on Pocket Boroughs at
>   www.spartacus.schoolnet.co.uk/PRpocket.htm

32) See 1-2 section on Charles Fox at
>   www.spartacus.schoolnet.co.uk/PRfox.htm

33) See 3 section on William Pitt at the same website.

34) Ibid. 3

35) Ibid. 5 A 'bob' is English slang for a shilling – the expression is still quite common 40 years after decimalisation.

36) See 2 section on Lord Liverpool at Spartacus.schoolnet

37) See 1 section on Six Acts at Spartacus.schoolnet.

38) See 1 section on George IV at
>   www.spartacus.schoolnet.co.uk/PRgeorgeIV.htm

39) See 1 section on The Luddites at
>   www.spartacus.schoolnet.co.uk/PRluddites.htm

40) Ibid. 1-2

41) See 2 section on George IV at Spartacus.schoolnet

42) See 1 section on Gagging Acts at
>   www.spartacus.schoolnet.co.uk/PRgagging.htm

43) See 3 section on Lord Byron at
>   www.spartacus.schoolnet.co.uk/PRbyron.htm

44) See 3 section on Industrial Unrest at Spartacus.schoolnet

45) Hywel Williams 144

46) Clive Emsley *LEVIATHAN* BBC

47) Ibid. *LEVIATHAN* BBC

48) Ibid. *LEVIATHAN* BBC

49) Ibid. *LEVIATHAN* BBC   By 1997 Antwerp was Europe's largest cargo port.

50) Ibid. *LEVIATHAN* BBC

51) See Wikipedia on George I, George II, George III and George IV

52) See 7 section on the Hessians on Wikipedia at
                    http://wapedia.mobi/en/Hessians

53) See 4 section on The Luddites at Spartacus.schoolnet

54) See 2 section on Peterloo Massacre at
                    www.spartacus.schoolnet.co.uk/PRpeterloo.htm

55) See article by Judy Hobson BBC News Online   Remember The Peterloo Massacre at
                    http://news.bbc.co.uk

56) Quotation from HERITAGE HISTORY Homepage on September 2nd 2009
                    www.heritage-history.com

NAPOLEON THE TAMBORA ERUPTION AND WATERLOO

As the last of the twilight faded, the heroic remnants of the Old Guard held back the flood of refugees. Chaos was endemic in the French ranks. All discipline and order had gone save for the superb bearing of a few battalions of Old Moustaches. The grognards marched south with pursed lips and heavy hearts. It was night on June 18th 1815 and their Emperor had just been defeated in battle.

Never had a contest been so equal, even though the valiant French Army had in the end faced a combined force that was nearly double their numbers. It seemed that fate itself had been against them. Perhaps even the weather? It seems at first a ludicrous assertion, a feeble excuse for defeat. But then those who might scoff obviously know knowing about Tambora.

There are over 17,000 islands in the Indonesian archipelago that stretch across thousands of miles of seas and oceans. They range in size from giants like Java and Sumatra to tiny insignificant dots, uninhabited and unfrequented. One of the islands is called Sumbawa.

A massive crater in the north of the island is called Tambora. Sumbawa itself is within the so-called Ring of Fire, one of the most volcanically active places on Earth. Tambora had a composite cone and was one of the most deadly types of volcano - a stratovolcano. Krakatoa is another island in the same chain.1

The molten fires from deep within the Earth's crust began to stir spectacularly in 1812 – a fateful year if ever there was one. Steam and smoke rose from the cone of the threatening volcano and ash was scattered over the surrounding jungle and seas. The local inhabitants and people on passing vessels must have cast a wary eye at the imminent menace.

On the other side of the world, the greatest man of the Nineteenth Century was about to take his greatest gamble. Napoleon's supposed ally, Tsar Alexander of Russia had deployed his forces to the border in 1811, threatening

Napoleon's empire. Unable to garner allies from the usual suspects, Austria and Prussia, Alexander backed down. Without the millions in gold that England could use to bribe continental armies to fight the French, Alexander's enterprise was seen as just too risky by both Francis of Austria and Frederick-William of Prussia.

Napoleon had had enough. He had been extremely lenient with Alexander at Tilsit in 1807 and became very fond of the handsome, cultured but very impressionable young Tsar. The French Grand Army had defeated the Russians decisively at Friedland and the western provinces of the great colossus were at Napoleon's mercy. Not for the first time, nor for the last, Napoleon was magnanimous in victory. Alexander had told him he hated the English as much as Napoleon did, to which the French Emperor replied that in that case peace was assured between them. They got on so famously that they joked they would be each other's secretaries during the peace negotiations.

Like many a political love affair, this one was not going to last. Napoleon had been assured by Alexander that Russia would close its ports to English goods. A trade ban was the only way in which Napoleon could retaliate against the British Cabinet's and the younger brother of the exiled French King Louis XVIII, d'Artois', repeated plots against his life and fomenting of wars and strife on the continent. Britannia not only ruled the waves, she was determined to stick her trident wherever it might do the French the most damage.

The Tsar who had been captivated by Napoleon's charm when he finally met him in person, went back to Saint Petersburg only to discover that the Treaty of Tilsit was either loathed or hated by the Russian ruling class and seen as a pact with the devil by members of his own family, who were not best pleased with him. As a consequence, the backsliding began almost immediately. At Erfurt in 1808, Alexander promised to send troops to aid Napoleon if the Austrians provoked yet another war, but in 1809, when Francis launched a surprise attack on Bavaria, Napoleon's ally, Russian soldiers were conspicuous by their absence on the battlefield of Wagram.

Despite this, Napoleon allowed Alexander to annexe some territory in the following peace dealings.

As Napoleon gathered his forces in 1812 for what he knew would be an epic struggle, steam and smoke billowed from Tambora's hungry mouth. A giant was re-awakening from a sleep that had lasted 5,000 years. The famous comet that presaged the invasion of Russia had already scared the living daylights out of superstitious folk in many European countries. As the renewed devastation of war threatened innumerable peasant farmers and townspeople alike, no one dreamt that their lives were about to be rocked by a force of nature that made even Napoleon's army of over 500,000 men seem inconsequential.

As if the god Vulcan was juggling with the plates of the earth, molten magma seethed and rolled beneath the buckling crust of Sumbawa. There were rumblings and outpourings of black smoke. A force that, when unleashed would be the equivalent of thousands of atomic bombs, was being marshalled beneath Tambora's proud, austere façade.

On the surface of the thin crust thousands of miles away in Europe, tiny humans were toying with their destiny. For two weeks in 1812 Dresden was the centre of the world. Having arrived on May 16th, Napoleon quickly established himself in the palace of his ally the King of Saxony and from there he saw to the final preparations for the invasion of Russia. By his side, fluttering like moths around a flame, gathered the rulers of the states that he had vanquished: the Emperor and Empress of Austria; the King, Queen and Crown Prince of Prussia; dozens of German princes and a myriad of minor nobles. In his honour grand receptions were held, gala performances at the theatre; boar hunts; firework displays; illuminations and torchlight processions. At the age of forty-two, the Emperor of France was at the height of his power and the fate of Europe seemed to lie in his hands.

The fires of Moscow, the result of a maniacal plan by Rostopchin, the Governor of the city, were as nothing when compared to the seething cauldron of volcanic lava about to be unleashed in the southern hemisphere.

General Winter destroyed Napoleon's Grand Army, along with starvation, disease, mismanagement and bad luck. Napoleon's cavalry vanished almost overnight. He had his back to the wall in 1813 and 1814 but it was treachery that finally removed him from power, not the military might of the Allies.

When he returned from Elba to popular, if not universal acclaim in France, he was able to march on Paris without a drop of blood having been shed. The Emperor had come home. Louis XVIII waddled into his coach and that should have been the end of that. However, the Royalists in Europe and the parasitic aristocrats in many countries, were hell bent on either regaining all of their privileges if they were French and had lost them in the Revolution, or on keeping their 'birthrights' and perquisites if they were from other countries, especially Britain. So Napoleon's plea for peace – he sent letters to all the monarchs – went unanswered.

Men like Jean-Roch Coignet flocked to Paris to serve Napoleon in any capacity they could. In 1815 he was to have his best army since 1809 as many veterans came back to the colours. But morale was fragile. The common soldiers were loyal with adamantine steadfastness, but there were many 'loyal' traitors like Bourmont, one of d'Artois' agents, just waiting for their chance in the officer corps.

The cry 'Vive l'Empereur' was heard in the streets and boulevards and then on the way to the frontier, the chorus of thousands willing to die for the man whom even his enemies called a genius. But it would be all to no avail for on the other side of the world, the roar of Tambora had been heard on April 10th 1815.

It had taken centuries for the magma chamber beneath the volcano to fill. Then a series of titanic explosions rent the air sending streams of volcanic ash high into the stratosphere. The pyrotechnics went on for seven days and a chunk of Tambora a mile wide was vaporized. With a rating of seven on the Volcanic Explosivity Index, the only one ever with such a high figure, Tambora was the loudest and largest volcanic eruption in the whole of human history. Clouds of ash fell on distant Borneo, Java and nearby Sulawesi. Some 71,000 people died, around 11,000 as a direct result, the rest from starvation and disease.2

Its effects were global. Once the ash got into the stratosphere the dust and detritus was caught up in the jet stream and shunted around the Earth. Steven Cary of the University of Rhode Island states that: "The Tambora eruption, which is the largest historic eruption we know of, caused a global cooling of about 1 degree Centigrade... it had very serious implications"3 - including regional differences in temperature of up to 10 degrees. There was a loss of up to 90% of light leading to a weird daytime twilight and there were frosts in New England in the summer of 1816. Indeed, 1816 was widely known as 'the year without a summer' and there was widespread starvation. The global darkness was at its worst in September 1815. As Byron put it: "the bright sun was extinguish'd... morn came and went – and came, and brought no day".4

An estimated 100-150 cubic *kilometres* of ash and debris were thrown skywards along with a massive sulphur dioxide discharge of 200 million tons and a dark cloud enveloped creation in a Biblical apocalypse leading to widespread global cooling.5 Rain drops form around miniscule drops of dust that float in the atmosphere – imagine what happens when there are trillions of dust particles to form such nuclei. The resultant downpours were enough to please even the Storm God of the Hittites. And some of these unprecedented and hitherto unheard of storms occurred on the night before Waterloo.

In the dreary damp and dismal summer of 1816 Mary Shelley wrote 'Frankenstein'. To many, Napoleon had been cast as the monster, in Britain his name was even used to frighten wayward children. But what really died the year before on the sodden fields around Mont Saint-Jean was equality of opportunity and careers open to talent. They were replaced by the undead, the returning vampires from the former Ancien Regime that just would not lay down and die. It took further revolutions in 1830 and 1848 to drive the last stakes into the heart of privilege.

The eruptions could not have come at a worst time for Napoleon. Ten weeks after Tambora, ample time for the dust to be scattered across the globe, he was looking through the driving rain at Wellington's army on Mont Saint-Jean. The atmosphere holds most water at the height of summer and Waterloo was fought only three days before the longest day – June 21st.

The tremendous monsoon like rains held up the French forces for a crucial three hours on the 18th, having already slowed down their pursuit of Wellington the day before. These hours were critical as they allowed the Prussians to arrive and play their vital part in the battle.

Jacques Logie in *Waterloo- the 1815 Campaign* is very dismissive of all this. He states: "Some writers, basing themselves on the declarations of General Drouot, explain this delay by arguing that the state of the ground, made sodden by the previous day's storm and the overnight rain, would not have allowed the movement of artillery before the end of the morning." He goes on, revealing his attitude further by saying: "The attempted vindication lacks foundation, for in his *Memoires*, Napoléon acknowledged '... that at eight o'clock that morning, the gunnery officers, who had gone over the ground, announced that the artillery could be manoeuvred. Albeit with a certain difficulty which in an hour would be reduced.' "[6]

Logie, as well as being as fine an apologist for Wellington as ever existed this side of the Channel, gives the impression that the cataclysmic Tamboran downpours were little more than the sort of summer storms that might hold up a Wimbledon final and were simply an *excuse* for Napoleon's defeat.

The English artillery officer Captain Mercer, who was *there* as the French pursued Wellington's fleeing army after Ligny and Quatre Bras, remarks: "I had longed to see Napoleon, that mighty man of war – that astonishing genius who filled the world with his renown. Now I saw him, and there was a degree of sublimity in the interview rarely equalled. The sky had become overcast since the morning, and at the present moment presented a most *extraordinary appearance.* Large isolated masses of thundercloud, *of the deepest, almost inky black,* their lower edges hard and strongly defined, lagged down, as if momentarily about to burst, hung suspended over us, involving our position and everything on it (in) deep and gloomy obscurity..."7

David Hamilton-Williams describes what followed: "Just as Napoleon prepared to set off up the Brussels road after Wellington, the heavy clouds massed overhead broke forth with a violent thunderstorm which brought sheets of rain on to the stage of human events. The game was escape and pursuit; the quarry had a long lead; but the hunter was driven; and the rain assigned a handicap to both parties."8

Logie enthuses about Wellington being 'everywhere' at Waterloo exposing himself to danger and infers Napoleon no longer got so personally involved in battle. Yet during this pursuit according to Dumaine, one of officers in the French Guard artillery: "he was constantly near the pieces, exciting the gunners by his presence and by his words, and more than once in the midst of the shells and bullets which the enemy's artillery showered upon us".9

Uxbridge had to order a British withdrawal at Genappe and: "Throughout this dogged retreat rain fell in torrents with thunder and lightning, and men and horses were reduced to a walking pace because of the mud."10 And this was only the *start* of the Tamboran storm.

Light faded very early on that night of June 17th, so much for extended summer nights. This, and roads that had become quagmires, hampered the French far more than the English who, at that stage, just wanted to escape and hide: "Nightfall would favour the hunted not the hunter".11

Wellington got to Mont Saint-Jean and Napoleon soon realized that he meant to defend the position. He had wanted the Englishman to stand and fight, but his own army was now very extended. As Hamilton-Williams makes clear: "Now that all Wellington's men had closed up on Mont St-Jean it was *only the French* who were impeded by the foul weather".12

At his headquarters at Le Caillou Napoleon soon realized how much time the storms had already cost him. Sergeant de Mauduit of the Guard wrote: "The tracks were so deep in mud after the rain that we found it impossible to maintain any order in our column... One by one the regiments of his Guard came up, but each arrived there in a state of exhaustion. During all the marches and countermarches of that *frightful night* there was a real helter-skelter. Regiments, battalions, even companies became muddled… our greatcoats and our trousers were caked with several pounds of mud. A great many of the soldiers had lost their shoes and reached the bivouac barefoot".13

Anyone for tennis Monsieur Logie?

Captain Fritz of the Prussian Landwehr on his way to Wavre, wrote in his journal: "In very bad weather we set off again in the morning to cross the Dyle…"14 And Napoleon wrote in his Memoirs that in the early hours of the 18th the rain continued to fall in torrents: "I returned to my headquarters well satisfied with the great error which the enemy commander was making and very anxious lest the bad weather should prevent my taking advantage of it".15

By 8 a.m. on June 18th only d'Erlon's corps was in line of battle, Reille's was still in the process of positioning itself. Despite Logie's abrupt dismissal above, Hamilton-Williams counters that: "When Napoleon had dictated general movement orders for his attack formations, he had timed them for 6 a.m. But several officers had complained that the deep mud and general softness of the ground from the recent downpour would make very difficult the movement of men, horses and especially artillery pieces, each weighing several thousand pounds".16

Furthermore, some of the men had been bivouacked some distance from the battlefield at Genappe and Glabais and would obviously need time to trudge through the mud to their stations: "Napoleon's own reconnaissance of the terrain confirmed this. *At this moment the main road was the only passable route forward*".17 For these reasons, Reille's corps had not left Le Caillou before 9 a.m. Hence the Emperor had to change the general orders to the same time – 9 a.m.

Already, at least three hours had been lost because of Tambora's storms. Thus Mars, the god of war had had to wait in the wings while Tlaloc the Aztec god of rain prepared the stage for battle.

There were further delays for: "It was not until 10-30 that the formations had been completed; the battle would be starting rather late in the day because of the mud and the distance many units had had to march from their bivouacs". [19]

For some, the Battle of Waterloo will always be Wellington's greatest victory and how with 15,000 infantry, 5,840 cavalry and 2,967 Ordnance personnel (less than 24,000 *British*) he managed to defeat Napoleon's 72,000 men.[20]

More objectively, the role of the German soldiers of all arms ought to be accorded much more importance and, especially, the pathological hatred that Blücher bore towards Napoleon. Having been knocked off his horse at Ligny and nearly captured by the French, the old man still insisted on honouring his commitment to provide Wellington with at least one Prussian corps when he came to face Napoleon. Gneisenau would have been only too happy to have returned to Prussia asap, until his muddy, bedraggled superior resurfaced.

This makes a nonsense of Marxist history – which seeks to make the individual totally unimportant in the grander scheme of things. Similarly, it was Napoleon's own personal charisma that earned him the undying devotion of his soldiers. And yes, Wellington deserves recognition for his leadership on the field of battle. But without the Prussians there would have been no victory.

Another person who was sorely missed and who could have prevented many of the errors on the French side, was Berthier, Napoleon's former Chief-of-Staff and right hand man. Very little is said about him today and he is a far more important historical personage than many other popular historical figures. Without

Louis Alexandre Berthier there might not have been a United States because it was his military talents that ensured victory for Washington and his French allies over the British at the siege of Yorktown in 1781. Had Berthier been at Napoleon's side during the Waterloo campaign, the British might well have faced a defeat as ignominious as that of Yorktown.

The great Tamboran eruption of 1815 and its effect on the weather is another element in the run-up to the great battle that deserves further study. A rare diary belonging to a farmer called John Andrew from the North-West of England has recently come to light. He kept a detailed weather record: " 'Hail as large as eggs', 'deep snowdrifts' and 'sky as red as blood' are all carefully documented in the well-preserved 'weather books' written around the time of the Battle of Waterloo."21 Although these specific comments probably refer to 1816 'the year without a summer' it indicates that global climate change was a real event after Tambora. And, that the outpourings of ash that clouded the atmosphere affected the weather at the most crucial point of the Waterloo campaign, there can be no doubt.

NOTES

1. See Mount Tambora map and further details on Wikipedia
                http://en.wikipedia.org/wiki/Mount_Tambora
2. Ibid. Wikipedia.
   See also article on Physical Geology 2005 website - Tambora, The year without a summer.
3. Steven Cary of the University of Rhode Island quoted in BBC programme *EARTH AND LIFE* an Open University series, in an episode called *Above the Volcano* (1997).
4. Byron quoted in Tambora The year without a summer, above.
5. See Wikipedia and Physical Geology as above.
6. Jacques Logie *Waterloo The 1815 Campaign* (Stroud, England: Spellmount, 2003) 171
7. Quoted in Hamiliton-Williams *Waterloo New Perspectives* 251-252 (My italics)
8. Ibid. 252
9. Ibid. 253
10. Ibid. 253
11. Ibid. 253
12. Ibid. 254 (My italics)
13. Ibid. 254 (My italics)
14. Ibid. 255
15. Ibid. 258
16. Ibid. 261
 17.Ibid. 261 (My italics)

18. If the Battle had started at 9am the outcome might well have been very different.

19 Hamilton-Williams 265

20. Ibid. 268

21. Lancaster University England - LU News 19th Century Weather Diaries Shed Light on Climate Change - Dr Rob Mackenzie, Deborah Lee and Christine Valentine. See Dec 2007 section on Lancaster University website.

HAIRSAY AND HERESY: THE MURDER OF NAPOLEON

In March 1995 a single lock of human hair was sold to an American for £3,680.[1] This was no ordinary relic. It came from the head of an exile who spent the last six years of his life upon a lonely speck of rock in the South Atlantic. For decades those frail strands of hair had kept a dark secret. Each contained minute traces of arsenic, a clear indication that the donor had been poisoned. The lock still exists today as mute testimony to the crime of the century – the murder of Napoleon.

History is written by the victors. During his time as First Consul, and then Emperor of the French, Napoleon was castigated by the British press and by its corrupt Establishment. He was the Corsican Ogre, the cause of all wars, an evil man who had to be destroyed at all costs. Mothers threatened their children with his name and his face appeared inside chamber pots.

Black propaganda has coloured innumerable subsequent histories written over a period of one hundred and ninety years and, as a result, errors, misinformation and downright lies have come to be accepted as fact. In England he has been dubbed a "monster genius" by one 'historian', and "a great, bad man" by another. Many English writers dismiss him merely as the general who lost at Waterloo.[2]

In France, after his fall from power, the Royalists printed anything that might sully his name. During the so-called White Terror, officers and men who had fought for him were hunted down and executed without trial, at the express demand of Lord Liverpool, the British Prime Minister, who was determined to wreak a fanatical revenge upon those misguided French nationals who had dared to support Napoleon.

We know of Trafalgar and Waterloo, but how many British people know about this?

Napoleon embodied the principle that the individual mattered, that careers should be open to talent and should not just be the province of the highborn and the well-to-do. This was anathema to the British ruling class and their counterparts, the French aristocracy who clung to a belief in the divine right of kings. To them there was no such thing as the Rights of Man, only the Right of Might.

Following the spread of the doctrine of democracy after the American War of Independence, the French Revolution of 1789, the death knell of privilege, was bound to provoke a furious reaction from the courts of Europe. They would do anything to nip the concept of individual freedom in the bud. Hence common cause was made against the figurehead of the new ideas – Napoleon. The huge bribes secretly paid by the British Government to foreign powers to entice them into wars against France certainly helped this process along.

In Napoleonic France, advancement was possible for gifted people of all ranks. The Emperor was a pragmatist. He even allowed hundreds of former aristocrats back into France if they were prepared to serve him. In the process he unwittingly welcomed his would-be assassins.

The ordinary Frenchman did much better under Napoleon than they had ever done under the Bourbons. Napoleon restored peace within France; his Concordat with the Pope re-established Catholicism as the religion of the majority of the French people; his Napoleonic Code instituted a body of laws that confirmed the property rights of the millions of peasants who had gained land after the Revolution – it is still the basis of the French legal system today.

His soldiers worshipped him. One has only to read the memoirs of Sergeant Bourgogne and Captain Coignet to see that. Under Napoleon, every soldier believed there was a baton in his knapsack. Anything was possible, they had seen it happen. Men of humble birth like Ney and Murat became marshals, princes, even kings. Napoleon's personal charisma was almost magical. When he was a boy, Heine, the German poet, saw him: "high on horseback, the eternal eyes set in the marble of that imperial visage, looking on, calm as destiny, at his guards as they march past. He was sending them to Russia, and the old grenadiers glanced up at him with so anxious a devotion, such sympathy, such earnestness and lethal pride: *Ave Caesar, morituri te salutant!*".3

Napoleon supported French industry and provided political stability after the chaos of the Revolution. As a result, the peasants and the middle-classes prospered and France became a great nation once again. Compared to the days of the old monarchy, the French people had never had it so good. What else had Europe to offer?

In England, Old Farmer George, King George III, after losing the American colonies because of his asinine inability to compromise, went mad and spent his time shaking hands with trees and talking to them. His son "Prinny", the Prince Regent, convinced himself he had actually led the charge at Waterloo, when the only charge he did lead was the one for the dinner table. Prinny was loathed by the British public because of the way he treated his estranged wife, Princess Caroline. The Royals lived in a world of their own, blind to the misery endured by ordinary Britons at a time of economic hardship and depression.

Wellington was short of cavalry at Waterloo because the politicians at Whitehall relied on mounted troops to keep the people down in Britain and Ireland. They were even more concerned with quelling internal dissent than they were in defeating France. Some 78,400 people were transported to Australia in only nine years, 1816-1825, many for merely daring to question the way the country was being governed.4

Napoleon was three times acclaimed by national plebiscite in France. No one ever voted for Louis XVIII who succeeded him. If Napoleon became the heart and soul of France, Louis can be said to have been its stomach. A political lightweight, he made up for it on the personal level, weighing in at 310 lbs. Twice he returned to Paris in the baggage train of the Allies – he needed it, no horse could carry him. Waddling along, limping, plagued by gout, and with his penchant for blond young men, he was yet mystified by the fact that the populace preferred Napoleon to himself.

It was Louis' sinister brother and heir Charles, Comte d'Artois, who began making plans for the murder of Napoleon.

D'Artois could execute 'traitors' every day of the week and still go to Mass on a Sunday. He was a true scion of the Old School.

In 1792, with the blessing of Pitt's government, d'Artois began planning the Bourbon restoration from a base on Jersey. Living there were 7,500 émigré priests and nobles, all eager to regain privileges and sinecures swept away by the Revolution. There, in the greatest secrecy, with the knowledge of just a few men in the British Cabinet, d'Artois set up his infamous Chevalier de la Foi. This nest of spies and death squads was given the task of restoring Louis to the throne. From Jersey, British vessels could easily land agents on the mainland at the dead of night.5

When Napoleon overthrew the French Directory in 1799, the issue became personalized. D'Artois' pathological hatred of the Corsican Usurper knew no bounds. To him, Napoleon was evil incarnate, the Antichrist.

Royalist guerrillas fought in Brittany and Normandy and when his troops defeated them, Napoleon had the magnanimity to offer one of their leaders, Georges Cadoudal, a commission in the Army. Cadoudal fled to Jersey instead. Once there he organized a plot to kill Napoleon with a bomb.

On December 24th 1800, Cadoudal's man, Saint-Regent, abandoned a wine cart in the rue Saint-Nicaise in Paris. A thirteen-year-old girl was left holding the horse's reins. Napoleon was due to pass on his way to the opera. However, his coachman was suspicious. Whipping his horses on, he careered past the cart. The people in the carriages behind were not so lucky. The innocent girl was blown to bits, more than a dozen others were killed, and over 200 were wounded. Cadoudal slunk back to Britain.

D'Artois had backed the plot. His agent, d'Auvergne, who was also the British naval commander in Jersey, provided the gunpowder, the money for the operation, and the vessel necessary to land Cadoudal on the French coast – all on the orders of William Pitt. It was nothing less than state sponsored terrorism.

Two years later, during the Peace of Amiens, Captain d'Auvergne went to Paris to meet fellow agents. He wore his

British uniform in case he was arrested as a spy. He was caught and imprisoned, but when the British Ambassador intervened, Napoleon had him released after thorough questioning.

Parliament was in uproar. Napoleon had dared to arrest a British officer with a valid passport at a time of peace. The French Ambassador in London leaked the real reason for d'Auvergne's arrest to prominent political figures. With the possibility of "Chants D'Auvergne" ringing in their ears, the Cabinet panicked. The thought that the British public might find out about their illicit dealings with d'Artois, which were still continuing despite the peace, terrified them. Thus, with delicious irony, Lord Liverpool was forced to speak up in Parliament on Napoleon's behalf. Perhaps that is why, after Waterloo, he was determined to have killed as many people as possible who had ever supported Napoleon.

Napoleon's military career is well known. More than 300,000 books have been written about him, more than any other individual in history. After his final defeat, with misplaced trust, he threw himself upon British justice, seeking asylum upon these shores. There was precious little freedom and justice for ordinary Britons, still less was there to be for the fallen Emperor.

Betrayed by numerous Frenchmen he had elevated to prominence, Napoleon took passage with Captain Maitland of *HMS Bellerophon* – 'Billy Ruffian'. Naively assuming he would be allowed to settle in England, he was taken to Torbay where crowds of people came from all over Britain just to catch a glimpse of him. However, it was imperative for the Cabinet that he did not land. The public, far more noble than their self-seeking politicians, had sympathy for Napoleon and would have allowed him to stay in England. On August 3rd 1815 an article appeared in *The Times* stating that an Act of Parliament was necessary to detain Napoleon and another would be necessary to intern him in a British colony.6 Frightened by this growing support for him, Lord Liverpool gave the order to have Napoleon transported to Saint Helena on board *HMS Northumberland*. With him was a certain Comte de Montholon.

Montholon had attached himself to Napoleon after Waterloo and asked to share his exile. He was, in fact, d'Artois' agent, and murder was on his mind.[7]

Napoleon's death had to be seen as an accident. Any obvious action would have led to widespread insurrection in France and, at the very least, extremely awkward questions being raised in a Parliament that was already greatly concerned with the growing republican movement in Britain. So Montholon began to lace Napoleon's wine with arsenic. The body's natural reaction is to disperse the poison where it will do the least harm, hence it got into his hair.

Montholon arranged for the removal of most of Napoleon's faithful companions after inveigling his way into the Emperor's affections. Montholon was soon the only person Napoleon trusted. His fate was sealed. With his health failing rapidly, Napoleon stated in his will: "I die before my time, murdered by the English oligarchy and its hired assassin." To the very end, he never suspected Montholon. He died on May 5th 1821, leaving Montholon 2,000,000 francs in his will. For the final time, Napoleon had been betrayed by someone he trusted. A lock of hair was taken from his corpse and eventually found its way to Phillips' Saleroom in London.

A French delegation arrived at Saint Helena to reclaim Napoleon's body in 1840. When his grave was opened the onlookers were stunned. Napoleon's sightless eyes stared back at them, for the arsenic which had poisoned the Emperor had also preserved his body. His remains now lie in a splendid mausoleum in Paris.

In June 1994 Professor Maury of Montpelier University announced that he had Montholon's written confession to Napoleon's murder. This corroborates the findings of Dr Sten Forshufvud and Ben Weider. Tests done on samples of Napoleon's hair at Glasgow University have revealed traces of arsenic *inside* the hair follicles. There is no way that arsenic from wallpaper or hair pomades could get inside the hair. Furthermore, Sten Forshufvud, a trained toxicologist who had studied the Emperor's mysterious symptoms for years, proved that the levels of arsenic *inside* the strands of hair, coincided with bouts of illness described in the memoir of Marchand, Napoleon's trusted valet. Whenever the levels of arsenic reached critical levels, Napoleon became ill. The work of Sten Forshufvud and Ben Weider has proved beyond a doubt and with scientific certainty, that Napoleon was poisoned on Saint Helena.

Does Napoleon's corpse continue with its victory over death even to this day? If a lock of hair was worth £3,680 in 1995, an intriguing question remains – what is his body now worth? Napoleon's signature alone fetched £150 back then and its value increases every year.[8] His reputation meanwhile, needs to be reassessed and revalued.

NOTES

1. *The Sunday Times* London March 26th 1995. It also reported that there were more than 100 other Napoleon lots up for auction in March 1995 alone. In the article by Peter Johnson it says: "In a multitude of forms from portrait miniatures to life-sized statues, from love letters to battlefield autographs, he is revered by collectors." He also adds: "by contrast a lock of hair from the Duke of Wellington's (head) was a snip at £598."
Napoleon's popularity with collectors is phenomenal. On September 18th 1988 *The Sunday Telegraph* London reported a: 'Brush with history – No plaque is expected to mark the spot, but Napoleon's silver and gold-plated toothbrush goes under the hammer next month at the Munich auction house of Herman Historica.'
2. Napoleon was called a "monster genius" by the English journalist Nigel Nicholson, in an article in the *Daily Telegraph* London of September 3rd 1988. Nicolson's twisted portrayal of Napoleon is far too ludicrous ever to be called history. Napoleon was called a "great bad man" by David Chandler in the video series called *The Great Commanders*. Chandler, who was a great historian, shortly before his own death came to accept that Napoleon had been murdered by Montholon – for years he would not accept the fact.
3. Quoted in Paul Britten Austin *1812 The March on Moscow* 29
4. David Hamilton-Williams *The Fall of Napoleon* 330
5. Ibid. APPENDIX II The Royalist Underground and the Chevaliers de la Foi, 302-308
6. Ibid. 271
7. Ibid. 273
8. Peter Johnson article in *The Sunday Times* March 26th 1995. See above.

Appendix One
Two Book Reviews

THE WARS AGAINST NAPOLEON
By Ben Weider and General Michel Franceschi (2008)

I wrote the following review on Amazon in 2008 and it was after reading it that Ben Weider got in touch with me and invited me to join the International Napoleonic Society. That led to a series of articles for the INS that formed the basis for my own book *The Real Napoleon*. Sadly, I never got to meet Ben for he died later that year, just days before his own Napoleonic Collection was officially added to the Montreal museum.

—

The greatest threat to peace in Europe in the early nineteenth century was the British Cabinet. With its millions in subsidies it fought a mainly proxy war against France before Napoleon, and France under Napoleon. It was other countries that basically did the dying for British ends. England had been fighting France for decades and, still smarting under the loss of the American colonies, who won their freedom with crucial French backing, the last thing it wanted was for ideas of freedom and equality to spread amongst its own down-trodden people.

The British population was held in contempt by its autocratic, aristocratic, oligarchic masters. The French Revolution was a match hovering over the keg of liberty and the British Cabinet was determined to put it out.

Napoleon solidified the gains of the Revolution. He was the only one strong enough and pragmatic enough to heal the wounds of French society and under him France became a serious player in the field of international relations once again. The ancient monarchies were terrified that under his leadership, the liberalisation fostered by revolutionary ideas would spread to their own realms. Hence they pocketed the English bribes and fostered a series of coalitions that were to expunge the French leader and all he stood for from the map of Europe.

In their excellent book, Michel Franceschi and Ben Weider raise dozens of points, particularly in regard to the diplomacy of the time, that will be a real eye-opener to British readers. Especially telling are the references to the British press and Opposition in 1815 who said that the war of that year against Napoleon was totally unjustified. And Marie-Louise's letter to her father, expressing her anguish that he could be contemplating war against his own son-in-law is very revealing - especially as she says the English were probably behind it.

One reviewer has stated sneeringly that the authors blame the loss at Waterloo on a bad thunderstorm. They do not say that: they rightly comment that the French were outnumbered. In fact, although Wellington hung on grimly, it was the arrival of 45,000 Prussians, 7,000 of whom died at the hands of the Young Guard at Placenoit, that sealed the Emperor's fate. Not many of those Prussians went to Eton by the way.

As a reader of dozens of books on this period, I can honestly say that this is the first one that I have come across that looks at things from Napoleon's perspective. Far from being called The Napoleonic Wars, the period 1799-1815 would be better dubbed The English Mercenary Wars. Five stars!

—

The second review concerns a book by a writer who was very hostile to Napoleon, yet I nevertheless found it riveting reading.

NAPOLEON
By Georges Lefebvre (1936)

Although Lefebvre was a Marxist historian writing in 1935-1936, his book is nevertheless the 'Great Man' type of work that the Marxist school were very much against. He wrote while Hitler was in power in Germany and there are conscious and subconscious allusions to the dictator throughout this book. He uses the Nietzschean phrase '*the will to power*' several times in reference to Napoleon as if it was simply Napoleon's unbridled ego that led to the many wars of the early C19th. He lays the blame for war squarely at Napoleon's feet.

Few people realize that after Nietzsche died in 1900, his sister Elisabeth gathered together his unfinished notebooks and published them as *The Will to Power: Attempt at a Revaluation of all Values.* She was feted by the Nazis and told Hitler that her brother would have welcomed him and Nazis philosophy. Nothing could have been further from the truth. Yet the philosopher's views as espoused by his sister, were very much in favour with Hitler and his cronies. This support with such a highly regarded academic background appealed to the dictator's vanity. In return for this endorsement, Elisabeth became a virtual sainted grandmother of the Third Reich. However, she reinterpreted many of Nietzche's ideas and warped his views in order to please her powerful new patron.

Elisabeth inferred that her brother Friedrich would have been a supporter of Hitler's anti-semitism. In fact, Nietzsche ended his friendship with Wagner because of the latter's anti-semitism and spoke of the anti-semite as being the lowliest type of person - the exact opposite of what Elisabeth was saying to Hitler. The Nazi dictator's own philosophy of Social Darwinianism - that the strongest should survive and that the devil could take the hindmost - could be bolstered by the now warped ideas behind the theory of *the will to power,* hence Hitler made use of it. Thus Nietszche became the so-called 'Philospher of the Third Reich' and has often been unfairly denigrated subsequently because of this.

Hitler persecuted and murdered the Jews - Napoleon gave them equal rights, and freed them from unfair restrictions throughout the territories under his control. And he was the first person to suggest that they should be given a homeland of their own in the Holy Land.

Napoleon was unlike Hitler, Stalin and Mao in other respects.

Those three dictators eliminated all opposition. Despite repeated treachery from Talleyrand, Fouche, Bernadotte and many others, Napoleon did not have them executed. Indeed, he even invited Cadoudal - who have been plotting to murder him - to become an officer in his Army. Also, despite innumerable assassination attempts upon his life by D'Artois, the 'legitmate' heir to the vanished Bourbon throne, paid for by English gold, Napoleon did not respond in kind by trying to murder the British monarch.

Lefebvre goes out of his way to blame Napoleon for 'all the wars' and states that the Coalitions against him were only *reacting* to his plans of conquest - this despite the fact that Napoleon was usually attacked first by the other powers before he crushed them in battle. Neither does Lefebvre mention that after 1805, Napoleon could easily have deposed Francis of Austria; after 1806 he could have deposed Frederick William of Prussia - but he did neither; and after 1807 he could have really put the Tsar in his place - yet Alexander was treated incredibly leniently at Tilsit.

Lefebvre, despite his main Orwellian thesis i.e. 'Napoleon bad - Allies good', then goes on to describe Tsar Alexander's ambitions and empire-building plans and his unsated desire for more and more territory to add to his beloved Russian homeland. (Long before Alexander, the Russians sent the Second Kamchatka expedition to Alaska from 1733-1743 and soon had vessels trapping sea otters off the Alaskan coast and subsequently down the Pacific Northwest as far south as California.) In fact, Lebevre goes into great detail about the Tsar's plan to **attack** France in 1811 - the very best and most detailed explanation of Alexander's treachery - when he was supposed to be an ally of Napoleon - I have ever read. This casts Napoleon's invasion of 1812 in a completely new light. In the end, both powers were determined upon war and it was simply a question of who could get their strike in first.

Lefebvre states that Napoleon wanted a quick battle in 1812 and then a new settlement with Alexander to ensure the success of his Continental System. Lefebvre's grasp of the economic, social and cultural aspects of this period in

European history is superb - be it about Prussia, Russia, Austria, 'Germany' or even the minor states. His use of detailed records of imports, exports and trade statistics add to the fullest explanation of each powers diplomatic and trading status I have ever come across. His conclusion that England greedily viewed the seas as totally its own domain should come as a surprise to no one. He could have made more of the fact that with its command of the seas, no other power was able to grab as much land and as many colonies as the British, then and subsequently, even outdoing Russia in the end.

Lefebvre's *Napoleon* is an erudite and scholarly work that still reads like a novel - it is exciting, thought provoking and stimulating. Certainly five stars.

Appendix Two

As a confirmation of the enduring fascination that Napoleon excites throughout the world and the vast sums that people are prepared to pay for anything connected with him, here is a clip from a recent story dated June 11th 2012 in *The Daily Telegraph* in England:

SOLD, NAPOLEON'S ENGLISH HOMEWORK

"A rare letter in English by Napoleon has been sold at auction for £262,000, five times its estimate. The document went under the hammer in Fontainebleau and sold after a bidding war."

Napoleon's letter, sealed with his imperial eagle stamp, was written on Saint Helena in 1816 and was a homework exercise sent to a teacher in England. There are only three such English letters written by the former Emperor still in existence according to the Osenat auction house.

So, despite being beaten by Britain and the Prussians at Waterloo, and despite being an extremely reluctant prisoner on Saint Helena (he had hoped for asylum in England's green and pleasant land), the Emperor had the humility and common sense to want to learn the language of his jailers!

Appendix Three

And now for something completely different...

SEX AND THE CITY

SCANDALS IN LONDON AND PARIS

Every Thursday between 8 pm and midnight, men and women gathered in a darkened room at 102 Rue de Vaugirard. Clutching their prized introductions, they would pay their 12 francs and tremble in anticipation of a visit to seventh heaven. As the lamps were extinguished, partners were chosen and couples would act out their own sexual fantasies. This black market of love had only one rule: no one was allowed to find out who their partners were.

When this den of iniquity was finally discovered by the police, three marquises, a banker, a head clerk, a barrister and a lawyer were exposed, as it were. With Parisian tact, the men were allowed to go free and only the women were arrested! The Prefect of Police was an understanding man. When Barba's bookshop was raided and smutty volumes were confiscated, he had the good taste to keep them to show his friends after dinner parties.

In another part of the city, in a house in Rue Campagne-Premiere, a former priest called 'Bonjour' had founded a rather dubious religion in which strange ceremonies were performed in various degrees of undress. No doubt all the participants were assured beforehand of having a 'good day'.

An English visitor in 1806 estimated there were 75,000 prostitutes in Paris. However, he did not say if he knew them all personally. There were certainly many possibilities for dangerous liaisons in this city of sin.

Once a female streaker was whistled at in the Elysee Gardens, yet most women wore clothes designed to catch the eyes of male admirers. It was said that the transparent gowns of muslin left nothing to the imagination. Trying to dress like Grecian goddesses, the so-called "marvellous ones" of Paris had plunging necklines, see-through bodices and gowns split to the thigh. One lady of fashion, Madame Tallien, went to the Opera dressed as the goddess Diana with one breast completely bare. At this time, the Emperor Napoleon was trying to restore decency to his Court and he was furious with her.

On another occasion, Josephine and her friends paraded in semi-nudity in his presence. Grabbing the tongs and piling wood onto the fire, Napoleon shouted at the servants: "We need more heat, can't you see the ladies are naked!"

Napoleon was far from being a puritan himself, however. Parisians were immensely entertained when they heard that he had passed-out whilst making passionate love to the famous actress Mademoiselle George.

Paris was riddles with scandal and gossip. There were two types of candle in those days, the normal and the bastard. Wags said it was the same with the children. Paul Barras, leader of the French Government in the 1790s had dozens of mistresses, all of them ladies of refinement and quality. One of them, Josephine de Beauharnais, he eventually tired of and 'gave' to Napoleon.

With his male lovers, Barras was not so particular, and he paraded publicly with the riff-raff from the streets. He liked a 'bit of rough' in modern parlance. Another public figure, Jean-Jacques Cambaceres put the gay into Gay Paris. His little failing was notorious. Once, when he blamed a "fair visitor" for making him late to a meeting with Napoleon, the Emperor said: "Next time, my friend, you will have the goodness to say to this lady, 'Take your hat and stick and buzz off!' "

Talleyrand, the famous diplomat, was the greatest lover of his day. Despite having a limp in one leg, a complexion like that of a corpse, and a face described as lizard-like, he was far from cold-blooded. It was certainly true to say that Talleyrand had connections with many noble families, particularly in the female line, and the number of his mistresses was legion, including his own niece. When he became Vice Grand Elector in

Napoleon's empire, it was said that it was the only vice he did or previously have.

Yet, when he eventually married, this clever and treacherous statesman chose a woman who was as stupid as she was beautiful. Catherine Grand was blonde and blue-eyed with dark lashes, a truly ravishing creature. At the age of 15 she became the mistress of a British civil servant in India. Less than a year after marrying him, he found her in bed with another lover and she had to flee to France in disgrace. Talleyrand and Catherine were obviously made for each other.

Things were even more lively when the troops were at home. One soldier's idea of fun was to urinate through a grating onto the tables and guests in an underground café called *The Cave*. An officer accosted a shopkeeper's daughter. The man reproached him and said: "Monsieur, my daughter is an honest girl." The officer replied: "So much the better, that's how I like them!"

Massena, one of Napoleon's marshals, actually took his mistress with him on campaign dressed as a hussar. Their night-time manoeuvres were known of by everyone. Many a female corpse was found on bloodstained battlefields during those momentous years – some had actually fought, but others were victims of love, captive to their feelings for some dashing young man in a bright uniform.

Meanwhile, in London, life was far from dull thanks to Caroline of Brunswick, the wife of George, the Prince Regent. Caroline, the Princess of Wales, shocked English society with her sexual goings-on. After falling out with Prinny her husband, she scoured Europe looking for lovers and a good time. She could even have been the original good time had by all. With her hair dyed, wearing a see-through bodice and a short skirt that revealed her fat little legs, this lady in her Forties waltzed the night away.

Looking at their portraits, it isn't exactly Brad Pitt meets Jennifer Lopez, although the British Prime Minister was William Pitt – a confirmed bachelor who drank a bottle of port a day.

In 1820, the year George became King, Caroline had her lover Pergami installed as her Chamberlain. The same year she was said to have frolicked naked on a beach in Greece. She would have enjoyed the package holidays of today – she was obviously a woman ahead of her time.

Caroline's escapades were recorded by spies and kept in a notorious green bag in London. When he was later tried in court for her scandals the bag had grown to sack-like dimensions. On one occasion, Italian servants had found Caroline and Pergami asleep in a carriage with their hands on each other's private parts.

Although very fat, George was himself renowned for his series of lovers. For the unfortunate victims it must have been a bit like being tackled by an ardent elephant seal. His favourite mistress at this time, Lady Conyngham, was a plump woman aged 54. Being unpopular, George had to suffer ridicule at the hands of unknown verse makers. One wrote:

"Tis pleasant at seasons to see how they sit,
First cracking their nuts, and then cracking their wit,
Then quaffing their claret – then mingling their lips,
Or tickling the fat about each other's hips."

Some years before the Prince Regent had been visited by Tsar Alexander of Russia whose armies had helped defeat Napoleon. With him, Alexander brought to London the Grand Duchess Catherine. She was both his sister, and his mistress. Being able to satisfy Alexander's lusts she had great influence over him. However, she did not please Prinny. Every time the orchestra was about to play at one of the grand receptions, she would cry: "Music always makes me want to vomit!" and then the recital was over before it began.

The blond handsome Tsar, Alexander Ist was feted in England but his sister shocked the whole Court. Alexander had allowed his own father to be murdered and he was haunted by a guilty conscience all his life. Yet he was looked upon as a saviour by the aristocratic elites of the Continent because he had 'saved' Europe from Napoleon, from democracy, and from careers open to talent.

Anxious for an heir and to promote peace with Russia, Napoleon had asked for the hand of Catherine in marriage, but she was quickly married off to someone else to prevent this. It was probably just as well! However, Napoleon's sister Pauline was even more notorious for her sexploits. It was said that had the Emperor taken her into Russia in 1812 he wouldn't have needed his Grand Army – she could have worn out *all* the Tsar's men.

But in fairness to Pauline, when everyone else deserted Napoleon in 1814 including most of his family, she went to visit him on the island of Elba and even after Waterloo, she wrote to him on Saint Helena. She was both warm-hearted and a 'warm 'un' as they say in Yorkshire.

Sex and the City? You ain't seen nothing yet. In London and Paris in the early C19th they'd been there, done this, done that – and not bothered with the T-shirt (unless it was see-through).

Appendix Four

A VERY BRITISH CONCEIT

Here is what H.G. Wells said about Napoleon in his book *The Outline Of History* (1920):

"And now we come to one of the most illuminating figures in modern history, the figure of an adventurer and wrecker, whose story seems to display with an extraordinary vividness the universal subtle conflict of egotism, vanity, and personality with the weaker, wider claims of the common good. Against this background of confusion and stress and hope, this strained and heaving France and Europe, this stormy and tremendous dawn, appears this dark little archaic personage, hard, compact, capable, unscrupulous, imitative, and neatly vulgar..." (page 487)

AS FIRST CONSUL

"Now surely here was opportunity such as never came to man before... Had this man any profundity of vision, any power of creative imagination, had he been accessible to any disinterested ambition, he might have done work for mankind that would have made him the very sun of history. All Europe and America, stirred by the first promise of a new age, was waiting for him. Not France alone. France was in his hand, his instrument, to do with as he pleased, willing for peace, but tempered for war like an exquisite sword. There lacked nothing to this great occasion but a noble imagination. And failing that, Napoleon could do no more than strut upon the crest of this great mountain of opportunity like a cockerel on a dunghill. The figure he makes in history is one of almost incredible self-conceit, of vanity, greed, and cunning, of callous contempt and disregard of all who trusted him, and of a grandiose aping of Caesar, Alexander, and Charlemagne which

would be purely comic if it were not caked over with human blood..."
(page 490)

AS A MILITARY LEADER

"Since his military schemes were bound to provoke a war with England, he should, at any cost, have kept quiet until he had brought his navy to a superiority over the British navy...
(page 492)

"There seems to have been as little reason in the foreign policy that now plunged Europe into a fresh cycles of wars... At the same time his aggressions in south Germany forced Austria and Russia steadily into a coalition with Britain against him...
(page 493)

ON MEETING TSAR ALEXANDER AT TILSIT

"To Napoleon the meeting must have been extremely gratifying. This was his first meeting with an emperor on terms of equality. Like all men of limited vision, this man was a snob to the bone, his continual solicitude for his titles shows as much, and here was a real emperor, a born emperor, taking his three-year-old dignities as equivalent to the authentic imperialism of Moscow... After Tilsit there was a perceptible deterioration in Napoleon's quality; he became rasher, less patient of obstacles, more and more the fated master of the world, more and more intolerable to everyone he encountered...
(page 494)

ON NAPOLEON HIMSELF

"It would be difficult to find a human being less likely to arouse affection. One reads in vain through the monstrous accumulations of Napoleonic literature for a single record of

self-forgetfulness. Laughter is one great difference between man and the lower animals, one method of our brotherhood, and there is no evidence that Napoleon ever laughed... There is no proof that this unbrotherly, unhumorous egotist was ever sincerely loved by any human being... He had never even a dog to love him... He had never a gleam of religion or affection or the sense of duty. He was, as few men are or dare to be, a scoundrel, bright and complete...
(pages 499-500)

———

With such biased, ridiculous and unprecedented tosh was the British public and their children indoctrinated in the early part of the C20th. No wonder Napoleon has had a bad reputation in this country after oceans of such drivel has been sprayed over countless pages. Wells was full of it. He wrote only a year after Runciman, a proper historian, penned his life of Drake, Napoleon and Nelson. Runciman's Napoleon is light years away from the novelist's dark imaginary construct. But then H.G. Wells was a great writer of fiction wasn't he? Yes – a very great writer of fiction...

Appendix Five

HISTORY THROUGH A DISTORTING LENTZ

A PERSONAL VIEW BY
JOHN TARTTELIN

"No historian who believes strongly in their profession or their passion, having looked at the various arguments and seriously investigated the documents, can believe a word of these poisoning or substitution theories..." (Thierry Lentz)[1]

There exists today a conspiracy between Thierry Lentz et sa bande to muzzle opposition and confine to the outer darkness all those views and opinions that do not accord with their own. From his arrogant Olympian heights he descends like a new Moses with his tablets of stone and cries: "L'histoire c'est moi!" In an interview given to Delage Irène in April 2009, the new Messiah espouses his philosophy with a forthright and practiced brio. He states that: "Napoleon was poisoned! Despite historians' best efforts, Rumour(sic) continues to flourish, endlessly seeking to make the transition between Myth and History... In recent years, the poisoning and substitution hypotheses have resurfaced, driven by the death of Ben Weider..."

In a classic 'guilt by association' trick, Lentz tries to connect Ben Weider's life's work on the poisoning of the Emperor with nonsensical stories about a substitute for Napoleon's body having been placed in his tomb - as if the two cases were the same. Lentz looks through a glass darkly and refuses to countenance what he has not discovered himself. He literally 'won't see' what he doesn't want to know.

Then, in the same interview, in a phrase that could have come directly from the mouth of the Korean Great Leader he says: "Jacques Macé and I... want to close these debates, once and for all." So much for unrestricted historical enquiry and freedom of speech - it would appear that Lentz would burn those books that he disagrees with if only he had the chance.

Lentz continues: "What is important, and certainly the most worrying, about the substitution and poisoning theories is the way that the media coverage surrounding them has given them an air of validity, of incontrovertability. As a consequence these "false truths" have painted and continue to paint historians who do not believe in them as "has-beens"..." Here we have it: one protests a little too much Monsieur – are the Ugly Sisters whining because they haven't been invited to the Ball?

The late Ben Weider is not here to defend himself and speak out against such a travesty of his life's work. So I shall do it for him.

I might add at this stage that I wrote an article on the poisoning of Napoleon at Saint Helena in 1995 entitled *Hairsay and Heresy*, long before I had ever heard of Thierry Lentz. Theories, stories and evidence pertaining to the Emperor's early demise have been building up for decades. If Lentz thinks he can trash the research and study of a great number of historians and toxicologists with a few puerile comments in an interview, he has got another think coming.

Napoleon was a singular phenomenon, the greatest man of the C19th. Admired by Germans like Goethe, Heine and Nietzsche and Englishmen like Hazlitt and Byron, his early death was mourned even by his former enemies like the British Peninsular historian Napier, and Wilson, the British attaché to Kutozov's army during the Campaign of 1812. When graffiti appeared in the streets of London in 1821 asking people to mourn the passing of the greatest genius of their day, many Englishmen wept at the Emperor's passing.

Napoleon, that mass of energy, a one-man nuclear furnace, who was able to work for twenty hours a day, day after day, and who needed very little sleep, died at the age of 51, an early death even for the beginning of the C19th, let alone for someone so full of life. He died on an outcrop of rock lost in the South Atlantic, having often declared that he was being poisoned by his British jailors. Napoleon was no fool and he obviously had suspicions of his own. Indeed, the Governor of the island, the reptilian Hudson Lowe, was a creature of the night if ever there was one. However, the Emperor was actually poisoned by one of his own, betrayed yet again by someone he had trusted.

In 1982 Ben Weider and David Hapgood published *The Murder of Napoleon*. Perhaps Lentz has heard of David Chandler, the former doyen of Napoleonic scholarship in the English-speaking world? This is what Chandler said of the book: "Fascinating and deeply researched. The story the authors unfold and the scientific evidence they furnish are more than enough to justify careful thought and reconsideration. This book could well lead to considerable changes in the history of Napoleon's last years."[2]

Let's take a closer look at that assessment by a man who knew more about Napoleon than McDonald's knows about hamburgers. Chandler says the volume is "*deeply researched*" and he speaks of "*scientific evidence*". Lentz says the poisoning debate is a result of a "vast media circus". If that is the case then his contribution and that of his coterie amounts to little more than the entrance of the clowns. Chandler had more academic gravitas in his little finger than Lentz has in his whole body.

Chandler gave an interview to the British newspaper *The Daily Telegraph* on June 25th 2001. He was quoted by their reporter Thomas Harding as follows: "A leading British expert on Napoleon has given his backing to the theory that the deposed French Emperor was assassinated by his fellow countrymen."

"Dr. David Chandler, considered the foremost living authority on Napoleon, believes that history books should be re-written to include a final chapter on the conspiracy behind his death."[3] Before he died Chandler had become convinced that Napoleon has been poisoned.

Another commentator on Ben Weider's *The Murder of Napoleon*, Michael Baden, M.D., former chief medical examiner of New York City remarked that: "This fascinating account shows how modern forensic scientific techniques can be applied to help resolve old mysteries."[4]

In a germane contribution to this discussion, Jean-Claude Damamme, the Representative for France of the International Napoleonic Society said that: "Recently, various media reports have referred to a joint Swiss-Canadian-American study that rejects the "now largely discredited" (quotation) theories of Napoleon's poisoning by arsenic. In this regard, one must ask who discredited these theories?"[5] It wouldn't perchance be Lentz would it? And here the *media circus* is clearly *against* the poisoning of Napoleon, and not all for it as Lentz would have us believe.

As Jean-Claude Damamme goes on to say, the multi-national "study makes absolutely no mention of the work of Dr. Pascal Kintz, President of the International Association of Legal toxicologists, nor those of Prof. Robert Wennig of the University of the Grand Duchy of Luxembourg, whose analyses demonstrated – beyond question – a massive **concentration of rat poison in the core of the Emperor's hairs**. There is only one explanation for this presence: the toxic substance must have entered through the digestive tract."

Despite a by now decidedly large dose of Thierry ennui, I shall press on. Lentz says of his own book on the subject, *La Mort de Napoléon: Légendes, mythes et mystères* : "It is our refusal to allow such a noble and useful discipline as history to be taken hostage by these manipulators of public opinion that has driven us to write this book. We make no attempts to hide our surprise, nor our displeasure, in seeing those who at the same time as crying out "Freedom for History!", manipulate it for their own media-driven ends."

Physician heal thyself! It is Lentz who is warping and twisting the historically objective and scientific studies undertaken by Ben Weider and Sten Forshufvud, so as to discredit them in the eyes of the public and the mass media. He cannot be allowed to get away with this atrocious spin and manipulation. He himself is poisoning the discipline of history by his vile calumnies.

Just who does this man think he is?

On one side we have Weider, Forshufvud, Chandler, Damamme, Baden, Kintz and Wenning and on the other – Thierry Lentz. Who would a dispassionate reader believe I wonder?

The man who would like to "close these debates, once and for all" has bitten off more than he can chew. History is not written on tablets of stone proofread by Thierry Lentz. History is a fluid and inexact discipline, more Art than science, with natural ebbs and flows of belief and conjecture. Occasionally there is an historical tsunami when the views of the many are given spate, are widely accepted, and shortly after are to be seen in full-flood – thus is a paradigm created. Lentz has been whining and dining with the media to affect a seismic shift of his own – but his 'paradigm' isn't worth two cents, it is a plugged nickel as the Americans would say, counterfeit coin. It must not be allowed to be the accepted historical 'currency' amongst real historians and the public at large.

Napoleon *was* poisoned. "What proof do they have?" Lentz cries. Well Monsieur, proofread all the above and then read Ben Weider's book.

Yet another commentator on *The Murder of Napoleon*, 'Steven Ross, professor at the U.S. Naval War College; authority on Napoleonic History' adds: "An intriguing and well-written book. It makes a strong case and – unless someone has contrary medical evidence – compelling case that Napoleon was poisoned."[6]

One wonders if Lentz has ever *read* any of the books and articles that he would like to bury "once and for all"? It is a strange 'historian' who manages to open his mouth and blow off both of his feet at the same time. I shall not dwell any longer upon the antics of the clown prince of Napoleonic history.

When Ben Weider published *The Murder of Napoleon* in 1982 he was nearly sixty and he had devoted a lifetime of study to the subject. That same year Lentz was twenty-two and a total unknown. He still is, thankfully, in most of the English-speaking world.

There follows the article I wrote back in 1995, after having engaged in a lot of research of my own.[7] By coincidence it was the same year that Ben Weider formed the International Napoleonic Society. Many years later in 2008 he read my review of his book *The Wars Against Napoleon* on Amazon and invited me to become a member of the INS.

I was lucky enough to know Ben for five brief months. I only ever had two phone conversations with him and never met him in person. He was a kind and generous man, especially with his time – despite being incredibly busy. I will not suffer his memory to be impugned and dishonoured by a person who seems immensely jealous of the organization Ben inaugurated and who has none of Ben's integrity and sense of honour.

© 2011 John Tarttelin
M.A. FINS (Legion of Merit)

NOTES

1.   See www.napoleon.org/en/fondation   THE MAGAZINE/NEWS THIERRY LENTZ: THREE QUESTIONS ON THE "MYSTERIES" OF ST. HELENA (Interview by Delage Irène, April 2009) All Lentz's quotes are taken from this article.

2.   Quoted on the back of the book *The Murder of Napoleon* (New York, Congdon & Lattès, Inc., 1982).

3.   See INS website www.napoleonicsociety.com under Poisoning and *Doctor David Chandler, FINS, on the poisoning of Napoleon*. The Telegraph article is posted here.

4.   Quoted on the back of *The Murder of Napoleon*.

5.   See INS website under Poisoning and *The Poisoning of Napoleon, Correction* – By Jean-Claude Damamme.

6.   Quoted on the back of *The Murder of Napoleon*.

7.   The article became Chapter Sixteen of this book.

IMPORTANT NAMES

ALEXANDER TSAR (1777-1825) Indecisive, mystical Russian leader who knew about the murder of his father Tsar Paul – an ally of Napoleon. Came under the spell of Napoleon at Tilsit in 1807 but soon turned against him. The war with Russia of 1812 led to Napoleon's disastrous retreat from Moscow.

AUGEREAU PIERRE (1757-1816) The hero of the Battle of Castiglione, he was very tardy in 1814 at Lyons when he could have attacked the Austrians and relieved Napoleon's embattled forces.

BERNADOTTE JEAN-BAPTISTE (1769-1844) Republican whose 'support' for Napoleon was always tenuous. Often dallied in plots and intrigue. Married Desiree Clary and later became Crown Prince of Sweden. Traitor to France and Napoleon.

BONAPARTE CARLO (1746-1785) Christened Charles-Marie. Napoleon's father. Because he died of stomach cancer, many people assume Napoleon must have died of the same ailment – even though Joseph and Jerome lived to a ripe old age. Supporter of Paoli's quest for Corsican independence, but when Paoli went to England, Carlo threw in his lot with the French. He was a lawyer and a lover of books – Napoleon shared this bibliophilia.

BONAPARTE NAPOLEON (1769-1821) Born in Corsica, educated in France. Successful General, later Emperor in 1804. Faced implacable opposition from the British Government and the monarchs of Europe who believed in their God-given, divine right, to rule. Forced to abdicate in 1814 and was exiled to Elba. His return to France in 1815 was wildly popular but, after his peace overtures were rejected, he was defeated at Waterloo in 1815. Exiled to Saint Helena where he was poisoned by Montholon.

BONAPARTE FAMILY

JOSEPH (1768-1844)   NAPOLEON (1769-1821)   LUCIEN (1775-1840)
ELISA (1777-1820)   LOUIS (1778-1846)   PAULINE (1780-1825)
CAROLINE (1782-1839)   JEROME (1784-1860)

BOURRIENNE LOUIS (1769-1834) Wrote an infamous Memoir of Napoleon that is still widely used to this day by sloppy historians. He was his personal secretary from 1797-1802. He was twice dismissed by Napoleon for embezzlement. In 1814 he became a Royalist.

BYRON (1788-1824) Famous English poet. Napoleon was his hero. He loathed Wellington and ridiculed Castlereagh, the British Foreign Minister. Died fighting for Greek independence in 1824.

CANNING GEORGE (1770-1827) Had a famous duel with Castlereagh – British politicians hated each other almost as much as they hated the French. As Foreign Secretary he was responsible for the unprovoked attack on Copenhagen in 1807. This attack on neutral Denmark killed 2,000 innocent people. It was a war crime that will ever tarnish his reputation.

CAULAINCOURT ARMAND LOUIS (1773-1827) French General and diplomat. Always spoke his mind to Napoleon. French Ambassador to Russia. Represented France at the Treaty of Fontainebleau April 10th 1814. His *With Napoleon in Russia* was not published until 1933.

CLARY DESIREE (1777-1860) Had a romance of sorts with a young Napoleon, who considered marrying her. However, one Bonaparte in the family was enough for her parents. She later married Bernadotte and became Queen of Sweden – a place she disliked. Because of her, Napoleon spared her husband on many occasions despite his treachery.

COLOMBIER CAROLINE DU Born c. 1768. Napoleon's first love. He met her at Valence. She was the daughter of Madame Gregoire du Colombier.

D'ARTOIS (1757-1836) One of the most odious characters in French history. Younger brother of Louis XVIII known as 'Monsieur', future Charles X. His terrorist group the 'Chevalier de la Foi' plotted innumerable assassination attempts upon Napoleon's life. His man Montholon finally succeeded in poisoning Napoleon with arsenic on Saint Helena.

DAVOUT LOUIS-NICHOLAS (1770-1823) Napoleon's greatest general, 'the Iron Marshal'. Short-sighted, he was a strict disciplinarian. Greatest triumph was at Auerstädt in 1806 where with a single corps of 28,000 men he defeated the main Prussian Army with 63,000. Also the most loyal of Napoleon's marshals, beyond self-seeking. He was sorely missed at Waterloo. After the battle, however, he was persuaded by Fouché to distance Napoleon and refused to help his former master take on the dispersed forces of Wellington and Blücher. Napoleon had little choice but to abdicate a second time.

DES MAZIS ALEXANDRE (1768-1841) Became Napoleon's best friend at the École Militaire and afterwards at Valence. They were both in the Regiment de la Fere. He became his drill instructor because Napoleon took umbrage when his first instructor rapped him over the knuckles, which was against the regulations.

ENGHIEN (1772-1804) Bourbon Prince in the pay of the English. Fought with Suvarov against France. Under suspicion of plotting to take Napoleon's life, Talleyrand and Fouché argued for his arrest. Executed in 1804 by firing squad by over-zealous subordinate before Napoleon had a chance to pardon him – as he did many others. Ever since, Napoleon has been personally blamed for this debacle.

FRERON LOUIS-MARIE STANISLAS (1754-1802) Born in Paris to a wealthy family. Brutal man, infamous as enforcer of the Reign of Terror.

FOUCHÉ JOSEPH (1759-1820) Talleyrand's accomplice and notorious traitor. Calculating fanatic. Prominent Jacobin. During the Revolution arranged mass executions as 'The Executioner of Lyons'. A master of duplicity and deceit, his only loyalty was to himself. As Napoleon's Chief of Police he had double- and even triple-agents at his beck and call. Betrayed Napoleon after Waterloo in 1815.

FOX CHARLES JAMES (1749-1806) Arch-rival of William Pitt the Younger. He opposed George III and was on the side of the American revolutionaries.

Whig, who favoured peace with Napoleon. Briefly Foreign Secretary in 1806 before he died. Had he lived a little longer, history would have been very different.

GEORGE III (1738-1820) King from 1760-1820. Lost the American colonies because he couldn't compromise. Mad, bad and dangerous to know. He disliked Fox and backed Pitt, thereby ensuring that the British attacks on Napoleon would continue. The historian Walter Runciman said that even when he was not enduring a bout of madness, his decisions were insane. Originally against the attack on Copenhagen, he allowed himself to be talked round. Two thousand died as a result.

GEORGE THE PRINCE OF WALES (1762-1830) Stood in for his insane father from 1810. A ridiculous figure, weighing 245lb, he had to wear a corset. The British public loathed him after his tumultuous relationship with his wife Caroline of Brunswick came to an end. He convinced himself he led the final charge at Waterloo. Like father, like son, but what a disaster for the British nation. He ran up personal debts of £650,000 by 1795 – *millions* in today's money! Addicted to laudanum and alcohol.

ILARI CAMILLA A tough Corsican peasant girl and daughter of a Ajaccio sailor. Napoleon's wet-nurse. Treated as another member of the family by the Bonapartes.

LAS CASAS EMMANUEL (1766-1842) Soldier and historian, followed Napoleon into exile on Saint Helena. Published Napoleon's memoires as *Memorial of St Helena* in 1823 and began the Napoleonic legend.

LANNES JEAN (1769-1809) One of Napoleon's most able and bravest Marshals. Always said exactly what he felt. Died at Wagram. Napoleon wept at the death of his favourite.

LIVERPOOL (1770-1828) Harsh, reactionary British Prime Minister (1812-28), dead set against political reform at home. After Waterloo, he insisted on a punitive retaliation against former supporters of Napoleon in so-called White Terror. Many executions followed. He was just as brutal to his own people.

LOUIS XVIII (1755-1824) Younger brother of Louis XVI of France, this 310lb Bourbon returned to Paris in the baggage-train of the Allies – twice, in 1814 and 1815. An ineffectual ruler who proved that the Bourbons had learnt nothing and forgotten nothing. Easily swayed by d'Artois and Lord Liverpool.

MADEMOISELLE DE LAUBERIE DE SAINT-GERMAIN Napoleon had his second romantic attachment with her. She was from one of the County families of Valence in whose society he was entertained. She became a lady-in-waiting to the Empress in 1806 even though she stipulated that she must have plenty of time for her husband and children!

MAITLAND FREDERICK (1777-1839) Captain who commanded the British vessel *HMS Bellerophon* – 'Billy Ruffian' – on which Napoleon sailed from Rochefort to England in July 1815.

MACKINTOSH SIR JAMES (1765-1832) Historian, philosopher, doctor of medicine, and British author of *Vindiciae Gallica*, reflections on the French Revolution.

MADAME MERE (1750-1836) Maria Letizia Ramolini, Napoleon's mother, was extremely beautiful in her youth. She had her son's undying respect throughout his life. Careful with money, she once said that her favourite child was the one who was in the most trouble!

MARIE LOUISES Nickname, from Napoleon's second wife the Austrian Princess, given to the young soldiers who fought bravely for Napoleon in 1813 and 1814. Some were little more than boys of 16. Few knew even how to fire a musket when they were enlisted. Many fought fanatically for their Emperor. Despite adverse propaganda, Napoleon was loved by most people in France and these boys were prepared to die for him.

MARMONT (1774-1852) Early and seeming life-long friend of Napoleon and one of his Marshals, but he betrayed him by surrendering his Corps to the Allies in 1814. As Duke of Ragusa his title became a verb – raguser, a synonym for treachery. Wherever he went, little children pointed him out as 'the man who betrayed Napoleon'.

MOORE SIR JOHN (1761-1809) British General who fought in the Spanish Peninsula. He was chased out of Spain by Napoleon and died at Corunna in 1809. His men escaped, after leaving their women and children behind. The French soldiers returned them unharmed.

MURAT JOACHIM (1767-1815) Greatest cavalry commander of his age, fearless in the charge, but hopeless when it came to caring for his men and their mounts. Made a Marshal in 1804. His leadership of the cavalry at Eylau in 1807 saved the day for Napoleon. Richly rewarded, he became King of Naples, but he regretted that he was not given Spain to rule. Given command of the remnants of the Grand Army after the disastrous retreat of 1812, he fled to Naples. Turned against Napoleon in 1814 and was not used therefore the following year at Waterloo - had he been, the French cavalry would not have been wasted by Ney.

NELSON HORATIO (1758 -1805) Believed in the divine right of British seapower. The great victory at Trafalgar in 1805, after the French Admiral Villeneuve set sail contrary to Napoleon's orders, and his glorious death, made him an English hero, but in his private life he was a very arrogant man. He also ordered the cold-bloodied execution of Caracciolo and other republican prisoners in Naples in 1799, despite a signed treaty permitting them the honours of war. He once said that even his mother hated the French.

NEY MICHEL (1769-1815) Le Rougeaud as the troops called him, on account of his ruddy complexion, he was 'the bravest of the brave' in 1812 and a great personal leader of men. Son of a master barrel cooper, his wife was slighted by the Bourbons he served in 1814. As a result, he rallied, belatedly to Napoleon in 1815. To this day, it is not known why he threw his cavalry at the British squares time after time at Waterloo without bothering to bring up his infantry or horse artillery.

PITT WILLIAM (THE YOUNGER] (1759-1806) Prime Minister in 1804-1806, had an obsessive hatred for France and Napoleon. He formed the Third Coalition, bribing Russia and Austria to attack France in 1805. Some consider him to be a great PM but not Walter Runciman. A weird fish, he drank himself to death. He owed £40,000 when he died, despite a salary of £10,500 as PM– the epitome of decadent 'privilege'. Parliament paid off his debts. To the manor born.

ROBESPIERR**E** (1758-1794) Provincial lawyer who presided over the most revolutionary phase of the French Revolution. Fanatical follower of Rousseau's social theories. Member of the Committee of Public Safety. Butcher of Reign of Terror. Some 28 guillotine beheadings a day occurred at the height of this bloodbath.

SOULT (1769-1851) Marshal Soult was a brooding figure who resented not being made Duke of Austerlitz after his part in that victory. Wellington's opponent in the Peninsula. Went over to the Bourbons in 1814. Rallied to Napoleon in 1815 but his lacklustre performance at Waterloo, failing to emulate Berthier's role was one of the reasons for defeat.

TALLEYRAND CHARLES MAURICE DE (1754-1838) Early supporter of Napoleon who became his Foreign Minister but later betrayed him. Gave Paris to the Allies in 1814 which led to Napoleon's abdication. Helped Allies at the Congress of Vienna 1815 against Napoleon and France. Extremely influential diplomat and inveterate womaniser. "Treason is a matter of dates," he once said to Tsar Alexander. Traitor to his country and to Napoleon. His chief aim and intention in life was to enrich himself with bribes and foreign subsidies. In this he succeeded admirably.

WELLINGTON (1769-1852) Fought the French in the Spanish Peninsular War. Defeated Napoleon at Waterloo with the help of 45,000 Prussians under Blucher. Prime Minister 1828-30. Opposed Reform Bill 1831-32. Aristocrat who believed in power remaining with an elite.

WILSON SIR ROBERT (1777-1849) British General who fought with the Russians against Napoleon in 1812. Yet, during the White Terror, he spoke out against the murder of Bonapartists and was jailed for three months by Louis XVIII because of it.

WURMSER (1724-1797) Austrian Field Marshal, but a Frenchman born at Strasbourg. Defeated by Napoleon at the Battle of Castiglione on August 5th 1796. Surrendered to Napoleon at Mantua.

FINAL NOTE

During the period France was led by Napoleon, England was ruled by aristocratic politicians and a mad King. Castlereagh killed himself – Canning would have cheerfully done the deed for him; Pitt drank himself to death; Nelson craved adulation at every turn – even Wellington said Nelson was fond of approbation – an in joke if ever there was one, for the Duke was a lover of the trowel; while the general population devoid of political representation was left mired in poverty and destitution. If ever this country needed a Napoleon, it was during the period 1800-1820.

BIBLIOGRAPHY

Abbott John.S.C. *The History of Napoleon Bonaparte* (New York: Harper & Brothers, 1885)

Adair John *By The Sword Divided* (London: Century Publishing, 1983)

Adam Albrecht *Napoleon's Army In Russia* Translated by Jonathon North (Barnsley, England: Pen and Sword Military, 2003)

Austin Paul Britten *1812 The March On Moscow* (London: Greenhill Books, 1993)

Austin Paul Britten *1812 Napoleon In Moscow* (London: Greenhill Books, 1995)

Austin Paul Britten *1812 The Great Retreat* (London: Greenhill Books, 1996)

Austin Paul Britten *1815 The Return Of Napoleon* (London: Greenhill Books, 2002)

Bernard J.F. *Talleyrand: A Biography* (London: The History Book Club, 1973)

Black Jeremy Ed. *Great Military Leaders And Their Campaigns* (Stroud, England: Spellmount, 2008)

Blaze Elzéar *Life In Napoleon's Army* (London: Greenhill Books, 1995)

Blond Georges *La Grande Armée* Translated by Marshall May (London: Arms And Armour Press, 1995)

Bourgogne Sergeant Adrien *The Retreat From Moscow* Translated by J.W. Fortescue (London: Folio, 1985)

Bowle John *Napoleon* (London: Weidenfeld And Nicolson, 1973)

Brett-James Antony *1812 Eyewitness Accounts Of Napoleon's Defeat In Russia* (London: Book Club Associates, 1966)

Cate Curtis *The War Of The Two Emperors* (New York: Random House, 1985)

Caulaincourt Armand de *With Napoleon In Russia* (New York: Dover Publications Inc., 2005)

Chair Somerset de (Ed) *Napoleon On Napoleon* (London: Brockhampton Press, 1992)

Chandler David *The Campaigns of Napoleon* (London: Weidenfeld & Nicolson, 1966)

Chandler David *The Campaigns of Napoleon In Three Volumes* (London: The Folio Society, 2002)

Chandler David *Waterloo The Hundred Days* (London: Osprey, 1980)

Chandler David Ed. *Napoleon's Marshals* (London: Cassell, 2000)

Clark John *The Life And Times Of George III* (London: Book Club Associates, 1972)

Coignet Jean-Roch *Captain Coignet* www.leonaur.com Leonaur 2007)

Cronin Vincent *Napoleon* (Harmondsworth, England: Penguin, 1971)

Damamme Jean-Claude *Les Aigles En Hiver* (Paris: Plon, 2009)

Delderfield R.F. *The March Of The Twenty-Six* (Barnsley, England: Pen & Sword, 1962)

Dougherty Kevin J. et al *Battles Of The American Civil War* (Stroud, England: Spellmount, 2007)

Dwyer Philip *Napoleon The Path To Power 1769-1799* (London: Bloomsbury, 2007)

Elting Colonel John R. *Swords Around A Throne* (London: Weidenfeld and Nicolson, 1989)

Epton Nina *Josephine And Her Children* (London: Weidenfeld And Nicolson, 1975)

Faur Major Faber du *With Napoleon In Russia* Edited And Translated By Jonathon North (London: Greenhill Books, 2001)

Forrest Alan *Napoleon's Men* (London: Hambledon & London, 2002)

Franceschi General Michel And Weider Ben *The Wars Against Napoleon* (New York: Savas Beatie, 2008)

Fregosi Paul *Dreams Of Empire* (London: Hutchinson, 1989)

Glover Michael *The Legacy Of Glory* (New York: Charles Scribner's Sons, 1971)

Hamilton-Williams *Waterloo New Perspectives* (London: Arms And Armour Press, 1993)

Hamilton-Williams David *The Fall Of Napoleon* (London: Arms And Armour Press, 1994)

Haythornthwaite Philip J. *Die Hard* (London: Arms And Armour Press, 1996)

Haythornthwaite Philip J. *Napoleonic Cavalry* (London: Cassell, 2001)

Headley J.T. *The Imperial Guard Of Napoleon* (New York: Charles Scribner, 1851)

Hibbert Christopher *Napoleon His Wives And Women* (London: Ted Smart, 2002)

Hohendorf Horst *The Life And Times Of Goethe* (London: Paul Hamlyn, 1967)

Horricks Raymond *Marshal Ney* (Tunbridge Wells, England: Midas Books, 1982)

Hoyos Dexter *Hannibal's Dynasty* (London: Routledge, 2003)

Johnstone R.M. Ed. *In The Words Of Napoleon* (London: Greenhill Books, 2002)

Jonge Alex de *Napoleon's Last Will And Testament* (London: Paddington Press, 1969)

Keegan John *The Face Of Battle* (London: The Folio Society, 2008)

Kemble James *Napoleon Immortal* (London: John Murray, 1959)

Labaume Eugéne *Through Fire And Ice With Napoleon* (Solihull, England: Helion & Company, 2002)

Lachouque Henry And Brown Anne S.K. *The Anatomy Of Glory* (London: Greenhill, 1997)

Lee Christopher *Nelson And Napoleon* (London: Headline, 2005)

Lefebvre Georges *Napoleon* (London: The Folio Society, 2009) First published in 1936.

Logie Jacques *Waterloo And The 1815 Campaign* (Stroud, England: Spellmount, 2006)

Macdonell A.G. *Napoleon And His Marshals* (London: Prion, 1996)

Mackenzie Norman *The Escape From Elba* (Oxford: O.U.P., 1982)

Mansel Philip *The Eagle In Splendour* (London: George Philip, 1987)

Markham Felix *Napoleon* (New York: New American Library, 1963)

Markham J. David *The Road to St Helena* (Barnsley, England: Pen & Sword Military, 2008)

Markham J. David *Imperial Glory: The Bulletins of Napoleon's Grande Armée 1805-1814 (London: 2003)*

Martineau Gilbert *Napoleon's Last Journey* Translated By Frances Partridge (London: John Murray, 1976)

McLynn Frank *Napoleon* (London: Pimlico, 1998)

Muir Richard *The Lost Villages Of Britain* (London: Michael Joseph, 1982)

Munch-Petersen *Defying Napoleon* (Stroud, England: Sutton Publishing, 2007)

Napier William *History Of The War In The Peninsula* (London: Frederick Warne And Co., 1828)

Nicolson Nigel *1812* (London: Weidenfeld And Nicolson, 1985)

Palmer Alan *Napoleon In Russia* (London: Constable, 1997)

Palmer Alan *Russia In War And Peace* (London: The History Book Club, 1972)

Palmer Alan *The Life And Times Of George IV* (London: Book Club Associates, 1972)

Priestley J.B. *The Prince Of Pleasure* (London: Sphere Books Ltd., 1969)

Rolt-Wheeler Francis William *The Boy with the U.S. Weather Men* (Boston, Lothrop, Lee & Shepard Co. 1917).

Rosebery Lord *Napoleon The Last Phase* (London: Arthur L.Humphreys, 1900)

Runciman Walter *Drake, Nelson And Napoleon* (London: T.Fisher Unwin Ltd, 1919)

Smith Digby *Napoleon's Regiments* (London: Greenhill Books, 2000)

Solé Robert, Valbelle Dominique, Davies W.V. *The Rosetta Stone* (London: The Folio Society, 2006)

Sun-Tzu *The Art Of War* Translated By Roger T. Ames (London: Folio Society, 2007)

Strawson John *The Duke And The Emperor* (London: Constable, 1994)

Thompson J.M. *Napoleon's Letters* (London: Prion, 1998)

Tulard Jean *The Myth Of The Saviour* Translated By Teresa Waugh (London: Weidenfeld And Nicolson, 1984)

Uffindell Andrew *Great Generals Of The Napoleonic Wars* (Staplehurst, England: Spellmount, 2003)

Uxkull Boris *Arms And The Woman* (New York: The Macmillan Company, 1966)

Watson J.Steven *The Reign Of George III 1760-1815* (Oxford: At The Clarendon Press, 1960)

Weider Ben And David Hapgood *The Murder Of Napoleon* (New York: Congdon And Lattès Inc. 1982)

Wells H.G. *The Outline Of History Volume II* (London: The Waverley Book Company Limited, 1920)

Whiting Charles *'45* (London: Guild Publishing, 1985)

Williams Hywel *Fifty Days That Changed The World* (London: The Folio Society, 2008)

Zamoyski Adam *1812* (London: Harper Collins, 2004)

INTERNATIONAL NAPOLEONIC SOCIETY PUBLICATIONS

www.napoleonicsociety.com

ARTICLES

Cazottes Pascal *Napoleon and America*
Damamme Jean-Claude *Did Napoleon Merit The Reputation That Surrounds His Name?*
Damamme Jean-Claude *Iena 1806, The Battle That Napoleon Did Not Want*
Markham J.David *Was Napoleon an Anti-Semite? Napoleon, the Jews and Religious Freedom*

OTHER PUBLICATIONS

Franceschi General Michel *Austerlitz (2005)*
Franceschi General Michel *Bonaparte In Egypt (2006)*
Franceschi General Michel *The Duke Of Enghien Affair: A Plot Against Napoleon (2005)*
Franceschi General Michel *The 18th Brumaire Rescuing The Republic And Civil Peace (2007)*
Franceschi General Michel *The 13 Vendémaire Republican Coronation Of Napoleon (2006)*
Franceschi General Michel *Austerlitz (2005)*
Weider Ben And Kintz Dr. Pascal *The Poisoning Of Napoleon (2005)*

Picture on back cover part of *The Evening of Waterloo* by Earnest Crofts (1879)
Starburst added by author to represent the end of Napoleon's Empire.

Printed in Great Britain
by Amazon

28620262R00137